Consulting Editors

Michael Barton
Associate Professor of American Studies and History
Pennsylvania State University at Harrisburg, Capital College

Nancy A. Walker
Professor of English
Vanderbilt University

This unique series consists of carefully assembled volumes of seminal writings on topics central to the study of American culture. Each anthology begins with a comprehensive overview of the subject at hand, written by a noted scholar in the field, followed by a combination of selected articles, original essays, and case studies.

By bringing together in each collection many important commentaries on such themes as humor, material culture, architecture, the environment, literature, politics, theater, film, and spirituality, American Visions provides a varied and rich library of resources for the scholar, student, and general reader. Annotated bibliographies facilitate further study and research.

Volumes Published

Nancy A. Walker, editor
What's So Funny? Humor in American Culture (1998).
Cloth ISBN 0-8420-2687-8   Paper ISBN 0-8420-2688-6

Robert J. Bresler
*Us vs. Them: American Political and Cultural Conflict
from WW II to Watergate* (2000).
Cloth ISBN 0-8420-2689-4   Paper ISBN 0-8420-2690-8

Jessica R. Johnston, editor
The American Body in Context: An Anthology (2001).
Cloth ISBN 0-8420-2858-7   Paper ISBN 0-8420-2859-5

Richard P. Horwitz, editor
The American Studies Anthology (2001).
Cloth ISBN 0-8420-2828-5   Paper ISBN 0-8420-2829-3

Chris J. Magoc
*So Glorious a Landscape: Nature and the Environment
in American History and Culture* (2002).
Cloth ISBN 0-8420-2695-9   Paper ISBN 0-8420-2696-7

SO GLORIOUS A LANDSCAPE

SO GLORIOUS A LANDSCAPE

NATURE and the ENVIRONMENT in AMERICAN HISTORY and CULTURE

by
CHRIS J. MAGOC
with Documents and Readings

American Visions ❧ Readings in American Culture

Number 5

A Scholarly Resources Inc. Imprint ❧ Wilmington, Delaware

© 2002 by Scholarly Resources Inc.
All rights reserved
First published 2002
Printed and bound in the United States of America

Scholarly Resources Inc.
104 Greenhill Avenue
Wilmington, DE 19805-1897
www.scholarly.com

Library of Congress Cataloging-in-Publication Data

Magoc, Chris J., 1960–
    So glorious a landscape : nature and the environment in
American history and culture / by Chris J. Magoc
        p. cm. — (American visions)
    "With documents and readings."
    Includes bibliographical references (p.)
    ISBN 0-8420-2695-9 (alk. paper) — ISBN 0-8420-2696-7 (pbk. :
alk. paper)
        1. United States—Environmental conditions—History—Sources.
2. Human ecology—United States—History—Sources. 3. Landscape
changes—United States—History—Sources. I. Title. II. American
visions (Wilmington, Del.) ; no. 5

GE150 .M34 2001
333.73'0973—dc21   2001031070

To our children Ethan and Caroline

And my brothers

Ron, Gerard, Jim, and Dan

ABOUT THE AUTHOR

CHRIS J. MAGOC is assistant professor of history at Mercyhurst College in Erie, Pennsylvania. He is the author of *Yellowstone: The Creation and Selling of an American Landscape, 1870–1903* (1999) as well as a number of articles and reviews on popular culture and environmental and public history. Professor Magoc also is the writer and producer of *Tarentum: A History in the Making* (1996), a documentary film centered on an industrial town near Pittsburgh. Before joining Mercyhurst, he directed the Allegheny-Kiski Valley Historical Society in Tarentum and the educational program for the Erie Maritime Museum and the U.S. Brig *Niagara*; he is the author of *Erie Maritime Museum and the U.S. Brig Niagara: A Pennsylvania Trail of History Guidebook* (2001). Prior to becoming a historian, Professor Magoc spent nearly a decade organizing and lobbying for various nonprofit groups in Pennsylvania and the West. He lives in Erie with his wife, Mary Ellen, and their two children, Ethan and Caroline.

CONTENTS

PREFACE AND ACKNOWLEDGMENTS

One never refuses an invitation from a greatly admired and respected former professor. When Michael Barton of the American Studies program at Penn State Harrisburg graciously asked me to submit a proposal for a collection of readings on nature and the environment for Scholarly Resources' American Visions Series, I leapt at the opportunity. Here was a chance, he suggested, to bring together in one place my view of the far-flung interdisciplinarity of American nature and environmental studies. As always, Michael's persuasion was compelling. He sparked in me a desire to assimilate and synthesize the major themes of this vast field; to better understand how culture, science, politics, and social history are interwoven in the study of the American environment; and, further, to unravel the meaning and significance of nature in the larger context of our national experience. The following pages represent the result of that conversation.

Not surprisingly, it proved to be a daunting challenge. Perhaps even more than other broad themes of American life, "nature" both culturally and historically is boundless. Like the seemingly endless continental wilderness of seventeenth-century European Americans, four hundred years later the literary horizon of the American landscape is hard to comprehend. Where to begin? Where and how to draw lines between themes and disciplines? Is Henry David Thoreau a natural historian or a philosopher of the human experience in nature? What to select and, harder still, what to leave out? These were among the difficult questions faced in piecing together an anthology of this sort. Obviously, my answers to those questions differ greatly from other compilations of either nature writing or environmental history.

Part of what distinguishes this collection may be its universality. I tried to dodge the last question—"what to leave out?"—by simply trying to graze, if occasionally lightly, over the entire terrain. As I see it, that is in keeping with the all-embracing traditional reach of American Studies. Some readers may find it an improbably extended journey—it is a long way from Acoman Indian myth of the fifteenth century to the National Environmental Policy Act of 1969—but one that I believe reveals the core essentials of the American experience in and with the natural world.

A brief outline is in order. The introductory sections to each of the five parts of the book articulate the central themes and historical background for the readings that follow. Part I establishes the outlines of the encounter of Native and European Americans in the wilderness, one of the central themes of American history. Until fairly recently, the environmental dimensions of that narrative have been overlooked. This first part moves quickly, and admittedly lightly, across much ground, but does form the historical and cultural context for what is to come. Part II offers first, an overview of the American nature aesthetic that emerged in the nineteenth century; and second, a glimpse of one of its most eloquent literary expressions, the nature essay. With profundity and passion, writers from Thoreau to Annie Dillard shaped an American sense of place that went far beyond natural history and landscape narrative to probing the essential relationship of humans with nature in the modern age.

In Part III we encounter some of the critical events and chief intellectual voices that transformed the scientific study of nature in America. As we shall see, science, from having served exclusively as a buttressing force for the mechanistic and often rapacious development of nature, was redefined by modern practitioners. Scientists of varying specialties and sensibilities applied natural history and a variety of other empirical tools in trying to understand the degree of and proper response to human environmental impact. Their exploration bore rich fruit: expertly managed resource conservation, the emergence of ecology as a credible science, and, more generally, an ecological ethic that would continue to evolve and try to come to terms with severe environmental change.

That story—that is, the social and political history of some of the most telling and chilling episodes of environmental change in the twentieth century—is the focus of Part IV. We meet here citizens and organizations of renown, as well as ordinary Americans, fighting tenaciously to protect or restore a wide array of landscapes and their inhabitants: the industrialized city, the arid southwestern desert, Appalachian mountainsides, a typically suburban northern community, and a (often forsaken, even by environmentalists) rural region of the south. These examples illustrate how Americans of varying class, race, and region have fought the power structures controlling the environmental health and fate of valued landscapes—sometimes successfully, often not.

Perhaps Part V illustrates more than any other the ponderous breadth of this subject. It sketches the immeasurably wide-ranging literary, intellectual, and political responses of Americans to the deepening sense of environmental crisis in the second half of the twentieth century. To say that there is a lot contained here is an understatement: from a poetic elegy on the loss of the passenger pigeon to a singularly caustic critique of national park policy, to the legalistic, technocratic means by which environmental scientists and bureaucrats manage ecological problems, to, finally, several profoundly challenging philosophical and literary reflections on the environmental crisis. But that is as it should be—a reflection of the richly layered and wildly heterogeneous views and experiences of Americans trying to comprehend and remedy a seemingly endless stream of problems unprecedented in severity and scope.

I fully acknowledge here that I have found it impossible to keep my own views and experiences out of this writing. To this project I brought a life of environmental study, philosophical musing, and occasional political activism. Inevitably, those activities have informed my interpretation of the materials. I offer not apologies but rather a hopeful expectation that the reader's own understanding of and experience with nature and the "environment" (a distinctly different, modern notion, as we will see) might be enriched by my perceptions.

I am forever grateful to Professor Barton for giving me the opportunity to put this volume together. Years before, at Penn State Harrisburg, he helped to inspire my love of American Studies and to foster my interest in the particular study of the landscape. His thoughtful critiques of this manuscript from beginning to end strengthened it considerably.

In addition, the comments of Nancy Walker, co-editor of the series, were also valuable and much appreciated. I thankfully acknowledge the insightful comments and generous patience of Matthew Hershey, senior acquisitions editor at Scholarly Resources. His recommendations for revisions of an earlier draft very much sharpened my analysis. Even more, perhaps, I have deeply appreciated his willingness to wait (and wait) for the completion of this book while a series of life changes slowed its progress. The invaluable assistance of these individuals notwithstanding, I alone am responsible for any errors that may yet be contained herein. I also extend grateful acknowledgment to Lynn Falk at the Interlibrary Loan desk of the Mercyhurst College Hammermill Library. Her assistance at the twelfth hour in securing original copies of many of the readings in the book was essential to its completion. Finally, I extend great love and appreciation to my favorite environmentalist, my wife, Mary Ellen, whose loving stewardship of our little patch of nature has for the past fifteen years continually inspired my work.

—*CJM*

I | Indian Ecology, American Conquest

You know, our fathers had plenty of deer and skins,
our plains were full of deer, as also our woods, and
of turkies, and our coves full of fish and fowl. But
these English having gotten our land, they with
scythes cut down the grass, and with axes fell the
trees; their cows and horses eat the grass, and their
hogs spoil our clam banks, and we shall all be
starved.

—Narragansett Chief Miantonomo, 1642[1]

Americans have long insisted that what the first white settlers
found here in the sixteenth and seventeenth centuries was a "New
World" of "virgin wilderness."[2] In this view, the country lay before
the eyes of English colonists pure and untouched and, paradoxically,
wildly inhabited by savages. From either side of the contradiction, the
land begged for redemptive improvement. However, like other great
national beliefs that have withered under either experience or critical
examination, the notion of a virgin continent has unraveled a bit. We
now understand it to belong more accurately to the category of American Myth: those most enduring and powerful of national ideals that

Americans want and need to believe. Rooted as much in imagination and ambition as in actual experience, our great cultural myths nonetheless exert a profound impact upon not only society and the political economy, but also the biophysical world we call "nature." For several hundred years the Virgin Myth has propelled Americans ever onward to empty and unlimited lands.[3] The ideal of unblemished and endlessly bountiful lands still endures, far beyond the woods of seventeenth-century New England where we first confront it. It helps to explain, for example, the suburban sprawl that continues to ooze over our landscape.

As several of the selections in Part I illustrate, however, North America was neither new nor unaffected by human hands when Europeans arrived. Historians and anthropologists estimate in the tens of millions the total native populations living throughout the Americas in the early fifteenth century before the arrival of whites.[4] From the Narragansett and Abenaki of the Northeast to the Pueblo peoples of the Southwest, the continent was anything but vacant. On the contrary, in the centuries before European colonization linked this land to a global market economy, Native American consciousness, spirituality, and ways of living worked to actively shape regional ecosystems.

By every conceivable definition, what came to supplant that Indian ecological paradigm in the early seventeenth century was a universe apart. English colonists arrived on eastern shores and Spanish conquistadors journeyed to the Southwest with very different ideas about the natural and spiritual worlds and the proper structure of human societies. Colonization by the Spaniards would proceed slowly and erratically, if only because they were more interested in discovering gold and proselytizing souls than unloading an excess urban population. Ultimately the Spaniards, and then succeeding Mexican and American authorities, would accommodate at least a share of native belief systems, particularly in New Mexico. In the Chesapeake Bay region and in New England, however, the story was quite different. As Miantonomo's elegy testifies, within just a few decades the process of English colonization that disrupted and destroyed Indian ecologies— and, by definition, Indian societies—was well under way.

This introduction and the accompanying selections will focus on the contrast of Indian and European ideas about nature and the initial conquest of Indian ecology as it first unfolded in New England. It will outline the transformation that Carolyn Merchant calls "ecological revolutions,"[5] which changed forever not only Miantonomo's world but also lands far beyond it. The Englishmen who revolutionized the human relationship with nature in New England established a new ecological paradigm, the heavy imprint of which would soon track the entire continent. Selections 7–9 will sketch lightly the ideological underpinnings that brought the ecological revolution to a climax in the second half of the nineteenth century. These broad outlines of an epic three-hundred-year-old social-environmental history are inevitably thin, but they will provide the context for the more fully layered, multidisciplinary stories to follow in Parts II–V.

———

To generalize about the complex belief systems of hundreds of Native American tribes concerning nature is slippery business; the contours of culture are as variegated as the land itself. Yet there are common threads, foremost among them the indivisibility of the natural world from the human. In Native American thought, "nature" as a separate realm simply does not exist. Nature is all—the stuff of both material and spiritual sustenance. Plant and animal life is closely linked to that of humans. All of nature, from rocks and soil to the stars above, is alive. Native cultures have long held that human survival is best ensured by identifying with and imitating all that sustains life.

Those core animistic beliefs are deeply embedded in Native American creation myths such as that of the Acoma Pueblo Indians of present-day New Mexico (Selection 1). Creation myths like this one explain the origins of native peoples in the world, forever root them to their homelands, and imbue meaning to the natural features of those landscapes. Many of these tales feature an animal-into-human metamorphosis, which serves to link the spirit and well-being of one to the other. In the Acoman version printed here, a planted, nurtured seed becomes the sacred symbol of both the people's emergence from the underworld into this one, and of the linkage between human welfare and that of plants. Once brought forth embryonically from the earth, the people are integral to maintaining the vital cycles of life: light and dark, warmth and cold, sun and rain, production and reproduction.

Other expressions of Native American belief reinforce an essential reciprocity between humans and nature. For the Tewa people of New Mexico, the agricultural and hunting practices, festivals, dances, songs, and other art forms imitate and honor nature's life-giving ways. The Tewa song, "Sky Looms" (Selection 2), offers a vivid evocation of place that suggests a deeply intimate relationship with the natural world: the people bring earthy gifts and seek by prayers of supplication a "sky loom" common to the Southwest—that is, a thunderstorm that, on the distant, dry summer horizon, appears to weave sky and land. Sky looms bring renewed life to an arid region and reaffirm the people's sense of living appropriately in their world.[6]

From one end of the continent to the other, Native Americans' mythologies like these have long shaped their actions on the land. For other surviving Indian tribes of the Southwest such as the Navajo and Hopi, the Corn Mother figures prominently in creation myths. Sacred rituals guide the cultivation and harvest of corn as well as the proper uses of corn pollen to bring about life-giving rain. For centuries, the fishing-dependent Tlingit of the Northwest repeated tales in which "the lives of animals and fish intermingled with those of humans."[7] In the harsh environment of the northern plains, the Mandan people survived for nearly a millennium because they recognized every component of the land as sacred and vital to their existence.[8] As for countless other tribes, only Euro-American diseases brought the near demise of the Mandan.

It was in New England that the cultural and ecological impact of European colonization was first and most severely felt by native peoples. Like the tribes of the West, the Eastern Abenaki of New England believed every part of nature to be equally suffused with life and meriting reverence. Indeed, they thought themselves begotten from certain animals. The myth of a common earthly ancestry helped to ensure the mutual survival of hunter and hunted.[9] Beholden to deer, moose, and elk for their existence, Abenaki hunters mimicked their behavior and revered those animals who gave their lives for the survival of the tribe. Elaborate tribal rituals and taboos worked against the extirpation of species. One dare not upset the spirits of the moose by failing to say the proper prayer, or by taking down more than the tribe needed; violation of such beliefs and traditions might have meant no moose to hunt next fall.

As William Cronon has written, the Indians' seasonal migration and reluctance to store up extra goods for times of want were likewise essential to their ecological survival. As Miantonomo's 1642 speech suggests, some tribes were more dependent on the field, some on fishing, others on the hunt. The overall pattern, however, was consistent: New England natives lived by—and many moved with—the rhythm of the seasons, continually taking advantage of the resource abundance of each locale's habitat at particular times of the year. Guided by myths that chastised those who did not keep an eye on the future, Indians rarely drew more from the ecosystem than they knew it could provide in the most climatologically severe of seasons. And because they knew what to expect at the next locale, natives carried with them only what they needed, keeping the burden of travel light.[10] They accepted lean times and survived them by consuming less and reproducing less frequently, thereby keeping their population in check. In sum, Indian societies lived for need, esteemed trade items for their use (as opposed to market) value, and were intensely and respectfully conscious of all that provided for their well-being.

Most New England tribes (and countless more across the continent) burned sections of forest undergrowth to create what modern ecologists would call "edge effect"—boundary zones of meadow between forest and grasslands that served as prime habitat for a great diversity of species and therefore excellent hunting ground. Burning had other benefits, too, including the elimination of flies and ticks around Indian settlements and the regeneration of the soil's nutrient base to improve farming. New England Indians were polycroppers— that is, they planted a variety of crops in high density. Grown closely together, a snarl of cornstalks, squash, and beans provided high yields per acre, inhibited weed growth, preserved soil moisture, and supplied a highly balanced protein diet.[11]

On every level the precolonial New England landscape reflected the profound respect that Indians maintained for an environment that met their needs. The abundance and habits of an animal who could sustain the tribe at a certain time of year in a particular place gave spiritual meaning and practical identity to that habitat: "clam-place" or "place of overgrown eels." These animal-place attachments also marked the cyclical movement of the seasons.[12] Places were identified more by their natural features than by any sense of human possession. New England Indians owned not the land but the use of the land. Moreover, those rights were owned not by individuals but rather were held in usufruct by the village sachem, who dispensed parcels to families who were free to use them for the land's appropriate ecological value.[13]

———

All of this seemed quite absurd to the Englishmen who stepped ashore in the fall of 1620. By virtually every standard of Anglican-Christian society, Indians appeared barbaric, reinforcing the long-standing European association of uncivilized country with savage and evil beings. Folk mythology, the Judeo-Christian faith, and the Englishmen's experience in a well-tamed environment together formed clear definitions of what was virtuous and moral, what was rational and civilized, and what was not. Wilderness was not. In his history of the Massachusetts Pilgrims' Plymouth plantation (Selection 3), Governor William Bradford's reference to innumerable "wild beasts and wild men" recalls the sinister wooded regions of Greek and Roman mythology, inhabited by wildly sensual half-human, half-animal gods and demons. Preying on anyone who dared traverse their abode, these spirits cast the forests as dark and forbidding places. Such associations continued into the folklore of virtually every early European people. From the German Wild Huntsman to the Anglo-Saxon Beowulf, stories of human-beast creatures filled the woods of medieval Europe, as Roderick Nash has written.[14] In the minds of Englishmen back home, therefore, these were the images conjured up by Bradford's "savage barbarians."

The Englishmen's God, too, had marked the wilderness as a "wasteland" to which evil men were banished, a "cursed" place of "thistles and thorns." Many of the Bible's nearly three hundred references to wilderness juxtapose such places in opposition to the pleasantly cultivated garden. In the wilderness, civilized men reverted to savagery. Men survived the wilderness and set about taming it. Bradford's narrative reaffirms the Pilgrims' purpose to do just that: his is a religiously colored documentary of an oppressed people enduring extraordinary physical circumstances in order to create a suitable environment where a spiritually pristine community might flourish. Although Jesus, John the Baptist, and medieval monastics also made of wild land a place for contemplative redemption, there is no sense of that here. A century would pass before the late-Puritan preacher Jonathan Edwards posited the receding New England wilderness as a spiritual place that, in hindsight, had sanctified the people's mission from the beginning.[15] Standing on the rocky coast of New England in the 1630s, as Bradford was, the wilderness was no literary abstraction. Having abandoned their civilization and then living at the mercy of a savage forest-dwelling people, the English were left alone with their worst fears. Pilgrims and Puritans could muster nothing less than a defensive disposition to their new surroundings and a godly determination to subdue them.

What about the people who already lived there? It mattered little to most Englishmen that the natives' deliberate burning of the woods increased the supply of game animals at which the colonizers marveled. Indian mixed-crop agriculture impressed the settlers only so far as it helped them survive; it otherwise seemed a tangled mess planted by unknowing Neanderthals who did not know enough to plant in rows. Although they helped to ensure survival of the new settlements through the first difficult winters, these and other subsistence patterns appeared to most English observers to be chaotic and wasteful.[16]

Of greater consequence was the English perception of Indian mobility: to a people whose society was centered on fixed settlements, the seasonal movement of natives reinforced the belief of the invaders that the land was theirs for the taking. Indian migration and a striking lack of fences seemed to the English an invitation to possess it themselves—a presumption further reinforced by the decimation of Indian populations brought by European diseases. "It pleased God to visit these Indians with a great sickness," Bradford reports elsewhere in his narrative. When smallpox and other disease epidemics reduced Indian village numbers by as much as 90 percent, Puritan preachers believed these plagues to be signs that God was "making room for us there." By virtue of the epidemics, "[He] hath hereby cleared out title to the place," as John Winthrop put it.[17] In short, the newcomers saw what they were conditioned to see. (Even when reality should have told them otherwise: in the pueblos of the Southwest, Spanish conquistadors with their Franciscan missionaries kept seeing the mirage of gold and pagans in need of conversion when there was neither.) And they would create what their God, their commercial benefactors, and history seemed to ordain: "For wee must Consider that wee shall be as a City upon a Hill, the eies [eyes] of all people are upon us," as Winthrop famously declared.[18]

The English view of the New England wilderness was not monolithic. Many of Bradford's contemporaries had less a documentary or religious purpose than a commercial one. These writers therefore focused on the astonishing natural resource bounty of New England. Filtering out the unpleasant, feral aspects of the new continent that seemed to possess Bradford, these explorers found what those who sent them were looking for—the raw materials and natural goods that Europeans were increasingly depleting in their own countries. From cod and alewife fish that clouded the waters to an amazing abundance of timber, birds, and mammals, the bounty of "merchantable commodities" dazzled European readers and left many incredulous.[19] Their cataloging reports resemble stock inventories that were clearly designed to lure further investment in the colonial enterprise.

But from whence comes the *virgin* in virgin wilderness? Why a *New* World? The notion of the land's untrammeled virginity grew from the need to minimize, romanticize, or excise entirely the Native American presence in North America and to further validate the chivalrous righteousness of taking the continent. Perhaps most critically, as Carolyn Merchant has argued, there was the long-standing patriarchal impulse to dominate a natural world defined as female. The men who led the Scientific Revolution had conceived the notion of female earth as seductive, wild, and in need of mechanistic control.[20] In 1609, William Strachey described Maine as a female place of "fertility and pleasure" that would produce much bounty, once it was "cleansed" of trees and made into "goodly meadow."[21] In this view, the North American wilderness was virgin because indolent savages were wasting it. It would now be made to produce by virtuous, hardworking Christian men. Evoking both the virgin mythology and Canaan, a biblical place of astonishing bounty, Thomas Morton (Selection 4) suggests that English industrial enterprise and the arts of agricultural husbandry and pastoral stewardship could create a new promised land.[22] For him, Bradford's "hideous wilderness" is a copious and seductive female paradise begging for procreation. His view of the "Savages" is far less prejudicial than the governor's. He is, first, less predisposed to harshly dismiss native practices that seemed to enhance the land's productivity. Indeed, he notes with curious delight the value of Indian burning of forest undergrowth and acknowledges that some colonists have themselves taken up the practice. Morton then finds redeeming value in the natives' "contented," if austere, society.

Darkly forbidding, bountiful, and virgin—these were the large meanings affixed to the continent by the first white Americans. These values reflect well the past culture and history of the colonizers together with the contemporary commercial and spiritual currents of the English project to settle North America. They also foretold the future: from 1620 forward, Englishmen carried on the divinely inspired but furiously secular mission to "improve" the wilderness. By the middle of the seventeenth century, colonists had established permanent settlements based on familiar agricultural patterns. They drew mightily upon the forest, using the timber as well as the agricultural products grown on previously forested land, to trade with Europeans. Vessels from across the Atlantic brought the staples and manufactured items that they could not supply for themselves. Englishmen drained swamps, killed wolves, and built fences to protect domesticated live-stock. They drew the natives—catastrophically weakened by epidemic diseases and the concomitant loss of their shamans and religious be-liefs—into the momentous beaver trade. In the end, European trade brought Indians much more than they bargained for: dependence upon a market system that assigned abstract monetary value to creatures previously thought sacred, a process that undermined ecological bounty and balance. The ecology of Englishmen that supplanted Indian ecol-ogy was economically centered, commodifying resources for the mar-ket and subordinating the natural world to that of men.[23]

Carolyn Merchant chronicles parts of that story in her essay on the breakdown of Abenaki culture (Selection 5). Excerpted from a larger study, Merchant illustrates the destruction of the Abenaki way of life that epitomized the "ecological revolution" of colonial New England. She relates how the cycle of fur trade dependency, coupled with the devastating impact of disease, bore severe consequences for the Abenakis' spiritual life and their material survival. As William Cronon also has argued, as early as 1750 the effects of the first phase of the English ecological revolution on the New England landscape were clear. Environmental manifestations of the colonial economy—deforestation, intensive agricultural cultivation and pastoralism, over-hunting for the market—had led to changes in regional climate, increased flooding and erosion, and the decline of certain valued species.[24]

Merchant argues further on in her study that around the time of the American Revolution, the first phase of ecological transformation was followed by another, more starkly driven by global capitalism and bearing ecological consequences more severe. Colonial farmers, through at least the first half of the eighteenth century, still lived and planted by the rhythm of the seasons and the movement of the stars far more than by the machinations of the market. But the succeeding capitalist transformation, Merchant argues, further dissolved those beliefs and reduced nature to "passive female," a world of lifeless "scientific ob-jects and natural resources" that were so much fuel for ever more in-tensive and mechanized agricultural and industrial systems.[25] Rapidly developing in the first decades of the nineteenth century, the new in-dustrial order redefined the meaning of gender, home, cycles of pro-duction and reproduction, work, and liberty itself. Subsumed by the market, nature no longer was identified by its life-giving properties. In the first decades of the nineteenth century, greater numbers of Americans became more psychically and physically disconnected from nature and more reliant upon a market economy that further dissolved their connections to nature. Under the capitalist ecological paradigm, nature—that is to say, natural resources—was extracted and harvested, measured and quantified, bailed and bundled, sold and resold.

Land became the primary commodity—now mapped on parchment with a Cartesian grid of numbers, lines, and letters. Soon after the formation of the new country, Congress set forth mechanisms for the selling and political development of public lands in the territory northwest of the Ohio River. With subsequent modifications, the Land Ordinance of 1785 and the Northwest Ordinance of 1787 (the latter, Selection 6) became templates by which public lands all the way to the Pacific Coast were surveyed, sold, subdivided, politically organized, and incorporated into the union. The first square of earth surveyed, on the Ohio River at Pennsylvania's western edge, became, in the words of Elliott West, a "kind of polestar for national development, the anchored point of reckoning for more than a billion acres."[26] Moreover, the 1785 law made national policy the redefinition of land that began with the first exchange of property between English colonists and New England tribes. Carved into section and township squares, the value of the land would heretofore be measured by a rational market and a distant government. A simple linear system, as West writes, "presumed to impose a sameness on a magnificently diverse landscape," one that had been defined by natives for its life-giving properties.

And what of the natives who still occupied that land? The Northwest Ordinance answered with spectacularly contradictory language. Even as it promised to keep faith with Indians (Article 3), the law set forth the details of how their lands would be broken by farmers and made part of the United States. In "[setting] down a plan of settlement for land that was already occupied, . . . [the] policy . . . had moved," argues West, "beyond contradiction to schizophrenia."[27] Such perplexities could easily be deferred. Thomas Jefferson led those influential men of the era who believed in the moral and practical virtues of an agrarian life, holding that only a large base of independent, landowning, voting farmers could ensure the future of a democratic republic. As president, Jefferson rejoiced when in 1803 the Louisiana Purchase doubled the nation's acreage and seemed to ensure a perpetual source of land for yeoman farmers.

After the War of 1812 tens of thousands of Americans began to fill up that seemingly limitless horizon exponentially faster than Jefferson had predicted. The central project to take and improve the continent focused American energies westward. To create from the wilderness a "City upon a Hill" was still the mission of men on the continent, as Puritans had believed, but the divine purpose of the enterprise was being subsumed by its more materialist impulses. As the nation became fixed on continental development, the "City" took on a distinctly secular cast. More and more Americans set their eyes upon the marketplace that the world had become. Expansion across the previously impenetrable barrier of the Appalachian Mountains accelerated as increasing numbers of boatmen, timbermen, farmers, and planters were drawn into an expanding, market-based economy. By the middle of the nineteenth century what seemed divinely inspired to men was less a morally pristine society than a burgeoning, capitalizing civilization.[28]

In the South, the expansionist impulse and a slave-based agrarian economy exhausted lands at a furious pace. Eli Whitney's invention of the cotton gin in 1793, along with the flourishing international textile industry, would make cotton king and demand expansion of the region. A cotton- and tobacco-based economy quickened the pace of migration into the Old Southwest, and southerners soon eyed the territory beyond the Mississippi. In the 1820s, Anglo Americans moved in large numbers into Texas—a migration that triggered the movement for Texan independence in the 1830s, and ultimately the Mexican War. In 1845, as the country braced for a war of expansion in the Southwest, John L. O'Sullivan, the editor of the *Democratic Review*, captured the nationalist spirit of the day when he referred to westward movement as the nation's "Manifest Destiny." O'Sullivan spoke confidently of the "boundless future [that would] be the era of American greatness" once conquest was complete. Nothing would stop the "onward march" of Americans who, declared O'Sullivan, represented the pinnacle of human progress, individual achievement, and democratic ideals.[29]

Similarly zealously confident was William Gilpin, who for decades had been an active statesman of, and military champion for, the accelerating westward movement. In 1846, Gilpin articulated the national epoch of expansion in omniscient and benevolent terms (Selection 7). In this brief excerpt is the glorious mission of Manifest Destiny in all its self-righteously bombastic splendor, although it does lack one key element: the fervent, racially charged rhetoric that buttressed much of the mythology of continental conquest. Proponents of Manifest Destiny were certain that God bore a white, Anglo-Saxon face and had given divine sanction to the Christian mission of subjugating both the land and its native populations. As another venerable voice of Manifest Destiny, Missouri's Senator Thomas Hart Benton, had put it, "It would seem that the white race alone received the divine command, to subdue and replenish the earth: for it is the only race that has obeyed it—the only race that hunts out new and distant lands, and even a New World, to subdue and replenish."[30] Cloaked in such divine and indomitable language, the westering of Euro-American civilization could not have failed. Inspired by the immediate desire for Pacific lands sought in the Mexican War, expansionists argued that vanquishing a savage wilderness constituted nothing less than the righteous duty of Americans and the providential fate of God, just as it had from the beginning.

The course of empire transpired, however, in ways that likely would have made Jefferson sick at heart. On the matter of the natives, he had suffered from the same paradoxical thinking that suffused the Northwest Ordinance: the romantic in him had hoped that Native Americans, as people of the land, as living testimony to the antiquity of the landscape he loved so much, might survive in some form even as he rested his hopes for the future of the country in the yeoman farmers who would displace them. Presidents who followed Jefferson had less ambivalence about natives and their lands. Most notably, in the 1830s, Andrew Jackson ordered the westward removal of southeastern tribes along what became known as the Trail of Tears to make way for white farmers, white planters, and their black slaves.

Whether Jefferson would have regretted that tragedy may be arguable, but certainly he would have had greater hopes for the Homestead Act of 1862. Enacted in the second year of the Civil War by a government anxious to reassert its federal authority and expand the physical reach of the Union, the Homestead Act was designed ostensibly to people the trans-Mississippi West with exactly the kind of independent farm folk whom Jefferson had idealized. That law and the subsequent land legislation that stemmed from it did, in fact, allow millions of acres to be settled by farmers. Vastly more millions, however, were commandeered through both legitimate and suspect means by railroads, speculators, and cattle barons, many of whom never set foot on the tall-grass prairie of the Great Plains. The railroads alone, for example, sold more land at five dollars per acre than the total acreage conveyed under the Homestead Act. Manipulation and gross violation of the land laws, combined with generous land grants totaling 158 million acres to the transcontinental railroads, contributed to the incorporation of vast sections of the West after the Civil War. The immense "Bonanza Farms" that emerged in the 1870s in the Red River Valley of the Minnesota-Dakota border region testified dramatically to that phenomenon. Established as part of the financial reorganization of the Northern Pacific Railroad and worked by armies of wage earners, the 34,000-acre Bonanza Farm operation foreshadowed the coming of modern agribusiness that would impose a uniform system of linear, market-driven monocropping upon the once-diverse landscape of the Great Plains.[31] Further, land-management decisions were increasingly made from afar by men in corporate boardrooms whose immediate concern for healthy profits outweighed any considerations about the long-term health and productivity of the land itself.

In the mid-1880s, Native Americans were depicted in the popular press as passive and silent witnesses to the conquest of the West—profound testimony to the success of Manifest Destiny. Note the locomotive on the Bismarck Bridge across the Missouri River. *The Northwest* (February 1883): 1.

As this story rushes forward, it inevitably skims the surface. It is important to note in passing that most small farmers resisted tenaciously the machinations of a distant market economy. The first generations of American settlers might best be thought of as lying between the earth-bound ways of natives and the full-blown capitalization of nature. For colonial farmers of eighteenth-century New England, for Illinois plowmen of the early nineteenth century, and for Mennonite farmers of the 1930s, the land was life itself, the organic center of family and community.[32] But the world beyond was fast reducing nature to cold hard cash, a means to private wealth. Through numerous mechanisms—the control of prices and transportation and storage rates, the lure of newly manufactured goods that could not be made at home, the mounting burden of indebtedness—market capitalism steadily encroached, attaching itself to every locale by the end of the nineteenth century. Willingly or not, small farmers were inexorably pulled into ever more intensively extractive, mechanized systems of drawing a living from the earth. More swamps were drained, more wolves killed, more fences (eventually of barbed wire) constructed.

The upshot for nature and Indians was profound. The life-giving earth of the Pueblos and Abenakis had become dollarable squares on an expanding grid. Capitalizing, industrializing, westward-moving society drew heavily upon the country's natural "capital" and left diseased, displaced, and decimated Indian tribes in its wake. Consider a few of the ramifications of the capitalist ecological revolution in the nineteenth century: forests in every region were felled at increasingly rapid rates to supply shipbuilders and to build and heat the homes and businesses of an expanding population; rivers were diverted to power mills that produced an increasing bounty of manufactured products, along with thousands of miles of fouled rivers and streams; cotton and tobacco flourished in the South even as those crops heavily exhausted soils and relied upon the most brutal form of labor known to humanity, racially based chattel slavery; railroads linked the country and accelerated the extraction and delivery of resources to expanding markets; bison were slaughtered by the millions on the Great Plains between 1860 and 1883, an annihilation of staggering proportions that supplied industrial machinery, hastened the defeat of Indian tribes, and readied the range for cattle herds that were driven to Chicago slaughterhouses to feed the middle class. Finally, during and after the Civil War, new technological processes emerged that helped to make the United States the leading industrial nation in the world but also, in combination with other forces, brought unprecedented environmental and social transformations.

This brief overview concludes in California, witness to some of the most dramatic manifestations of the capitalist ecological revolution. In the mid-1840s emigrants by the hundreds and then thousands began heading west on the Oregon and Santa Fe Trails. Many of them were destined for California, the great prize sought most eagerly by President James K. Polk in the Mexican War.[33] Before the discovery of gold, before the winning of the Mexican War (indeed, helping to trigger it), there was the promise of rich and fertile California lands just waiting to be made productive and profitable by Anglo Americans. The editor of the Monterey *Californian* recalls the agricultural potential of the region that constituted the "great promise of California" (Selection 8). There is in this short passage the confident assurance that Anglo Americans, unlike Mexican and Native American populations of the Pacific Coast, could make something of these lands.

By 1883, all that remained in the wake of the bison slaughter were bleaching bones, waiting to be shipped east and pulverized into fertilizer. Martin S. Garretson, 1913.

Divine, immediate confirmation of the nation's Manifest Destiny came in the spring of 1848 with the discovery of gold at John Sutter's mill in northern California. At the very moment when the Mexican War came to an end—again greatly enlarging the size of the nation—the discovery of gold on the American River was further evidence that God and history were on the side of the Americans. This would prove to be just the first of a forty-year wave of mineral strikes across the West that brought great wealth to a few, new entrepreneurial opportunities to others, and disillusioning wage labor to many more of the tens of thousands of people who went there dreaming of a great strike.

It took only a few years for the placer deposits of gold to be exhausted by small-time prospectors working their claims with pan or pick and shovel. By the end of the 1850s, large infusions of capital and technology were necessary to bore and tunnel into and blast away the rock and soil that covered the gold that remained. The technologically driven development and incorporation of the mineral West displaced individual miners and increased the concentration of wealth and political power throughout the region.[34]

The Gold Rush was a pivotal event in the building of modern California and the West. But for both Anglo and Hispano farmers and for native populations, the event brought environmental and social degradation. Once developed beyond the romantic stage of pick and shovel, the mining industry became an environmental nightmare. Most notoriously, the hydraulic technique of using high-pressure, high-volume water hoses to expose the ore lying beneath rock and soil at times both flooded farmers' fields and sapped their sources of irrigable water. Further, the use of mercury, or "quicksilver," to amalgamate smaller particles of gold dust resulted in the poisoning of entire watersheds. It took decades for political courage and legal remedies to emerge that would challenge the economic and political power of the California mining industry.[35]

The successful climax of Manifest Destiny and the capitalizing of the West held other legacies. The discovery of gold in California, silver in Nevada, gold again in Colorado, copper in Montana, and other subsequent strikes across the West led to the establishment of the 1872 Mining Law that would lure more individuals to further develop the region's mineral resources. Just as the land laws bore a number of undemocratic consequences, likewise the 1872 Mining Law served to further concentrate wealth into the hands of those few who had the means to extract the riches from deep within the earth. It also would leave an appalling environmental legacy more than a century later. Because, of course, no environmental regulations were attached to the 1872 law, and because of the continuing political strength of the mining industry, by the close of the twentieth century more than 0.5 million abandoned hard-rock mining claims littered the landscape with a staggering cost of more than $50 billion for environmental cleanup.[36]

For Native Americans, the gold rush triggered a decimation of genocidal proportions. Through violent confrontations and disease, California's native population was reduced from around 300,000 to fewer than 25,000 by 1880. California native Joaquin Miller offers a grim survey of that environmental and social landscape at century's end (Selection 9). None of this escaped the eye of the Indians themselves, whose worlds lay largely shattered by the end of the nineteenth century. In 1925 a Wintu, Kate Luckie, recorded a prophesy of ecological doom for the people who had engineered the California mining industry (Selection 10). Luckie waxes elegiacally on this celebrated chapter of American history. She poignantly recalls the animistic world view that once prevailed among the human societies of North America but which had fallen before the march of a civilization with entirely different views of nature.

NOTES

1. "Leift Lion Gardener His Relation of the Pequot Warres," Massachusetts Historical Society Collections, 3rd series 3 (1833), 154–55, quoted in William Cronon, *Changes in the Land: Indians, Colonists, and the Ecology of New England* (New York: Hill and Wang, 1983), 162.
2. For a brilliant essay on the subject of the Virgin Myth, see Noel Perrin, "Forever Virgin: The American View of America," in Daniel Halpern, ed., *On Nature: Nature, Landscape, and Natural History* (San Francisco: North Point Press, 1987), 13–22.
3. Among the classic American Studies works to probe the connection of myth and environment are Peter J. Schmitt, *Back to Nature: The Arcadian Myth in Urban America*, with Foreword by John R. Stilgoe (Baltimore: Johns Hopkins University Press, 1969); Annette Kolodny, *The Lay of the Land: Metaphor as Experience and History in American Life and Letters* (Chapel Hill: University of North Carolina Press, 1975); Leo Marx, *The Machine In the Garden: Technology and the Pastoral Ideal in America* (New York: Oxford University Press, 1964); Carolyn Merchant, *The Death of Nature: Women, Ecology, and the Scientific Revolution* (San Francisco: Harper and Row, 1980); and Henry Nash Smith's *Virgin Land: The American West as Symbol and Myth* (Cambridge, MA: Harvard University Press, 1958).
4. William Brandon, narr., Alvin M. Josephy, Jr., ed., for the editors of American *Heritage, The American Heritage Book of Indians*, with Introduction by John F. Kennedy (New York: American Heritage, 1961), 110.
5. Carolyn Merchant, *Ecological Revolutions: Nature, Gender, and Science in New England* (Chapel Hill: University of North Carolina Press, 1989), see especially 1–26.
6. Marta Weigle and Peter White, *The Lore of New Mexico* (Albuquerque: University of New Mexico Press, 1988), 14.
7. Ibid., 22.
8. Peter Iverson, "Native Peoples and Native Histories," in Clyde A. Milner II, Carol A. O'Connor, and Martha A. Sandweiss, eds., *The Oxford History of the American West* (New York: Oxford University Press, 1994), 29.
9. Merchant, *Ecological Revolutions*, 44–50.
10. Cronon, *Changes in the Land*, 47–53.

11. Ibid., 42–46.
12. Merchant, *Ecological Revolutions*, 48–51.
13. Cronon, *Changes in the Land*, 62–67.
14. Roderick Nash, *Wilderness and the American Mind*, 3rd ed. (New Haven: Yale University Press, 1982), 11–13. Nash provides an excellent summary of the classical and folkloric roots of evil wilderness.
15. Ibid., 17–19; Perry Miller, *Errand into the Wilderness* (New York: Harper and Row, 1956), 153–66.
16. Cronon, *Changes in the Land*, 33–53, 58.
17. John Winthrop to Sir Simond D'Ewes, July 21, 1634, in Everett Emerson, ed., *Letters from New England* (Amherst, MA, 1976), 116, quoted in Cronon, *Changes in the Land*, 90.
18. John Winthrop, quoted in Perry Miller, *Errand into the Wilderness*, 11.
19. Cronon, *Changes in the Land*, 19–33. As Cronon notes on p. 20, the term "merchantable commodities" belongs to Richard Hakluyt's classic 1584 treatise on western exploration, *Discourse Concerning Western Planting*.
20. See Merchant, *The Death of Nature*.
21. For a brilliant explication of this myth as it applied to westward migration in the nineteenth century, see Richard Slotkin, *The Fatal Environment: The Myth of the Frontier in the Age of Industrialization, 1800–1890* (New York: Atheneum, 1985).
22. William Strachey's account of the colony of Sagadahoc, Maine, "Extract" (1609), quoted by Carolyn Merchant, *Ecological Revolutions*, 101; and Thomas Morton, "New English Canaan" (1632), quoted by Annette Kolodny, *The Lay of the Land*, 12.
23. Cronon, *Changes in the Land*, 127–56.
24. Ibid., 122–26.
25. Merchant, *Ecological Revolutions*, 24–25.
26. Elliott West, "American Frontier," in Milner, O'Connor, and Sandweiss, eds., *Oxford History of the American West*, 124.
27. Ibid., 125–26.
28. Miller, *Errand into the Wilderness*, title of Miller's brilliant book and essay; argument summarizes the final chapter, "The End of the World," 217–39.
29. John L. O'Sullivan, "The Great Nation of Futurity," *The United States Magazine and Democratic Review* 6 (November 1845): 2–3, 6.
30. Speech of Missouri Senator Thomas Hart Benton to the U.S. Congress in 1846.
31. Chris J. Magoc, *Yellowstone: The Creation and Selling of an American Landscape* (Albuquerque: University of New Mexico Press, 1999), 23–26; Alan Trachtenberg, *The Incorporation of America* (New York: Hill and Wang, 1982), 19–22. See also Slotkin, *The Fatal Environment*, 284–85; and Smith, *Virgin Land*, 190–93.
32. See Merchant, *Ecological Revolutions*, 149–97; John Mack Faragher, *Sugar Creek: Life on the Illinois Prairie* (New Haven: Yale University Press, 1986); and Donald Worster, *Dust Bowl: The Southern Plains in the 1930s* (New York: Oxford University Press, 1979).
33. Clyde A. Milner II, "National Initiatives," in Milner, O'Connor, and Sandweiss, eds., *Oxford History of the American West*, 167.

34. Keith L. Bryant, Jr., "Entering the Global Economy," in Milner, O'Connor, and Sandweiss, eds., *Oxford History of the American West*, 197–201.
35. J. S. Holliday, *Rush for Riches: Gold Fever and the Making of California* (Berkeley: Oakland Museum of California and the University of California Press, 1999), 142, 164, 246–60.
36. Natural Resources Defense Council, *http://www.nrdc.org/triv/mmet.html*, October 1999.

1 | Acoma Pueblo Creation Myth

In the beginning two female human beings were born. These two children were born underground at a place called Shipapu. As they grew up, they began to be aware of each other. There was no light and they could only feel each other. Being in the dark, they grew slowly.

After they had grown considerably, a Spirit whom they afterward called Tsichtinako spoke to them, and they found that it would give them nourishment. After they had grown large enough to think for themselves, they spoke to the Spirit when it had come to them one day and asked it to make itself known to them and to say whether it was male or female, but it replied only that it was not allowed to meet with them. They then asked why they were living in the dark without knowing each other by name, but the Spirit answered that they were nuk'timi (under the earth); but they were to be patient in waiting until everything was ready for them to go up into the light. So they waited a long time, and as they grew they learned their language from Tsichtinako.

When all was ready, they found a present from Tsichtinako, two baskets of seeds and little images of all the different animals (there were to be) in the world. The Spirit said they were sent by their father . . . and that he wished them to take their baskets out into the light, when the time came. . . .

[The women planted unseen seeds from their baskets, and the trees grew slowly toward the light. Before their emergence, when, thanks to

From "Acoma Pueblo Creation Myth," Matthew W. Stirling, *Origin Myth of Acoma and Other Records*, in U.S. Bureau of American Ethnology *Bulletin* 135 (Washington, DC: Government Printing Office, 1942), 1, 3–4.

their helpers Badger and Locust, they could see the light above, Tsichtinako "taught them the prayers and the creation song, which they were to sing," and the animals helped them to the surface.] . . .

The earth was soft and spongy under their feet as they walked, and they said, "This is not ripe." They stood waiting for the sun, not knowing where it would appear. Gradually it grew lighter and finally the sun came up. Before they began to pray, Tsichtinako told them they were facing east and that their right side, the side their best aim was on, would be known as kū'ā'mē (south) and the left ti dyami (north) while behind at their backs was the direction pūna'me (west) where the sun would go down. They had already learned while underground the direction nūk'ūm' (down) and later, when they asked where their father was, they were told tyunami (four skies above). . . .

They now prayed to the Sun as they had been taught by Tsichtinako, and sang the creation song. Their eyes hurt for they were not accustomed to the strong light. For the first time they asked Tsichtinako why they were on earth and why they were created. Tsichtinako replied, "I did not make you. Your father, Uchtsiti, made you, and it is he who has made the world, the sun which you have seen, the sky, and many other things which you will see. But Uchtsiti says the world is not yet completed, not yet satisfactory, as he wants it. This is the reason he has made you. You will rule and bring to life the rest of the things he has given you in the baskets." The sisters then asked how they themselves had come into being. Tsichtinako answered, saying, "Uchtsiti first made the world. He threw a clot of his own blood into space and by his power it grew and grew until it became the earth. Then Uchtsiti planted you in this and by it you were nourished as you developed. Now that you have emerged from within the earth, you will have to provide nourishment for yourselves. I will instruct you in this." Then they asked where their father lived and . . . why Tsichtinako did not become visible to them. . . . And they asked again how they were to live, whether they could go down once more under the ground, for they were afraid of the winds and rains and their eyes were hurt by the light. Tsichtinako replied that Uchtsiti would take care of that and would furnish them means to keep warm and change the atmosphere so that they would get used to it.

At the end of the first day, when it became dark they were much frightened, for they had not understood that the sun would set and thought that Tsichtinako had betrayed them. "Tsichtinako! Tsichtinako! You told us we were to come into the light," they cried. "Why, then, is it dark?" So Tsichtinako explained, "This is the way it will always be. The sun will go down and the next day come up anew in the east. When it is dark you are to rest and sleep as you slept when all was dark." So they were satisfied and slept. They rose to meet the sun, praying to it as they had been told, and were happy when it came up again, for they were warm and their faith in Tsichtinako was restored.

2 | Tewa Sky Looms

Oh our Mother the Earth, oh our Father the Sky,
Your children are we, and with tired backs
We bring you the gifts that you love.
Then weave for us a garment of brightness;
May the warp be the white light of morning,
May the weft be the red light of evening,
May the fringes be the falling rain,
May the border be the standing rainbow.
Thus weave for us a garment of brightness
That we may walk fittingly where birds sing,
That we may walk fittingly where grass is green,
Oh our Mother the Earth, oh our Father the Sky!

From *Songs of the Tewa*, trans. Herbert Joseph Spinden (1933; reprint Santa Fe, NM: Sunstone Press, 1976), 94. Reprinted by permission of Sunstone Press.

WILLIAM BRADFORD

3 A Hideous and Desolate Wilderness (1647)

Being thus arrived in a good harbor, and brought safe to land, they fell upon their knees and blessed the God of Heaven[1] who had brought them over the vast and furious ocean, and delivered them from all the perils and miseries thereof, again to set their feet on the firm and stable earth, their proper element. And no marvel if they were thus joyful, seeing wise Seneca was so affected with sailing a few miles on the coast of his own Italy, as he affirmed, that he had rather remain twenty years on his way by land than pass by sea to any place in a short time, so tedious and dreadful was the same unto him.[2]

But here I cannot but stay and make a pause, and stand half amazed at this poor people's present condition; and so I think will the reader, too, when he well considers the same. Being thus passed the vast ocean, and a sea of troubles before in their preparation (as may be remembered by that which went before), they had now no friends to welcome them nor inns to entertain or refresh their weatherbeaten bodies; no houses or much less towns to repair to, to seek for succour. It is recorded in Scripture[3] as a mercy to the Apostle and his shipwrecked company, that the barbarians showed them no small kindness in refreshing them, but these savage barbarians, when they met with them (as after will appear) were readier to fill their sides full of arrows than otherwise. And for the season it was winter, and they that know the winters of that country know them to be sharp and violent, and sub-

From William Bradford, *Of Plimoth Plantation* (Boston: Wright and Potter, 1901), 94–97.

ject to cruel and fierce storms, dangerous to travel to known places, much more to search an unknown coast. Besides, what could they see but a hideous and desolate wilderness, full of wild beasts and wild men—and what multitudes there might be of them they knew not. Neither could they, as it were, go up to the top of Pisgah to view from this wilderness a more goodly country to feed their hopes; for which way soever they turned their eyes (save upward to the heavens) they could have little solace or content in respect of any outward objects. For summer being done, all things stand upon them with a weatherbeaten face, and the whole country, full of woods and thickets, represented a wild and savage hue. If they looked behind them, there was the mighty ocean which they had passed and was now as a main bar and gulf to separate them from all the civil parts of the world. If it be said they had a ship to succour them, it is true; but what heard they daily from the master and company? But that with speed they should look out a place (with their shallop) [small open boat] where they would be, at some near distance; for the season was such as he would not stir from thence till a safe harbor was discovered by them, where they would be, and he might go without danger; and that victuals consumed apace but he must and would keep sufficient for themselves and their return. Yea, it was muttered by some that if they got not a place in time, they would turn them and their goods ashore and leave them. Let it also be considered what weak hopes of supply and succour they left behind them, that might bear up their minds in this sad condition and trials they were under; and they could not but be very small. It is true, indeed, the affections and love of their brethren at Leyden was cordial and entire towards them, but they had little power to help them or themselves; and how the case stood between them and the merchants at their coming away hath already been declared.

What could now sustain them but the Spirit of God and His grace? May not and ought not the children of these fathers rightly say: "Our fathers were Englishmen which came over this great ocean, and were ready to perish in this wilderness; but they cried unto the Lord, and He heard their voice and looked on their adversity,"[4] etc. "Let them therefore praise the Lord, because He is good: and His mercies endure forever." "Yea, let them which have been redeemed of the Lord, shew how He hath delivered them from the hand of the oppressor. When they wandered in the desert wilderness out of the way, and found no city to dwell in, both hungry and thirsty, their soul was overwhelmed in them. Let them confess before the Lord His loving kindness and His wonderful works before the sons of men."[5]

NOTES

1. Daniel ii.19.
2. Epistle 53 (Bradford). The sentence is in Seneca, *Epistulae Morales ad Lucilium* liii §5: *Et ego quocumque navigare debuero, vicesimo anno perveniam.*
3. Acts xxviii (Bradford); verse 2.
4. Deuteronomy xxvi.5, 7 (Bradford).
5. Psalm cvii.1–5, 8 (Bradford).

THOMAS MORTON

4 | Potential of the New English Canaan (1632)

The Author's Prologue

If art & industry should doe as much
As Nature hath for Canaan, not such
Another place, for benefit and rest,
In all the universe can be possest,
The more we proove it by discovery,
The more delight each objcct to the eye
Procures, as if the elements had here
Bin reconcil'd, and pleas'd it should appeare,
Like a faire virgin, longing to be sped,
And meete her lover in a Nuptiall bed,
Deck'd in rich ornaments t'advaunce her state
And excellence, being most fortunate,
When most enjoy'd, so would our Canaan be
If well employ'd by art and industry
Whose offspring, now shewes that her fruitfull wombe
Not being enjoy'd, is like a glorious tombe,
Admired things producing which there dye,
And ly fast bound in darck obscurity,
The worth of which in each particuler,
Who list to know, this abstract will declare.

From Thomas Morton, "The New English Canaan," in *Tracts and Other Papers Relating Principally to the Origin, Settlement, and Progress of the Colonies in North America from the Discovery of the Country to the Year 1776*, 4 vols., ed. Peter Force (Washington, DC: Peter Force, 1838), 2:10, 36–37, 38–39, 41–44.

Of their Custome in burning the Country, and the reason thereof

The Salvages are accustomed, to set fire of the Country in all places where they come; and to burne it, twize a yeare, vixe [viz.] at the Spring, and the fall of the leafe. The reason that mooves them to doe so, is because it would other wise be so overgrowne with underweedes, that it would be all a copice wood, and the people would not be able in any wise to passe through the Country out of a beaten path. . . .

And least their firing of the Country in this manner; should be an occasion of damnifying us, and indaingering our habitations; wee our selves have used carefully about the same times; to observe the winds and fire the grounds about our owne habitations, to prevent the Dammage that might happen by any neglect thereof, if the fire should come neere those howses in our absence.

For when the fire is once kindled, it dilates and spreads it selfe as well against, as with the winde; burning continually night and day, untill a shower of raine falls to quench it.

And this custome of firing the Country is the meanes to make it passable, and by that meanes the trees growe here, and there as in our parks: and makes the Country very beautifull, and commodious. . . .

That the Salvages live a contented life

A Gentleman and a traveller, that had bin in the parts of New England for a time, when hee retorned againe in his discourse of the Country, wondered (as hee said,) that the natives of the land lived so poorely, in so rich a Country, like to our Beggers in England: Surely that Gentleman had not time or leasure whiles hee was there, truely to informe himselfe of the state of that Country, and the happy life the Salvages would leade weare they once brought to Christianity. I must confesse they want the use and benefit of Navigation (which is the very sinnus [sinews?] of a flourishing Commonwealth,) yet are they supplied with all manner of needfull things, for the maintenance of life and lifelyhood, Foode and rayment are the cheife of all that we make true use of; and of these they finde no want, but have them in a most plentifull manner.

If our beggers of England should with so much ease (as they,) furnish themselves with foode, at all seasons, there would not be so many starved in the streets, neither would so many gaoles [jails] be stuffed, or gallouses [gallows] furnished with poore wretches, as I have seene them. . . .

The general Survey of the Country

In the Moneth of June, Anno Salutis: 1622. It was my chaunce to arrive in the parts of New England with 30. Servants, and provision of all sorts fit for a plantation: And whiles our howses were building, I did endeavour to take a survey of the Country: The more I looked, the more I liked it.

And when I had more seriously considered of the bewty of the place, with all her faire indowments, I did not thinke that in all the knowne world it could be paralel'd. For so many goodly groues of trees; dainty fine round rising hillucks: delicate faire large plaines, sweete cristall fountaines, and cleare running streames, that twine in fine meanders through the meads [meadows], making so sweete a murmering noise to heare, as would even lull the sences with delight a sleepe, so pleasantly doe, they glide upon the pebble stones, jetting most jocundly where they doe meete; and hand in hand runne downe to Neptunes Court, to pay the yearely tribute, which they owe to him as soveraigne Lord of all the springs. Contained within the volume of the Land, Fowles in abundance, Fish in multitude, and discovered besides; Millions of Turtledoves one the greene boughes: which sate pecking, of the full ripe pleasant grapes, that were supported by the lusty trees, whose fruitfull loade did cause the armes to bend, which here and there dispersed (you might see) Lillies and of the Daphnean-tree, which made the Land to mee seeme paradice, for in mine eie, t'was Natures Master-peece: Her cheifest Magazine of, all where lives her store: if this Land be not rich, then is the whole world poore. . . .

What trees are there and how commodious

Oakes are there of two sorts, white and redd, excellent tymber for the building, both of howses, and shipping: and they are found to be a tymber, that is more tough then the oak of England. They are excellent for pipe-staves and such like vessels; and pipe-staves at the Canary Ilands are a prime commodity, I have knowne them there at 35. p. the 1000, and will purchase a fraight of wines there before any commodity in England, their onely wood being pine, of which they are enforced, also to build shippinge; of oackes there is great abundance in the parts of New England, and they may have a prime place in the Catalogue of commodities.

Ashe there is store and very good for staves, oares or pipes, and may have a place in the same Catalogue.

Elme: of this sort of trees, there are some; but there hath not as yet bin found any quantity to speake of.

Beech there is of two sorts, redd and white very excellent for trenchers [platters for food], or chaires and also for oares and may be accompted for a commodity.

Wallnutt, of this sorte of wood there is infinite store and there are 4 sorts, it is an excellent wood, for many uses approved, the younger trees are imployed for hoopes, and are the best for that imployement of all other stuffe whatsoever, the Nutts serve when they fall to feede our swine, which make them the delicatest bacon of all other foode, and is therein a cheife commodity.

Chestnutt, of this sorte there is very greate plenty; the tymber whereof is excellent for building and is a very good commodity, especially in respect of the fruit, both for man and beast.

Pine, of this sorte there is infinite store in some parts of the Country. I have travelled 10. miles together, where is little, or no other wood growing. And of these may be made rosin, pitch, and tarre, which are such usefull commodities, that if wee had them not from other Countries in Amity with England, our Navigation would decline. Then how great the commodity of it will be to our Nation, to have it of our owne, let any man judge.

CAROLYN MERCHANT

5 Fate of the Abenaki in the Colonial Ecological Revolution

The breakdown of Abenaki subsistence was a process of interaction between the fur trade that disrupted traditional gathering and hunting production and introduced diseases that disrupted biological and social reproduction. Externally caused by ecological additions and withdrawals, it opened the way for a new symbolic system in which the transcendent God of Christianity replaced Abenaki animism.

The fur trade of New England that would devastate beaver and Indian began inauspiciously as an extension of regular fishing expeditions from Bristol, England, to the Newfoundland coast around 1480. The cod banks also attracted fishermen from France and Portugal as well as coastal explorers such as John Cabot (1497), Giovanni da Verrazzano (1524), and Jacques Cartier (1534). The Indians of Narragansett Bay received Verrazzano in the tradition of native reciprocity exchange patterns, trading mainly for decorative copper earrings and necklaces.

In the north, however, early exchanges involved tools and utensils. The shrewd Abenaki of present-day Maine, whose experience of the fur trade had included kidnappings by Portuguese and Spanish explorers, traded only off treacherous coastal rocks and demanded

From Carolyn Merchant, *Ecological Revolutions: Nature, Gender, and Science in New England* (Chapel Hill: University of North Carolina Press, 1989), 52–58, 60–61. © 1989 by the University of North Carolina Press. Reprinted by permission of the University of North Carolina Press.

from Verrazzano "knives, hooks for fishing, and sharp metal" for tools more durable than their own. To their north, Micmac Indians on the Saint Lawrence Gulf, who waved sticks with furs to attract Cartier in 1534, also wanted the metal tools that would facilitate hunting, fishing, cooking, and sewing. Far from being passive pawns at the hands of unscrupulous traders, these Indians recognized the advantages of the new tools for their own subsistence. But as iron arrowheads, axes, knives, and kettles gradually replaced decomposable bone hooks, wooden arrows, and bark baskets, the material base of the gathering-hunting economy was transformed by a technology the Indians themselves did not control. The adoption of utilitarian technologies absorbed into gathering-hunting production initiated a transition that would ultimately become an ecological revolution in northern New England.

In the mid-sixteenth century fishermen established salt-processing stations on shore in order to increase and lighten their cargoes, and began bargaining for pelts with the Indians of Labrador, Newfoundland, and Nova Scotia. Trade quickened in the 1580s when the Indians of the Saint Lawrence River provided sufficient furs to lower the price of the new beaver hats described by Philip Stubbes.[1]

While the earliest exchanges of commodities for furs were a by-product of fishing expeditions, mercantile capitalists financed explorers who scouted the New England coast for profits from the beaver trade. Martin Pring, who set out to look for fish, furs, timber, and sassafras (a reputed cure for syphilis), explored the Massachusetts coast in 1603 and enthusiastically envisioned profits from the furs of the many "wild beasts" he saw there. In the year 1604 alone, Pring reported, the French had imported from Canada beaver and otter skins amounting to 30,000 crowns. On his visits to the Maine coast in 1604, 1605, and 1606, Samuel de Champlain offered the Penobscot Indians the opportunity to "hunt the beaver more than they had ever done, and barter these beaver with us in exchange." Captain John Smith identified New England's potential for furs, as well as fish and timber, on his voyage of 1614 from the Penobscot to Cape Cod. Here he "got for trifles near eleven hundred beaver skins, one hundred martins, and as many otters." He estimated "of beavers, otters, martins, black foxes, and furs of price may yearly be had 6 or 7000 [pelts] and if the trade of the French were prevented, many more: 25,000 this year were brought from those northern parts into France."[2]

English exploitation of Abenaki furs commenced in earnest with George Weymouth's expedition to the coast of Maine in 1605. When three Abenaki dressed in beaver skins approached his ship, Weymouth signaled his desire to trade for pelts. Twenty-eight Indians returned the following day with forty beaver, otter, and sable pelts which they exchanged for "knives, glasses, combs, and other trifles to the value of four or five shillings." Seemingly eager for additional trading, an assemblage of 283 Indians with bows, arrows, and dogs encouraged the crew of fifteen to proceed farther up the river where more furs were allegedly stored. Instead, the now suspicious Weymouth kidnapped five Indians as insurance against future mischief and soon afterward set sail for England with glowing reports of abundant timber, fish, and furs in the new land.[3]

Two years later the English colonists George Popham and Raleigh Gilbert returned to establish a trading center at the mouth of the Kennebec, bringing with them one of Weymouth's Indians as a guide. Indian women, barely visible during Weymouth's visit, were now actively engaged in trading beaver. Having received higher prices from the French, the women demanded more than the English were willing to pay and were rejected. By spring, however, the colonists had traded a fairly good supply of furs and completed a fort. They were enthusiastic about the fertility of the land, the abundance of spruce trees for masts, and the "goodness" of the oak and walnut trees that grew open and free of thickets as in "our parks in England." Despite these successes and the eagerness of the Abenaki to trade, the harsh winter forced the colonists to return home. Nevertheless, both the English and the French continued to send trading vessels every year, exchanging iron knives, fishhooks, hatchets, kettles, and food for pelts. Faced with attacks by the Micmac to the north, who had greater access to European weapons and tools, and fated with a short growing season with sparse crop yields, the Abenaki soon came to depend on the Europeans for bread, peas, beans, and prunes and on the southern New England tribes for corn. Furs provided the exchange values needed for the European tools and food required for subsistence. What had begun as adaptation and absorption became dependency.[4]

Indians, with their access to a resource in demand as a symbol of status by upwardly mobile Europeans, were thus drawn into a system of worldwide mercantile exchange. Mercantile capitalism soon linked European capital with American natural resources and African labor in a pattern of money-mediated trading relationships often involving triangular voyages. The integral components of balanced ecosystems in the colonies became natural resources yielding fish, furs, and timber. Enslaved Africans were transported to the New World to become human resources helping to produce the profitable monocultures of tobacco, rice, sugar, and eventually cotton. Gold and silver extracted from the American earth fueled the process and financed the voyages of the adventurers. The dependency of native American production on mercantile capitalism was the first phase of the colonial ecological revolution in northern New England.

While the first impact of Europeans had affected the relations of production, offering the Indians the means to hunt beavers and other animals more efficiently for subsistence and exchange, the second altered the relations of reproduction. In 1616 disease struck the villages. From a population of about 10,000 in 1605, the Abenaki were within a few years reduced to 3,000, resulting in abandonment of over half the villages. The disease was probably either smallpox or a type of bubonic or pneumonic plague, originating along the shores of Massachusetts Bay in 1616 and spreading northward over the next four years to the Kennebec River and Penobscot Bay, leaving fields and villages barren in its wake. Plague is transmitted by rats and fleas as well as human contagion. By the time of Champlain's voyages of 1603–6 rats had been observed leaving European ships, while infestations of fleas in Indian summer wigwams were noted in colonial accounts. A letter of 1619 describes the epidemic's effect on the peoples of the Maine coast: "in other places a remnant remains, but not free from sickness. Their disease the plague, for [so] we might perceive the sores of some that had escaped, who described the spots of such as usually die."[5]

The impact of this crisis in reproduction on Indian subsistence was drastic. Women too weak to plant or gather and men unable to hunt lay helpless in their wigwams. Hunting band cohesion on which the success of the hunt depended was destroyed. Family hunting grounds evolved into trapping territories as tribes gave up winter hunting in small family bands and remained in permanent villages near the coast. The regulatory role of chiefs and shamans was also undercut. By 1624 only seven Abenaki sagamores remained to lead their people. The traditional power of shamans to assign rewards and punishments was rendered ineffective in the face of the unknown illnesses. A second major epidemic in 1638, this time smallpox, accentuated the changes initiated by the devastations observed in 1619.[6]

The demographic catastrophes that rendered the Abenaki more dependent on exchange for their own subsistence afforded the colonists an opportunity for trading expansion. The Plymouth Pilgrims, who themselves needed a resource to exchange for European merchandise, turned to the fur trade. By 1621 they had already obtained from the Massachusetts Bay Indians two hogsheads (each weighing 400 pounds) of beaver and other skins worth £500. Expanding northward, they traded a boatload of corn to the Abenaki for 700 pounds of beaver pelts. After the discovery by the Dutch in 1628 of the value of wampum (strings of white and purple shell beads produced by the Pequot and Narragansett for religious ceremonies) among the more distant tribes, the Pilgrims, aided both by their easy access to wampum and by their corn surpluses, established successful trading houses on the Kennebec River. In 1636, Pilgrim exports to England since the time of settlement had reached some 12,000 pounds of beaver pelts and 1,000 pounds of otter.[7] . . .

The devastating changes in biological reproduction were soon followed by equally momentous changes in social reproduction that altered land tenure. In place of the Indian view of the habitat as tribal home, the English imposed a legal concept of private property that would convert Indian lands to trapping territories. To the Indian, white pressure to cede territory meant extending hunting and fishing privileges on tribal homelands to the newcomers. To the English, however, it meant release of all tribal rights. Thus, two different interpretations of land tenure were operating when, in 1646, Nutahanada, son of the sagamore of the Kennebec River, transferred his lands to William Bradford, "to have and to hold to them and their heirs forever with all the woods, waters, soils, profits, liberties, and privileges any way belonging thereunto or arising from the same for and in consideration of two hogsheads of provisions, one of bread, and one of peas, two coats of cloth, two gallons of wine and a bottle of strong waters."[8]

Home to the English would mean the family farm on which colonists reproduced the family's subsistence through property inheritance by male sons and on which resources such as potash and lumber could be obtained for exchange. Massachusetts Bay merchants who bought land from the Maine Indians in the 1640s began cutting pines and shipping them to England. English settlements appeared at the mouths of rivers along the Maine and New Hampshire coasts where white pine masts, yards, spars, bowsprits, and naval stores could be cut and shipped to England. Sawmill owners soon realized lucrative profits and were able to add general stores and gristmills. The estate of Major Nicholas Shapleigh of Kittery, Maine (d. 1682), for example, included an elaborately furnished farmhouse with several Irish and black servants, farmlands with outlying marshes and fields, a grist-mill, a blacksmith shop, a sawmill, 10,000 feet of boards, timber chains, mast wheels, mast chains, shallops, canoes, eleven oxen, and yokes all related to the timber trade. Henry Sayword, who died in 1679, owned a sawmill valued at £150 and 347 acres of land at £314, for a net worth of nearly £600. Less wealthy men such as John Batson (d. 1685), with holdings worth £130, claimed half a sawmill. The estate of Sarah Tricky and her deceased son, whose total worth was £153, revealed two hand-saws, a whipsaw, and a crosscut saw—all items of use in the lumber trade.[9]

By the 1640s, the relations of production and reproduction in Abenaki subsistence had been drastically altered. Withdrawals of animals and trees as commodities changed the ecology of ponds, rivers, and forests. In turn, the loss of traditional habitats in the Indian homeland meant fewer resources for subsistence production. Moreover, additions of European pathogens and people undercut patterns of biological and social reproduction, further disrupting the relations of production. These dialectical processes between production and ecology and between reproduction and production changed material life for Indians. With these changes traditional forms of consciousness also began to break down. The myths, rituals, and taboos inherited from Gluskabe* and his animal ancestors that had regulated a viable gathering-hunting economy were now vulnerable to replacement. . . .

By the end of the seventeenth century, the Abenaki, who were now almost entirely converted to Catholicism, found themselves caught between the French, who provided them with a religion that seemed to offer help for their illnesses, and the English, who supplied the food and trade items on which they now depended. An Abenaki spokesman put it to the English thus: "Thy Ministers, [never] spoke to me of prayer or of the Great Spirit. They saw my furs, my beaver- and elk-skins, and of those alone did they think. . . . I was not able to furnish them enough. On the contrary, . . . one day I landed at Quebec, . . . I was loaded with furs, but the French black Robe [priest] did not deign even to look at them; he spoke to me first of the great Spirit, of Paradise, of Hell, and of Prayer, which is the only way of reaching Heaven. . . . I asked for Baptism, and received it."[10]

*Gluskabe is a trickster figure in the Abenaki oral tradition who often assists the Great Spirit by teaching people valuable lessons.—Ed.

The substitution of the Christian ethic for the Abenaki ethic altered the symbolic superstructure of the Indians' economy. An ethic of moral obligation between human and God replaced the ethic of reciprocity between human and animal. While the older practices of divination, taboos, and disposal of remains continued, they ceased to function as a restraining environmental ethic in an economy in which survival now depended on the sale of animal furs in the marketplace. The Abenaki could now combine the teaching of both European cultures they had adopted. By convincing the Indians to give up manitous [charms] and fetishes endowed with life and spirit and to embrace instead a transcendent God above nature, the Jesuits prepared the way for the fetishism of commodities. Under capitalism, the properties of life, growth, and development associated with organic life would be transferred to money and the products of the market. The market would exhibit strength, weakness, depression, and death, obscuring the underlying death of the animals and their Indian equals.

The process of ecological breakdown began at the level of material culture. Production relations were altered as tools and utensils obtained in the fur trade created inequalities among neighboring tribes, and dependency relations were substituted for reciprocity. The relations of reproduction were altered by diseases and property rights that further destroyed traditional patterns of subsistence. Finally, a new religion injected by Jesuit missionaries, who consciously set out to undermine Indian animism, seemed to offer rational explanation and solace in a time of crisis and confusion. The colonial ecological revolution in northern New England that began with the fur trade was essentially complete by the end of the seventeenth century.

NOTES

1. Neal Salisbury, *Manitou and Providence: Indians, Europeans, and the Making of New England, 1500–1643* (New York: Oxford University Press, 1982), pp. 50–56; quotation on p. 52.
2. Martin Pring, "A Voyage Set Out from the Citie of Bristol, 1603," in *Early English and French Voyages, Chiefly from Hakluyt, 1534–1608*, ed. Henry S. Burrage (New York: Charles Scribner's Sons, 1906), p. 350; Salisbury, *Manitou and Providence*, p. 61; John Smith, *A Description of New England* (London: Humphrey Lownes, 1616), pp. 1, 12, and idem, "New England's Trials (London, 1620)," in *Proceedings of the Massachusetts Historical Society, 1871–1873* (Boston: Massachusetts Historical Society, 1873), p. B3; Dean R. Snow, "Keepers of the Game and the Nature of Explanation," in *Indians, Animals, and the Fur Trade*, ed. Shepard Krech III (Athens: University of Georgia Press, 1981), pp. 59–71; Charles A. Bishop, "Northeastern Indian Concepts of Conservation

and the Fur Trade: A Critique of Calvin Martin's Thesis," in ibid., pp. 39–58.

3. James Rosier, "A True Relation of the Voyage of Captain George Weymouth, 1605," in *Early English and French Voyages*, ed. Burrage, pp. 368–71, 373–79, 385; quotation on p. 371.

4. [James Davies], "A Relation of a Voyage to Sagadahoc, 1607–1608," in *Early English and French Voyages*, ed. Burrage, pp. 403, 416, 419.

5. Dean R. Snow, "Abenaki Fur Trade in the Sixteenth Century," *Western Canadian Journal of Anthropology* 6, no. 1 (1976): 3–11; idem, "Wabanaki Family Hunting Territories," *American Anthropologist* 70, nos. 4–6 (August–December 1968): 1143–51; Samuel Purchas, "The Description of the Country of Mawooshen, Discovered by the English in the Yeere 1602, 3, 5, 6, 7, 8, and 9," in *Hakluytus, Posthumus, or Purchas His Pilgrimes*, 19 vols. (Glasgow: James MacLose and Sons, 1906), 19:400–405; Sherburne F. Cook, "The Significance of Disease in the Extinction of the New England Indians," *Human Biology* 45, no. 3 (September 1973): 489–90, quotation on p. 489; Alfred W. Crosby, "God . . . Would Destroy Them, and Give Their Country to Another People," *American Heritage* 29, no. 6 (October–November 1978): 38–43.

6. Snow, "Abenaki Fur Trade," pp. 8–9.

7. Francis X. Maloney, *The Fur Trade in New England, 1620–1676* (Cambridge, MA: Harvard University Press, 1931), pp. 25–31; Anonymous, "Edward Ashley: Trader at Penobscot," *Proceedings of the Massachusetts Historical Society*, 3d ser. 45 (October 1911–June 1912): 493–98.

8. Sister Mary Celeste Leger, *The Catholic Indian Missions in Maine, 1611–1820* (Washington, DC: Catholic University Press, 1929), quotation on pp. 69–70.

9. Charles F. Carroll, *The Timber Economy of Puritan New England* (Providence, RI: Brown University Press, 1973), pp. 71–72, 112; William M. Sargent, ed., *York Deeds, 1642–1738* (Portland, ME: J. T. Hull, 1887–96), bk. 5, pt, 1, fols. 16, 31, 36, 39; William Willis, *History of Portland from 1632–1864* (Portland, ME: Baily and Noyes, 1865), pp. 249–55; Fannie H. Eckstrom, "Lumbering in Maine," in *Maine: A History*, 5 vols., ed. Louis Clinton Hatch (New York: American Historical Society, 1919), 3:689–95.

10. Father Sebastien Rasles, "Letter from Father Sebastien Rasles, Missionary of the Society of Jesus in New France, to Monsieur His Brother, October 12, 1723," in *The Jesuit Relations and Allied Documents: Travels and Explorations of the Jesuit Missionaries in New France, 1610–1791*, 73 vols., ed. Reuben Gold Thwaites (Cleveland: Burrows, 1896–1901), 67:211. On the fetishism of commodities see Michael Taussig, "The Genesis of Capitalism amongst a South American Peasantry: Devil's Labor and the Baptism of Money," *Comparative Studies in Society and History* 19 (April 1977): 130–53.

6 The Northwest Ordinance (1787)

An Ordinance for the GOVERNMENT of the TERRITORY of the UNITED STATES, NORTH-WEST of the RIVER OHIO

BE IT ORDAINED by the United States in Congress assembled, That the said territory, for the purposes of temporary government, be one district; subject, however, to be divided into two districts, as future circumstances may, in the opinion of Congress, make it expedient.

Be it ordained by the authority aforesaid, That the estates both of resident and non-resident proprietors in said territory, dying intestate, shall descend to, and be distributed among their children, and the descendants of a deceased child in equal parts; the descendants of a deceased child or grand-child to take the share of their deceased parent in equal parts among them: And where there shall be no children or descendants, then in equal parts to the next kin, in equal degree; and among collaterals the children of a deceased brother or sister of the intestate, shall have in equal parts among them their deceased parents' share; saving in all cases to the widower of the intestate, her third part of the real estate for life. . . .

Be it ordained by the authority aforesaid, That there shall be appointed from time to time, by Congress, a governor, whose commission shall continue in force for the term of three years, unless sooner

From "An Ordinance for the Government of the Territory of the United States, North-West of the River Ohio," *Documents from the Continental Congress and the Constitutional Convention, 1774–1789*, Washington, DC, Library of Congress, Rare Book and Special Collections Division.

revoked by Congress; he shall reside in the district, and have a free-hold estate therein, in one thousand acres of land, while in the exercise of his office.

There shall be appointed from time to time, by Congress, a secretary, whose commission shall continue in force for four years, unless sooner revoked; he shall reside in the district, and have a freehold estate therein, in five hundred acres of land, while in the exercise of his office; it shall be his duty to keep and preserve the acts and laws passed by the legislature, and the public records of the district, and the proceedings of the governor in his executive department; and transmit authentic copies of such acts and proceedings, every six months, to the secretary of Congress. . . .

The governor and judges, or a majority of them, shall adopt and publish in the district, such laws of the original states, criminal and civil, as may be necessary, and best suited to the circumstances of the district, and report them to Congress, from time to time . . .

For the prevention of crimes and injuries, the laws to be adopted or made shall have force in all parts of the district, and for the execution of process, criminal and civil, the governor shall make proper divisions thereof—and he shall proceed from time to time, as circumstances may require, to lay out the parts of the districts in which the Indian titles shall have been extinguished, into counties and townships, subject, however, to such alterations as may thereafter be made by the legislature.

So soon as there shall be 5,000 free male inhabitants, of full age, in the district, upon giving proof thereof to the governor, they shall receive authority, with time and place, to elect representatives from their counties or townships, to represent them in the general assembly; provided that for every 500 free male inhabitants there shall be one representative, and so on progressively with the number of free male inhabitants, shall the right of representation increase, until the number of representatives shall amount to 25, after which the number and proportion of representatives shall be regulated by the legislature; . . .

The governor, judges, legislative council, secretary, and such other officers as Congress shall appoint in the district, shall take an oath or affirmation of fidelity, and of office, the governors before the president of Congress, and all other offices before the governor. As soon as a legislature shall be formed in the district, the council and house assembled in one room, shall have authority by joint ballot to elect a delegate to Congress, who shall have a seat in Congress, with a right of debating, but not of voting, during this temporary government.

And for extending to all parts of the confederacy the fundamental principles of civil and religious liberty, which form the basis whereon these republics, their laws and constitutions are erected; to fix and establish those principles as the basis of all laws, constitutions and governments, which forever hereafter shall be formed in the said territory;—to provide also for the establishment of states, and permanent government therein, and for their admission to a share in the federal councils on an equal footing with the original states, at as early periods as may be consistent with the general interest.

It is hereby ordained and declared by the authority aforesaid, That the following articles shall be considered as articles of compact between the original states and the people and states in the said territory, and forever remain unalterable, unless by common consent, *to wit*:

Article the First. No person demeaning himself in a peaceable and orderly manner shall ever be molested on account of his mode of worship or religious sentiments in the said territory.

Article the Second. The inhabitants of the said territory shall always be entitled to the benefits of the writ of habeas corpus, and the trial by jury; of a proportionate representation of the people in the legislature, and of judicial proceedings according to the course of the common law; . . .

Article the Third. Institutions for the [?] of religion and morality, schools and the means of education shall forever be encouraged. . . . The utmost good faith shall always be observed towards the Indians; their lands and property shall never be taken from them without their consent, and in their property, rights and liberty, they never shall be invaded or disturbed, unless in just and lawful wars authorised by Congress; but laws founded in justice and humanity shall from time to time be made, for preventing wrongs being done to them, and for preserving peace and friendship with them.

Article the Fourth. The said territory, and the states which may be formed therein, shall forever remain a part of this confederacy of the United States of America, subject to the articles of confederation, and to such alterations therein as shall be constitutionally made; and to all the acts and ordinances of the United States in Congress assembled, conformable thereto. . . .

Article the Fifth. There shall be formed in the said territory, not less than three nor more than five states; and the boundaries of the states, as soon as Virginia shall alter her act of cession and authorise the same, shall become fixed and established as follows . . .

Article the Sixth. There shall be neither slavery nor involuntary servitude in the said territory. . . .

Be it ordained by the authority aforesaid, That the resolutions of the 23d of April, 1784, be, and the same are hereby repealed and declared null and void.

WILLIAM GILPIN

7 | The Untransacted Destiny of the American People (1846)

The calm, wise man sets himself to study aright and understand clearly the deep designs of Providence—to scan the great volume of nature—to fathom, if possible, the will of the Creator, and to receive with respect what may be revealed to him.

Two centuries have rolled over our race upon this continent. From nothing we have become 20,000,000. From nothing we are grown to be in agriculture, in commerce, in civilization, and in natural strength, the first among nations existing or in history. So much is our *destiny* —so far, up to this time—*transacted*, accomplished, certain, and not to be disputed. From this threshold we read the future.

The *untransacted* destiny of the American people is to subdue the continent—to rush over this vast field to the Pacific Ocean—to animate the many hundred millions of its people, and to cheer them upward—to set the principle of self-government at work—to agitate these herculean masses—to establish a new order in human affairs— to set free the enslaved—to regenerate superannuated nations—to change darkness into light—to stir up the sleep of a hundred centuries—to teach old nations a new civilization—to confirm the destiny of the human race—to carry the career of mankind to its culminating

From William Gilpin, *Mission of the North American People: Geographical, Social, and Political* (Philadelphia: J. B. Lippincott and Company, 1874), 130 (quoting a report to the U.S. Senate of 1846).

43

point—to cause stagnant people to be re-born—to perfect science—to emblazon history with the conquest of peace—to shed a new and resplendent glory upon mankind—to unite the world in one social family—to dissolve the spell of tyranny and exalt charity—to absolve the curse that weighs down humanity, and to shed blessings round the world!

Divine task! immortal mission! Let us tread fast and joyfully the open trail before us! Let every American heart open wide for patriotism to glow undimmed, and confide with religious faith in the sublime and prodigious destiny of his well-loved country.

8 Americans Spread All Over California (1846)

EMIGRATION.—Emigrants from the United States are daily flocking into California; their landmark, after crossing the Rocky Mountains, is the Sacramento valley; amongst them are mechanics and labourers of all descriptions, and altho' they invariably strike for the Sacramento valley, still not one half of them will settle there; they will, as soon as they get acquainted with the country, and the winter season is over, spread all over California, and as many of these are people, who understand agriculture in all its branches, they will undoubtedly spy out thousands of acres of land, which are now considered as useless, except for grazing, and will in a short time prove to the old inhabitants that there is more land fit for cultivation in California, than ever has been imagined, by the natives; and many vegetable substances will be planted, and brought to maturity, which heretofore have never had a fair trial.

We have already had sufficient proof in various instances that the grape vine flourishes, in California, to the northward of San Luis Obispo, if not in an equal degree to that of the Angeles, at most, very little inferior, and there can be little doubt, that the industry, and intelligence of the agriculturists, which are daily emigrating to this country, will improve the nature of the soil to such a degree, as to greatly augment both the produce, and improve the flavour of this most delicious fruit, and the same may be said of all the other production of this country.

From the Monterey *Californian*, "Spread All Over California," November 7, 1846.

9 Social and Environmental Degradation in the California Gold Country (1890)

As lone as God, and white as a winter moon, Mount Shasta starts up sudden and solitary from the heart of the great black forests of Northern California.

You would hardly call Mount Shasta a part of the Sierras; you would say rather that it is the great white tower of some ancient and eternal wall, with nearly all the white walls overthrown.

Ascend this mountain, stand against the snow above the upper belt of pines, and take a glance below. Toward the sea nothing but the black and unbroken forest. Mountains, it is true, dip and divide and break the monotony as the waves break up the sea; yet it is still the sea, still the unbroken forest, black and magnificent. To the south, the landscape sinks and declines gradually, but still maintains its column of dark-plumed grenadiers, till the Sacramento Valley is reached, nearly a hundred miles away. Silver rivers run here, the sweetest in the world. They wind and wind among the rocks and mossy roots, with California lilies, and the yew with scarlet berries dipping in the water, and trout idling in the eddies and cool places by the basketful. On the east,

From Joaquin Miller, *My Life Amongst the Indians* (Chicago: Morril, Higgins and Company, 1892 [1890]), 18–22, 54–55.

the forest still keeps up unbroken rank till the Pitt River Valley is reached; and even there it surrounds the valley, and locks it up tight in its black embrace. To the north, it is true, Shasta Valley makes quite a dimple in the sable sea, and men plow there, and Mexicans drive mules or herd their mustang ponies on the open plain. But the valley is limited, surrounded by the forest, confined and imprisoned.

Look intently down among the black and rolling hills, forty miles away to the west, and here and there you will see a haze of cloud or smoke hung up above the trees; or, driven by the wind that is coming from the sea, it may drag and creep along as if tangled in the tops.

These are mining camps. Men are there, down in these dreadful cañons, out of sight of the sun, swallowed up, buried in the impenetrable gloom of the forest, toiling for gold. Each one of these camps is a world of itself. History, romance, tragedy, poetry, in every one of them. They are connected together, and reach the outer world only by a narrow little pack trail, stretching through the timber, stringing round the mountains, barely wide enough to admit of footmen and little Mexican mules, with their aparejos [equipment], to pass in single file.

But now the natives of these forests. I lived with them for years. You do not see the smoke of their wigwams through the trees. They do not smite the mountain rocks for gold, nor fell the pines, nor roil up the waters and ruin them for the fishermen. All this magnificent forest is their estate. The Great Spirit made this mountain first of all, and gave it to them, they say, and they have possessed it ever since. They preserve the forest, keep out the fires, for it is the park for their deer.

This narrative, while the thread of it is necessarily spun around a few years of my early life, is not of myself, but of this race of people that has lived centuries of history and never yet had a historian; that has suffered nearly four hundred years of wrong, and never yet had an advocate.

Yet I must write of myself, because I was among these people of whom I write, though often in the background, giving place to the inner and actual lives of a silent and mysterious people, a race of prophets, poets without the gift of expression—a race that has been often, almost always, mistreated, and never understood—a race that is moving noiselessly from the face of the earth; dreamers that sometimes waken from their mysteriousness and simplicity, and then, blood, brutality, and all the ferocity that marks a man of maddened passions, women without mercy, men without reason, brand them with the appropriate name of savages.

I have a word to say for the Indian. I saw him as he was, not as he is. In one little spot of our land, I saw him as he was centuries ago in every part of it perhaps, a Druid and a dreamer—the mildest and tamest of beings. I saw him as no man can see him now. I saw him as no man ever saw him who had the desire and patience to observe, the sympathy to understand, and the intelligence to communicate his observations to those who would really like to understand him. He is truly "the gentle savage"; the worst and the best of men, the tamest and the fiercest of beings. The world cannot understand the combination of these two qualities. For want of truer comparison let us liken him to a woman—a sort of Parisian woman, now made desperate by a long siege and an endless war.*

A singular combination of circumstances laid his life bare to me. I was a child, and he was a child. He permitted me to enter his heart. . . .

All this city [Sacramento] had been built, all this country opened up, in less than two years. Twenty months before, only the Indian inhabited here; he was lord absolute of the land. But gold had been found on this spot by a party of roving mountaineers; the news had gone abroad, and people poured in and had taken possession in a day, without question and without ceremony.

And the Indians? They were pushed aside. At first they were glad to make the strangers welcome; but, when they saw where it would all lead, they grew sullen and concerned. . . .

I hurried on a mile or so to the foot-hills, and stood in the heart of the placer mines. Now the smoke from the low chimneys of the log cabins began to rise and curl through the cool, clear air on every hand, and the miners to come out at the low doors; great hairy, bearded, six-foot giants, hatless, and half-dressed.

They stretched themselves in the sweet, frosty air, shouted to each other in a sort of savage banter, washed their hands and faces in the gold-pans that stood by the door, and then entered their cabins again, to partake of the eternal beans and bacon and coffee, and coffee and bacon and beans.

The whole face of the earth was perforated with holes; shafts sunk and being sunk by these men in search of gold, down to the bed-rock. Windlasses stretched across these shafts, where great buckets swung,

*Paris in 1890 was under siege by the Prussians.—Ed.

in which men hoisted the earth to the light of the sun by sheer force of muscle.

The sun came softly down, and shone brightly on the hillside where I stood. I lifted my hands to Shasta, above the butte and town, for he looked like an old acquaintance, and again was glad.

10 The Soreness of the Land (1925)

Prophecy of Kate Luckie (ten years ago).—People talk a lot about the world ending. Maybe this child [pointing to her eldest child] will see something, but this world will stay as long as Indians live. When the Indians all die, then God will let the water come down from the north. Everyone will drown. That is because the white people never cared for land or deer or bear. When we Indians kill meat, we eat it all up. When we dig roots, we make little holes. When we build houses, we make little holes. When we burn grass for grasshoppers, we don't ruin things. We shake down acorns and pine nuts. We don't chop down the trees. We only use dead wood. But the white people plow up the ground, pull up the trees, kill everything. The tree says, "Don't. I am sore. Don't hurt me." But they chop it down and cut it up. The spirit of the land hates them. They blast out trees and stir it up to its depths. They saw up the trees. That hurts them. The Indians never hurt anything, but the white people destroy all. They blast rocks and scatter them on the earth. The rock says, "Don't! You are hurting me." But the white people pay no attention. When the Indians use rocks, they take little round ones for their cooking. The white people dig deep long tunnels. They make roads. They dig as much as they wish. They don't care how much the ground cries out. How can the spirit of the earth like the white man? That is why God will upset the world—because it is sore all over. Everywhere the white man has touched it, it is sore. It looks sick. So it gets even by killing him when he blasts. But eventually the water will come.

From Wintu Indian Kate Luckie, in Cora Du Bois, *Wintu Ethnography* (Berkeley, CA: University of California Press, 1935), 75–76. Reprinted by permission of the University of California Press.

This water, it can't be hurt. The white people go to the river and turn it into dry land. The water says: "I don't care. I am water. You can use me all you wish. I am always the same. I can't be used up. Use me. I am water. You can't hurt me." The white people use the water of sacred springs in their houses. The water says: "That is all right. You can use me, but you can't overcome me." All that is water says this. "Wherever you put me, I'll be in my home. I am awfully smart. Lead me out of my springs, lead me from my rivers, but I came from the ocean and I shall go back into the ocean. You can dig a ditch and put me in it, but I go only so far and I am out of sight. I am awfully smart. When I am out of sight, I am on my way home."

II | Nature's Nation

The American Landscape and the Nature Writing Tradition

> All this is perfectly distinct to an observant eye, and
> yet could easily pass unnoticed by most.
> —Henry David Thoreau, *Walking*[1]

How, the question must come, did nature become something other than the fuel for an expanding, industrializing civilization? It arose, logically enough, from the anxieties provoked by what appeared to some observers as rapacious exploitation of seemingly every inch of American ground. By the midnineteenth century a new romantic nature aesthetic emerged in response to all that Manifest Destiny had wrought. Part II will sketch the outlines of that sensibility and focus on the development of one of its clearest expressions, the nature essay.

Originating in the eighteenth-century English countryside, the nature essay assumed particularly American qualities in the nineteenth century. The five authors whom we examine here—Henry David Thoreau, John Muir, John Burroughs, Mary Austin, and Annie Dillard— collectively represent what Thomas Lyon has called the "three main dimensions" of nature writing on the whole: "natural history information, personal responses to nature, and philosophical interpretation of nature."[2] They speak as much of the human relationship with nature as of the details of landscape. Highly introspective, the essays nevertheless speak to one of the appealing attributes of the nature essay: its capacity to evoke a *sense of place*. An elusive term, it might be described in this literary context as both the feeling and understanding of a particular locale inscribed over time by those who live or travel there.

These writers take divergent paths of inquiry across an assortment of landscapes: in a woodsy cabin outside Concord, Massachusetts, Thoreau broods over the growing distance between nature and civilization. Muir leaves that civilization to celebrate a euphorically sublime mountaintop, while Burroughs investigates an unlikely urban environment. Austin lands us in an inhospitable but mesmerizing desert wilderness, and finally Dillard's bucolic greensward opens up into a journey through regions of the mind. These five exemplary essays helped to establish a sense of place for the particular regions that are their focus. In a larger sense they suggest the rich texture of American nature writing, a literary form that shaped the redefinition of nature in modern America.

In 1820, English critic Sydney Smith asked dismissively, "Who reads an American book? or goes to an American play? or looks at an American picture or statue?"[3] Although such remarks stung the pride of genteel Americans who were conscious of such things, they need not have worried. Undoubtedly, Smith was aware that his fellow countrymen Coleridge, Wordsworth, and Blake were already immersing themselves in such literary works as William Bartram's *Travels* (Selection 16) and Thomas Jefferson's *Notes on the State of Virginia*.[4] And America's writers and artists would soon focus European and American attention on the spectacular and picturesque qualities of eastern landscapes such as Niagara Falls and the Catskill Mountains of New York. Washington Irving's folk-rooted stories romanticized the Catskill region, as did the paintings of Hudson River School artists such as Asher Durand and Thomas Cole. Novelist James Fenimore Cooper's Leather-stocking tales celebrated the nation's youthful but romantic and bloody frontier heritage. This body of nature-centered work emphatically answered European charges that America had nothing of antiquity or beauty to offer the rest of the world.[5] To be "Nature's Nation," as cultural historian Perry Miller would later characterize it, underpinned the self-conscious cultural nationalism of Americans.

Influenced, ironically, by European Romanticism, the American nature aesthetic that was crafted by the genteel largely embraced two complementary prisms of nature: sublime majesty and picturesque beauty. Romantics suggested that towering waterfalls, lofty mountain peaks, and deep canyons could bring one closer to God. These sublime landscapes inspired terror and awe and provoked an ineffable sense of nature's power. If the sublime touched the soul, then the picturesque—found in bucolic river valleys and gently rolling meadows—pleased the eye. With human intervention, a former wild place could be made inviting. Landscape architects, in particular, worked like landscape painters, placing just the right "natural" elements into the nation's first urban parks, cemeteries, and suburbs. As Jennifer Price has written, Andrew Jackson Downing, America's premier landscape designer, "made meadows roll, rivers meander and trees clump irregularly on country estates throughout the Hudson River Valley."[6] Both the sublime and the picturesque functioned to renew the spirit of an increasingly urban and harried upper class. And the growing infatuation with nature came in multiple forms, coloring the social and cultural life of the middle and upper classes. By the 1840s increasing numbers of people were commuting to cities from the first bucolic suburbs, purchasing dinnerware with a Niagara Falls motif, and papering their living room walls with floral designs. Nature became chic, a mark of good taste.[7]

It followed that having asserted nature as the nation's premier cultural asset, artists and writers would be among the first to recognize the darker side of rapid development. Cooper's hugely popular frontier novels contrasted villainous woodchoppers with ethical, sagacious backwoodsmen. His frontiersmen had their eye on the future, while his romanticized Indian characters bespoke America's deep natural history and prefigured the "noble, vanishing savage" counterstereotype that would dominate popular Indian imagery by century's end. William Cullen Bryant mourned the loss of the "wild and lonely woods" in the Great Lakes region. In his popular *Birds of America* (1827–1838), ornithologist and illustrator John James Audubon chastised the "greedy mills" as the cause of rampant deforestation. Artist Thomas Cole accused the more insidious "meagre utilitarianism" of Americans, which he said was a mark of their cold indifference to the virtues of the wilderness. Man had become "the destroyer," Cole declared.[8]

These were exceptional voices, to be sure. Most Americans celebrated the intrepid, continuous push of the frontier and the westering railroad as a colossal instrument of their country's progress. By midcentury the energy of a nation on the move was intoxicating, as evidenced by the words of William Gilpin (Selection 7). Cooper may have written elegies to the wilderness, but he recognized the inexorable force and righteousness of American civilization.[9] His fictional protagonists encouraged a conservationist ethic, but Cooper himself never softened his belief that wilderness and Indians had to give way to white men; they would simply have to be men of prudence and stature. This ambivalence grew more pronounced as Americans carried the romantic aesthetic into the West after the Civil War. Even as they tunneled through the region's mountains and forded its rivers with a transcontinental railroad, even as they called for furious unfettered development, promoters of westward migration trumpeted the cultural and touristic value of the grand natural wonders of the West.

In this there was no contradiction: Americans had little difficulty conjoining an appreciation of nature with the exhilaration of technological progress.[10] Walt Whitman and Ralph Waldo Emerson, the great celebrants of unblemished nature, wrote also of the genius of technology and the democratic energy of capitalism, reveling even in the opposition of the natural and technological sublime.[11] In the 1870s the first travelers to Yellowstone National Park marveled with equal fascination at the region's extractive and scenic resources. In the nineteenth century, America was expansive enough to exalt both "nature" and the civilization growing vigorously from it. Romantics and transcendentalists called not for the end of civilization, but for taking refuge from and beyond it.

And so we come to the shore of Walden Pond, where in 1845 Henry David Thoreau crafted the tension of nature and society into a work of brilliance. More than a century and one-half later, nature posters and coffee mugs celebrate Thoreau's tributes to the necessity for wildness and to individualism. We remember him less well for his sharp criticism of progress that seemed to him to be overrunning nature and the integrity of the individual—both of which for Thoreau constituted the very breath of life. That critique coursed throughout his writing and is a recurrent theme of much of the American nature essay. It was especially strong in the early chapters of *Walden*, from which our excerpt is taken (Selection 11).

From whence did such brilliant commentary on nature and civilization arise? Thoreau's early biography makes the two years at Walden seem less a bold "experiment" than a natural culmination of all he

The world's first such reserve, Yellowstone National Park embraces both pictur-esque scenes such as Hayden Valley and Kepler Cascade, and the more sublime, breathtaking grandeur of the Grand Canyon of the Yellowstone River. Frank Jay Haynes views, author's collection.

thought and believed. Thoreau heard Emerson advise the 1837 gradu-ates of Harvard to "cultivate the moral affections, [and] lead [an] inde-pendent life." Already predisposed to that philosophy, Thoreau would find utterly unacceptable anything other than a conscientious and conscious life of the mind. He refused to deliver corporal punishment

10111, KEPLER CASCADE, 100 FT., YELLOWSTONE PARK. Haynes-Photo

while teaching at a Concord public school and so dismissed himself. Thoreau declined long-term employment in his father's pencil business.

Before he went to Walden Pond, Thoreau had gone (at Emerson's suggestion) to New York, where he met editor and publisher Horace Greeley. Thoreau rejected the opportunity to begin a career in journalism because he could not suffer the pace of city life. He would not allow his writing to be directed by other men, nor his life to be reduced to making a living. If college yearbooks had existed in 1837, the caption under Thoreau's photo might have read "least likely to succeed," though not for lack of promise. Despite obvious erudition, literary talent, and middle-class position, Thoreau clearly lacked career "direction," according to his friends.[12] He could not, as he put it in *Walden*, resign himself to the "life of quiet desperation" led by most men. Rather, Thoreau chose a "broad margin" to his life, sustaining himself with short-term positions and the help of friends while spending most of his time on his real passions of walking, studying, and writing about the New England landscape. Thoreau eschewed what Emerson called the "Commercial Spirit," seeking instead to mimic the "deliberate" pace of nature.[13]

So he remained rooted near Concord and in March 1845 built the cabin he came to occupy on Independence Day—an unorthodox move, but not unprecedented. For decades a small but growing number of cultivated Americans had been retreating into the wilds. Like Thoreau, they went without any practical purpose, and some much farther than he: in a sincere attempt to discover "the advantages of solitude" and "the true interest of man," in the winter and spring of 1818 a New England lawyer named Estwick Evans walked four thousand miles into the wilds of the Old Northwest.[14] At the end of his century, Evans's retreat would become commonplace among the first generation of wilderness enthusiasts. More famous figures of the nineteenth century—both real and fictional—also lived, often alone, in the woods: Daniel Boone, Davy Crockett, and Natty Bumpo come to mind. What sets Thoreau apart? Those were rugged frontiersmen, archetypal figures of the Frontier Myth who left the evils of civilization behind only to remake it anew in the wilderness. Frontier heroes may have felt estranged from an overcrowding society, but never did they seriously question the meaning of that world. Indeed, they extended the physical reach of their society. Thoreau deconstructed it: "Men have an indistinct notion that if they keep up this activity of joint stocks and spades long enough all will at length ride somewhere, in next to no time, and for nothing; but though a crowd rushes to the depot, and the conductor shouts 'All Aboard!' when the smoke has blown away and the vapor condensed, it will be perceived that a few are riding, but the rest are run over—and it will be called, and will be, a 'melancholy accident.' "[15]

Although his life of nature study included more far-flung journeys into New England, in this instance Thoreau needed only to move to the outskirts of town. Indeed, his going into nature and his writing about it required that he stay within earshot of civilization. For this was no mere romantic piety, no primitivist ramble on nature's solitude and beauty, nor even a scientific study of its parts. *Walden* contains all of those elements, but Thoreau went to Walden Pond primarily because he believed intuitively that it would reveal to him higher truths about living in a rapidly changing world. Observed from a rustic cabin in the woods, the simple glories of nature and the change of the seasons offered Thoreau a prism through which the most essential meaning and moral purpose of life would become apparent. To see that with a clear eye meant living on the edge of the civilization that he had determined to be madly complex, frenetically paced, and overly materialistic. Throughout *Walden,* Thoreau's mind and senses are fixed toward both the pond and the village.

Although often interpreted as such, *Walden* is neither a decree nor a prescription for a primitivist life; Thoreau eschewed dispensers of such advice himself. At its core, the book profoundly affirms the essential republican values that Thoreau found rooted in the American woods—that much he shared with Boone and Bumpo. Even in 1845 the virtues seemed to be going the way of the fenceless pasture. The author vigorously extols the old American individualism: to seek happiness on a path of one's own choosing, free from the compulsions and machinations of the society at large. Herein lies both the author's motivation and the enduring, wide appeal of *Walden.* In this classically American cabin in the woods, Thoreau set out to discover one solitary, elemental, and unadorned answer to an increasingly complicated world. To see the essence of life and nothing more, as he had earlier when he ascended Mount Katahdin, Maine's highest peak, "Think of our life in nature,—daily to be shown matter, to come in contact with it,—rocks, trees, wind on our cheeks! the *solid* earth! the *actual* world! the common *sense! Contact! Contact!*"[16] Much of *Walden* is focused on this sense of what is most real and making oneself keenly alert to it.

As it is with great works of literature, these pages speak to our own age. To be truly alive, Thoreau argues, requires waking up from the exhilarating hum of commercial capitalism, symbolized then by the railroad. These days, Thoreau would find a remote-control society driven by microchips, megabytes, and tech stocks, a culture of immediate material gratification, and merciless sensory stimulation. We seem to have passed on Life and Liberty and settled for the Pursuit of Happiness. The "melancholy accident" rolls cheerfully on. Interestingly, the 1990s witnessed a sort of Thoreauvian movement toward voluntary "simple living" and widespread soul-searching. Best-selling books, Web sites, and videos testified to the notion that a goodly number of us were less than happy with the gratification-by-Visa Card model. Likely, Thoreau would have been encouraged and bemused by the mass organization and commercial trappings of what is at heart an austere, individual endeavor.

Notwithstanding our quiescent cravings for a more simple life, Thoreau's challenge grows more difficult every day. The seduction of things has grown far beyond the shop windows of Concord. Our postmodern world and desires are defined more cleverly than ever. It is harder than ever to find what simply *is*, to discover the essence of living, of anything. And the daily mad realities of most Americans render any sort of quest "to see"—Thoreau's prime motivation for going to the woods[17]—as either quaintly unnecessary or ridiculously impossible to achieve. This is why we return to Thoreau, because our irrepressible search for the essentials of life is more likely to begin in these pages than on the "Jerry Springer Show."

Walden will be read and read into for as long as Americans seek something apart from mass culture. We are still Thoreau's neighbors, yearning to be awakened by a rooster. To drive any beltway in America is to know that we still "live meanly," in more than one sense, "like ants." In our most desperate moments we still feel the need to awaken from the alluring and maddening paradigm of modernity—the same model for living that took hold in the years when its symbol was the railroad and few thought to question it. When the questions do come, the world beyond our door answers: if we can produce eight children in a bottle, we should; if we can have more information and faster, we will; if we can sprawl our consuming selves over old farms and plant cellular phone towers on the side of the road so that we can talk to ourselves whenever we please, well, by God, why even ask why? *Walden* dares to reopen the inquiry. It challenges our collective purpose as Americans, as individuals, and seeks to return us to *Common Sense.* "Should [we] live like baboons or like men?" Were he here today, Thoreau might rephrase the question in favor of the baboon.

Sounding a much further romantic retreat was John Muir, whose biographical journey into nature is the stuff of legend. Having emigrated in 1849 from Scotland to the Wisconsin frontier, Muir flirted briefly with a promising career as an inventor. But when a laboratory accident nearly cost him his eyesight, he went hiking, literally, into a life in the wild. Looking to go "just anywhere in the wilderness southward," he walked one thousand miles to the Gulf of Mexico. During the journey, Muir abandoned his father's devoutly Calvinist beliefs and pondered instead the spiritual qualities of untamed nature.[18] Early in 1868 a bout with malaria redirected Muir from his intended destination of the Amazon River to northern California. Muir arrived in San Francisco that spring and inquired of locals the quickest way into the wilderness. Within days, he found himself in the high country of the Sierra Nevadas.[19] He had come to the place that would give life to some of the most enduring nature writing in American literature. By 1892 the region had inspired him to establish the Sierra Club—initially an "outing" group of hikers, but ultimately becoming the most politically potent environmental organization of the second half of the twentieth century.[20]

Muir's account of his first summer in the Sierra (Selection 12) was not published until 1911, when he was in his seventies. By that time he had been hiking the place for forty years and had written extensively of the region's natural history (*Studies in the Sierra*, 1874–1875). The sciences are not the identifying characteristics of this essay, however. It is not the parts and processes of nature that inspired this work, but the wondrous power of whole, untainted wildness to enliven the human spirit. In these sweeping aesthetic impressions, we hear the emotive thrust of Muir's nature writing, the urgent language of a devout romantic caught up in the rapture of sublime nature.

Muir wrote elsewhere that "going to the woods is going home; for I suppose we came from the woods originally."[21] Of his sincerity on this matter we can be sure. Consider that Thoreau, whose work Muir greatly admired, fled to Walden Pond in part to test the degree and necessity of one's dependence on society. Yet Thoreau stayed close enough to civilization to maintain critical eye contact with it (and to get his laundry done); Muir, on the other hand, could not get far enough away from a modernizing culture that he thought was injurious to the natural free spirit. Even animals, Muir believed, suffered from the decadence of creeping modernity. He ennobles, for example, the wild sheep as "the bravest mountaineer of the Sierra" while disparaging the domesticated variety as a mere "fraction of an animal."[22]

Though indifferent to the society from which he took leave, Muir steeped his nature writing in its language: "noble walls—sculptured into . . . domes and gables, spires and battlements . . . all a-tremble with the thunder tones of the falling water." Such terminology, common practice among nature and travel writers since at least the midnineteenth century, derived from the ascension of nature in American culture and from the explorer's impulse to understand strange environments in the familiar terms of one's own civilization.[23] By 1911 the nature-romanticism that first made sense of American landscapes had become broadly popular among the middle class. Reduced to cliché, the prevailing nature aesthetic fostered both the preservation and consumption of nature. Yellowstone tourists of the 1890s "feasted" on the "eatable parts" of the park's standard guidebook tour, permeated with romantic language.[24] The language of romanticism had suffused touristic landscapes with cultural meaning, even as it increasingly prescribed what was to be seen and how.

Such popular commodification coexisted with and grew quite naturally from the genuine, spiritual love of wilderness that we hear in this excerpt. Indeed, Muir led the radical reconstruction of wildness for the modern age. His celestial vision of the wild illustrated the intellectual, spiritual, and material distance that he and his country had come from their Calvinist roots. Very unlike William Bradford (Selection 3), Muir found everywhere in the wilderness a godly presence. The fervor of Muir's prose is every bit as impassioned as that of the Pilgrim leader, but his sense of the moral virtue of wildness could not have been more different. This difference is embedded in context: far from the Pilgrims who nearly three centuries before had barely survived a "hideous and desolate" environment, Muir walked away deliberately from a rapidly modernizing society. He perceived it as having grown spiritually bereft. Even amid the terror of a booming thunderstorm, he sees a "divine manuscript" that can reinspire an overly civilized society. With a boundless sense of wonder, John Muir articulated the brave idea that wild places have the capacity to make modern men, if not holy, then whole again by returning them to their origins.

———

The naturalist John Burroughs once referred to John Muir as "mountain drunk," an altogether reasonable assessment. Burroughs, the most popular of all turn-of-the-century nature writers, bemoaned Muir for being "crazy about trees and wild scenes."[25] Although his influence on Muir extended only as far as the wilder man's vision would allow, to see Burroughs's work in the afterglow of one of his "students" is to glimpse the diversity of American nature writers. To be sure, their nature sensibilities differed markedly. While Muir immersed himself in the godly wonder of a wild scene, Burroughs listened in on the delicate conversations of birds hidden among its many species of trees: in one, the divine, universal power of nature; in the other, its exquisite particularity. In contrast with the western sublime, Burroughs looked mostly to the kind of rather ordinary, eastern places familiar to most Americans. Muir abandoned the world's discontents for a long walk in the wild; Burroughs, on the other hand, never seemed far from the affairs of the world. Indeed, he believed that the great purpose of nature study lay in helping humans better understand themselves, thereby helping to redeem society.[26]

"Spring at the Capital" (Selection 13) is drawn from *Wake-Robin* (1871), a book that followed *Walden* in establishing the "ramble" genre of the nature essay—a "classic American form," as Thomas Lyon has described it. In the ramble, "the author goes forth into nature, usually on a short excursion near home, and records the walk as observer-participant."[27] In his rambles, Burroughs had the gift of allowing personality—his and nature's—to shine through. In the walking vignette to "the capital of grasshopperdom," we see a man who brought both intensity of purpose and frivolous delight to his study of the landscape.

Burroughs believed that animals, in general, and birds, in particular, reflected the most noble traits of humanity and could shed insight on human behavior. And to better understand nature was to better understand ourselves. He took seriously his responsibility to educate his readers, indeed taking vehement issue with those writers whom he decried as "Nature Fakers." Burroughs argued that in their popular short stories and books, men such as Ernest Thompson Seton and the Reverend William J. Long took overly romantic and outright fictional liberties with animals, ascribing to them heroic or villainous attributes. Worse still for Burroughs, Nature Fakers maintained that their stories, however fictionalized, were grounded in actual observation and the natural sciences. "Wild Animals I Have Known," Seton boasted in one title. While Seton's chief literary goal—to "emphasize our kinship with the animals by showing . . . [their] virtues most admired in men"— seems little removed from that of Burroughs, it was the means, the animal fable, that troubled him. He led a chorus admonishing such works, arguing that wildlife needed no further romancing in order to teach us valuable lessons.[28]

Burroughs's own writing adheres to the ideals and language of nature romanticism that were well established by 1871. His burning desire that spring "to be off" sounds the familiar retreat from urban life into untainted nature. To envision Washington, DC, as Burroughs saw it certainly challenges the postmodern imagination. He takes us there with eloquent and exacting detail There is Burroughs, deep in the woods of pre-Beltway Washington, listening for the exotic sounds of the bobolink and, though less drawn to the sublime than Muir, eliciting enthusiasm for nature's "savage" look. More typically he embraces Washington's picturesque locales and at one wilder location calls for a "few touches of art" to perfect it. The landscape tradition called for a winding path here, a few less trees there to convert an unruly visage into a scene that could satisfy the eye and enrich civilization.

Where and exactly when could one find liverwort in 1871 Washington? Burroughs tells us. Like most of his life's work, his spring tour of the capital is both animated and meticulous. We move from the untouched ruggedness of Rock Creek Gorge to the bird life on the Capitol grounds, to the dying caterpillars in urban shop gutters. Weaving scientific with popular nomenclature, Burroughs narrates the landscape for nature lovers of all stripes. And as he reminds the reader, these are not conjectures made from the writer's window. Having traipsed this ground himself for eight years, Burroughs's erudite sense of this place is unimpeachable.

"Spring at the Capital" offers a middle landscape, a place somewhere between wild and civilized. The archetypal middle landscape—the working pastoral countryside—is glimpsed here only from afar. As cultural historians have noted, those who went "back to nature" in the nineteenth century did not go there to sweat. Romanticism called the middle and upper classes to taste the country in various ways "without being of it," as one early commuter put it. The pastoral landscape might please the eye, but actually working that land could never satisfy the soul.[29] To know nature was to soak it in visually, emotionally, and psychically, not to cultivate it.

Burroughs continued to do that for the rest of his life. In 1873, two years after *Wake-Robin*, he moved from Washington to a farm in New York's Hudson River Valley, where he built a retreat known as "Slabsides." For the next several decades he studied and wrote about it all, acquainting a generation of readers with the intimate details of that landscape. From there he became one of the most famous literary figures of his time, camping with such illustrious companions as Theodore Roosevelt and Henry Ford.

However learned a natural historian Burroughs made of himself, he grew more like John Muir with age—ultimately skeptical of the capacity of science to solve human ills and more drawn to the spiritual dimensions of nature. "Where there is no vision, no intuitive perception of the great fundamental truths of the inner spiritual world," he said late in life, "science will not save us." As he aged into the first decades of twentieth-century modernity, his enthusiasm for the science of nature yielded to the capacity of the woods to nourish his soul. "When I take a walk now," he said in his old age, "I suspect it is more to bathe the spirit in natural influences than to store the mind with natural facts."[30]

It is, finally, less for the natural history he imparted than for his graceful and lively detail of landscapes just beyond the front door that we most value Burroughs. Although he traveled widely and camped in exotic places, the bulk of his writing was inspired and grounded in the woods of home. He engaged his readers with those immediate environments by being attentive not only to their biology but also more vividly to their color, language, and movement. And by introducing middle-class Americans to the wonders of ordinary landscapes, John Burroughs suggested that similar small miracles might be found in their own corners of nature.

———

Mary Austin was no nature writer. Like William Bradford, whose life was bound up with more worldly affairs, Austin generally falls outside the canon of American nature literature. A number of passions fueled her writing career, most notably the early twentieth-century struggle of middle-class women for creative self-expression. For that theme her semi-autobiographical books had by the 1970s received overdue recognition.[31] Her most popular book, however, and the one with which she was most identified in her lifetime, was *The Land of Little Rain*, the opening pages of which appear here (Selection 14).

The extreme southwestern environment of Austin's text bears a stronger cultural link to Bradford's New England than the sublime and cheery landscapes of John Muir and John Burroughs. Variously feared, reviled, and ignored over the course of the westward movement, the California desert remained at the end of the nineteenth century largely *terra incognita*. By the time Austin was writing her book, Americans had established their civilization in most parts of the West. Most famously, the Great Plains region, labeled the Great American Desert in the 1820s, was popularly transformed into an Eden-like "garden" following the Civil War.[32] The "Country of Lost Borders," however, remained a place to avoid. And for very good reasons: the scarcity of life in this place rendered it entirely uninviting. The California desert, devoid of mountain grandeur and lush biotic diversity, lay utterly forbidding to all except Indian tribes, Hispanic enclaves, hard-core prospectors—and Mary Austin, who by 1903 had called it home for fifteen years.

From the fertile prairie of the Midwest, Mary Hunter Austin had come in 1888 when she was not yet twenty. Along with her mother and younger brother, she migrated to the high California desert to help an older brother scratch out a living as a farmer. Fifteen years later, therefore, she was writing not as a tourist but as someone who knew the limits of an unforgiving, seemingly barren environment. Like Burroughs, her credentials were well established by experience.[33] Austin carried no illusions about the place.

Yet her vision extended beyond the confines of the traditional landscape aesthetic. For Austin, there is a terrifying beauty in the desert that compels awful respect. Alluding to the history behind the foreboding Death Valley epithet, Austin recounts the foolishness of men who underestimated the arid power of the desert. Pity the unwitting traveler who does not know the desert environment and its scarce sources of water. She then locates them for the reader—moisture locked inside and under the various species that thrive here. With crisp, vivid language, Austin exposes the logic of the desert, centered simply on the paucity of water. Her account eloquently echoes the words of explorer John Wesley Powell, who in 1878 warned the U.S. Congress (alas, in vain) that the aridity of its western lands would not permit eastern-style development.[34]

As Powell had made clear, Austin illustrates that there is life in the southwestern desert, but it is of a much different sort than any other region of the United States. This land, while it may not easily support the twentieth-century American way of life, is permeated with color, movement, and rich biological diversity. Her narrative unravels the barren desert myth. Through her keen eyes we see a variety of desert species, hidden behind rocks and in the crevices of bush and tree, clinging tenaciously to life.

While Austin's work represents a new, rare desert strain of the "wilderness cult" growing at the turn of the century, she continues a tradition of spiritual retreat to desert environments common among ancient religions of the world.[35] Indeed, part of the author's redemption of this hellish place is to note its divine origins "out of God's hands." To her, the sense of place and time is so enchanting that one finds it hard to leave. Austin never did fully leave, returning again and again to residency in various parts of the Southwest until her death in 1934.

Austin parts again with some natural history writers in her appreciation for the human residents of this environment. Unlike John Muir, for example, who had little good to say of the native inhabitants of the High Sierra, Austin seems to hold genuine reverence for the indigenous peoples who long ago acquired the eye and spirit to live wisely in this landscape. *The Land of Little Rain* is permeated throughout with respect for the life-ways of Native and Hispanic American residents. The old Anglo miners, too, have become naturalized features of this landscape. They cut a romantic visage in Austin's narrative, although she tartly suggests that the tragic fate of many a lost gold miner was self-inflicted. The beguiling promise of mineral wealth for many men, she notes with a mix of sympathy and cold aversion, has become the kiss of death. This landscape is hypnotic; it does not breed especially good sense.

Austin is more optimistic that in the long run people will be lured to this place by the same mystical qualities that had her sophisticated sensibility so infatuated. The tormented denizens of the twentieth century will come here for healing. Austin could make such a prophecy in 1903 knowing that other locales in the Southwest, such as Santa Fe and the Grand Canyon, were developing as tourist meccas for the genteel classes of the urban East.[36] Although part of the region is now designated a national park, the more severe aridity of the Mojave has kept it largely uninhabited. (Never underestimate, however, the culture that roars behind the off-road vehicle, which has found its way into Austin's old haunts.)

Not satisfied with a narrative of the landscape itself, Austin probes incessantly the source of her love of the desert, likening herself to the hopelessly searching miner. Her expectations grow more distant the more she becomes cognitively aware of the place. She concludes that its ineffable beauty is only diminished with words. Beyond the physical features of the landscape, Mary Austin's desert aesthetic suggests the power of this appallingly desolate place to induce ecological humility. A starry desert night, pierced with the howl of the coyote, can inspire an appreciation for the smallness of humans and the vastness of the universe.

———————

This brief survey of American nature essayists ends with an author whose writing signifies the consciousness of her time as well as William Bradford's work did his. With an introspective sensibility of the 1970s, Annie Dillard offers in *Pilgrim at Tinker Creek* (Selection 15) both a narrative of place and a highly self-conscious geography of her own restlessly searching mind. Although Dillard writes of Tinker Creek, a real landscape in Virginia, her sense of place is universal. One gets the feeling that Dillard could have settled down beside any creek in America and produced the same insights into place and time. Her overriding purpose is to better understand her role in the world by thoroughly probing her home environment and her mind. This writing is, as Dillard calls it, as much "mental ramble" as natural survey. We hear modern reverberations of Thoreau, who likewise developed grand themes from his musings on a prosaic wooded landscape.

Dillard exemplifies that Thoreauvian strain of American nature writing that finds metaphysical wisdom by intensely focusing on nature in the here and now. Under a stately sycamore tree, drinking in the very ordinary view of a creek under a midday sun, Dillard sees in it extraordinary things. Like Mary Austin, she is keenly alert to the imagery, movement, and sensations of nature. If there is a singular meaning in the natural world, Dillard suggests, it lies in its capacity to awaken us from a mind-numbing, mediated culture. Turning our attention to a bend in the creek or a twist of a tree trunk, Dillard illustrates the meticulous watchfulness of the conventional natural historian. There convention ends, for she sees well not only the landscape of Tinker Creek, her present, but also the Squirrel Hill tunnel and busy sycamore-lined streets of Pittsburgh, her past. As it was for Emerson, nature for her is transcendentally linked—creek to desert, past, present, and future. And it is full of surprises. How can the sycamore thrive both amid a smoky city and beside a lush creek? Dillard answers her own query by reasoning toward the affinity of tree and human life. Hers is the quintessential open mind, at once unguarded and vigilant. Although she does not miss a pertinent detail of landscapes behind and before her, the natural history seems almost incidental to the more spiritual quest.

Dillard's prose is stamped with the same vintage American individualism that led Thoreau to eschew the possibility of organized social change and ponder the infinite meanings of Walden Pond. *Pilgrim at Tinker Creek* bespeaks the reincarnation of that impulse in the late 1960s and 1970s. Existential musing, soul searching, and consciousness raising entwined as another generation of Americans went "back to nature." Many of them were beleaguered civil rights and antiwar activists who resigned from trying to change a national politics that seemed beyond their control. They concentrated instead on the parochial, the individual, the immediate, and the *natural*. That impulse flavored much of the issue-oriented political activism and the music of the 1970s.[37] Bumper stickers of the period calling Americans to THINK GLOBALLY, ACT LOCALLY were a kind of activist's version of Dillard's desire to truly "live with trees." In the face of worsening national and global ecological problems that were surfacing in that decade, Tinker Creek is enough for Dillard to ponder. For many readers, perhaps it was a literary place to begin confronting those larger concerns.

Even for Dillard, though firmly grounded in the Virginia landscape, her sense of place and time cannot be contained there. Somehow this creek, this moment says something large about the planet and earthly perpetuity. Evoking one of the rules of ecology made popular in the 1970s by Barry Commoner, that "everything is connected to everything else,"[38] Dillard whirls us through the galaxy, aloft through the jet stream of global winds, across the tundra, atop the Andes Mountains, through river currents around the world, and back home again to Dead Man Mountain and Tinker Creek. Continually returning to the place she knows best, Dillard issues a casual challenge to her reader to do the same: "Where are *you* now?" (emphasis mine). And when, for Tinker Creek also provokes questions of time. Aroused from her dreamy Pittsburgh past that the sycamore evokes, Dillard looks up the creek toward the future.

What she ultimately finds in her patch of earth is an uncertainty that breeds the same humility discovered by Mary Austin in the desert: those of us who are sure we know our environment are in fact among the least aware.[39] We live in a culture impressed by certainty and dominance. Despite considerable daily evidence that should undermine our confidence, still we engineer environmental change with all of the authority and absolutism that has characterized the modern age. Annie Dillard counters our certitude with the uncomfortable adage that the more we learn of nature and the more contemplative time we spend there, the more we realize how little we know and how much there is to ponder.

NOTES

1. Henry David Thoreau, *Walking* (Cambridge, MA: Riverside Press, 1914), 62.
2. Thomas J. Lyon, "A Taxonomy of Nature Writing," in Cheryll Glotfelty and Harold Fromm, eds., *The Ecocriticism Reader: Landmarks in Literary Ecology* (Athens: University of Georgia Press, 1996), 276.
3. Sydney Smith, *Edinburgh Review* (1820), quoted by Alfred Runte, *National Parks: The American Experience*, 2d ed. (Lincoln: University of Nebraska Press, 1987), 32.
4. On the impact of Bartram on European romantics, see Michael Branch, "Indexing American Possibilities," in Glotfelty and Fromm, eds., *The Ecocriticism Reader*, 287; and N. Bryllion Fagin, *William Bartram* (Baltimore: Johns Hopkins University Press, 1933).
5. Roderick Frazier Nash, *Wilderness and the American Mind*, 3d ed. (New Haven: Yale University Press, 1982), 67–83; Hans Huth, *Nature and the American: Three Centuries of Changing Attitudes*, new edition, with Introduction by Douglas H. Strong (Lincoln: University of Nebraska Press, 1990), 30–53.
6. Jennifer Price, *Flight Maps: Adventures with Nature in Modern America* (New York: Basic Books, 1999), 119.
7. See Peter J. Schmitt, *Back to Nature: The Arcadian Myth in Urban America*, with Foreword by John R. Stilgoe (Baltimore: Johns Hopkins University Press, 1969, 1990), especially 3–19, 56–76; Huth, *Nature and the American*, 54–70; and Price, *Flight Maps*, particularly chapter 2.
8. John James Audubon, *Delineations of American Scenery and Character*, ed. Francis Hobart Herrick (New York, 1926), 9–10; Thomas Cole, "Essay on American Scenery," *American Monthly Magazine* 1 (1836): 3, 12; Cole, "Lament of the Forest," *Knickerbocker Magazine* 17 (1841): 518–19; Bryant, *Letters of a Traveller; or Notes of Things Seen in Europe and America* (New York, 1850), 302. All quoted in an excellent summary of this literature by Nash, *Wilderness and the American Mind*, 97.
9. Nash, *Wilderness and the American Mind*, 77; Henry Nash Smith, *Virgin Land: The American West in Myth and Symbol* (Cambridge, MA: Harvard University Press, 1957), 59–70 and 220–24.
10. Walt Whitman, "Leaves of Grass" (1855), line 1316. On the larger and related myth of endless American abundance, see David M. Potter, *People of Plenty: Economic Abundance and the American Character* (Chicago: University of Chicago Press, 1954), especially 128–65.
11. John F. Kasson, *Civilizing the Machine: Technology and Republican Values in America, 1776–1900* (New York: Penguin Books, 1976), 172–79. On Emerson and Thoreau, see Leo Marx, *The Machine in the Garden: Technology and the Pastoral Ideal in America* (New York: Oxford University Press, 1964), 227–65.
12. Joseph Wood Krutch, Introduction to *Walden and Other Writings by Henry David Thoreau* (New York: Bantam, 1981), 5. *Walden* was first published in 1854. For a premier interpretation of Thoreau, see Lawrence Buell, *The Environmental Imagination: Thoreau, Nature Writing, and the Formation of American Culture* (Cambridge, MA: Harvard University Press, 1995).
13. Ralph Waldo Emerson, "The Commercial Spirit," 1837 commencement address at Harvard College.

14. Estwick Evans, *A Pedestrious Tour of Four Thousand Miles through the Western States and Territories during the Winter and Spring of 1818* (Concord, NH, 1819).
15. Quoted from unnoted source by Krutch, *Walden and Other Writings*, 2.
16. Henry David Thoreau, *The Maine Woods* (Princeton: Princeton University Press, 1972), 71, quoted in SueEllen Campbell, "The Land and Language of Desire: Where Deep Ecology and Post-Structuralism Meet," in Glotfelty and Fromm, eds., *The Ecocriticism Reader*; originally in *Western American Literature* 24, no. 3 (November 1989): 199–211.
17. Scott Russell, "Speaking a Word for Nature," in Glotfelty and Fromm, eds., *The Ecocriticism Reader*, 188. For an extensive analysis of Thoreau's "psychology of awareness," see Scott Slovic's excellent piece, "Nature Writing and Environmental Psychology," in the same volume, 351–55.
18. Nash, *Wilderness and the American Mind*, 122–25.
19. Ibid., 125. See also Michael P. Cohen's excellent biography, *The Pathless Way: John Muir and American Wilderness* (Madison: University of Wisconsin Press, 1986).
20. See Michael P. Cohen, *The History of the Sierra Club, 1892–1977* (San Francisco: Sierra Club Books, 1988).
21. *John of the Mountains: The Unpublished Journals of John Muir*, ed. Linnie Marsh Wolfe (Boston, 1938), 315, 317, quoted in Nash, *Wilderness and the American Mind*, 128.
22. John Muir, "The Wild Sheep of California," *Overland Monthly* 12 (April 1874): 358–63, quoted in *Muir Among the Animals: The Wildlife Writings of John Muir*, ed. by Lisa Mighetto (San Francisco: Sierra Club Books, 1986), 18–19.
23. See Paul Shepard, *Man in the Landscape: A Historic View of the Esthetics of Nature* (New York: Alfred A. Knopf, 1967).
24. See, for example, Chris J. Magoc, *Wonderland: Yellowstone National Park and the Creation of an American Landscape, 1870–1903* (Albuquerque: University of New Mexico Press, 1998), chapter 4.
25. *John Burroughs Talks: His Reminiscences and Comments* as reported to Clifton Johnson (Boston: Houghton Mifflin, 1922), 188, 210, quoted in Huth, *Nature and the American*, 103.
26. Schmitt, *Back to Nature*, 22–25; Huth, *Nature and the American*, 102–3.
27. Lyon, "A Taxonomy of Nature Writing," 277.
28. Schmitt, *Back to Nature*, 42, 45–49; ibid., 47, quoting Seton from his *Lives of the Hunted* (New York: Scribner's, 1901), 9.
29. Eugene A. Clancy, "The Car and the Country Home," *Harper's Weekly* 55 (May 6, 1911): 30, quoted by Schmitt, *Back to Nature*, 17.
30. John Burroughs, *Field and Study*, quoted by Norman Foerster, *Nature in American Literature* (New York: Russell and Russell, 1958), 291, 294.
31. For a good summary of Austin's changing place in American letters, see Nancy Porter's Afterword to *A Woman of Genius* (New York: Old Westbury Press, 1985; original publication 1912 Doubleday).
32. Smith, *Virgin Land*, 174–83.
33. Vera L. Norwood, "Heroines of Nature: Four Women Respond to the American Landscape," in Glotfelty and Fromm, eds., *The Ecocriticism Reader*, 331.
34. John Wesley Powell, *Report on the Lands of the Arid Region of the United States* (Washington, DC, 1878), 25–45, quoted by Smith, *Virgin Land*, 196–200.

35. Norwood, "Heroines of Nature," 331.
36. Marta Weigle and Peter White, *The Lore of New Mexico* (Albuquerque: University of New Mexico Press, 1988), see especially 49–65; Earl Pomeroy, *In Search of the Golden West: The Tourist in Western America* (New York: Alfred A. Knopf, 1957), 3–30.
37. The numerous examples of this introspective, back-to-nature, existentialist body of music range from John Denver to the Grateful Dead.
38. Barry Commoner, *The Closing Circle: Nature, Man, and Technology* (New York: Bantam Books, 1972).
39. Scott Slovic, "Nature Writing and Environmental Psychology," in Glotfelty and Fromm, eds., *The Ecocriticism Reader*, 358.

11 Where I Lived and What I Lived For (1854)

When first I took up my abode in the woods, that is, began to spend my nights as well as days there, which, by accident, was on Independence Day, or the Fourth of July, 1845, my house was not finished for winter, but was merely a defence against the rain, without plastering or chimney, the walls being of rough, weather-stained boards, with wide chinks, which made it cool at night. The upright white hewn studs and freshly planed door and window casings gave it a clean and airy look, especially in the morning, when its timbers were saturated with dew, so that I fancied that by noon some sweet gum would exude from them. To my imagination it retained throughout the day more or less of this auroral character, reminding me of a certain house on a mountain which I had visited a year before. This was an airy and unplastered cabin, fit to entertain a travelling god, and where a goddess might trail her garments. The winds which passed over my dwelling were such as sweep over the ridges of mountains, bearing the broken strains, or celestial parts only, of terrestrial music. The morning wind forever blows, the poem of creation is uninterrupted; but few are the ears that hear it. Olympus is but the outside of the earth everywhere.

The only house I had been the owner of before, if I except a boat, was a tent, which I used occasionally when making excursions in the summer, and this is still rolled up in my garret; but the boat, after

From Henry David Thoreau, "Where I Lived and What I Lived For," *Walden* (Boston: Ticknor and Fields, 1854), 94–96, 100–103, 108–9.

passing from hand to hand, has gone down the stream of time. With this more substantial shelter about me, I had made some progress toward settling in the world. This frame, so slightly clad, was a sort of crystallization around me, and reacted on the builder. It was suggestive somewhat as a picture in outlines. I did not need to go outdoors to take the air, for the atmosphere within had lost none of its freshness. It was not so much within-doors as behind a door where I sat, even in the rainiest weather. The Harivansa says, "An abode without birds is like a meat without seasoning." Such was not my abode, for I found myself suddenly neighbor to the birds; not by having imprisoned one, but having caged myself near them. I was not only nearer to some of those which commonly frequent the garden and the orchard, but to those wilder and more thrilling songsters of the forest which never, or rarely, serenade a villager,—the wood thrush, the veery, the scarlet tanager, the field sparrow, the whip-poor-will, and many others.

I was seated by the shore of a small pond, about a mile and a half south of the village of Concord and somewhat higher than it, in the midst of an extensive wood between that town and Lincoln, and about two miles south of that our only field known to fame, Concord Battle Ground; but I was so low in the woods that the opposite shore, half a mile off, like the rest, covered with wood, was my most distant horizon. For the first week, whenever I looked out on the pond it impressed me like a tarn high up on the side of a mountain, its bottom far above the surface of other lakes, and, as the sun arose, I saw it throwing off its nightly clothing of mist, and here and there, by degrees, its soft ripples or its smooth reflecting surface was revealed, while the mists, like ghosts, were stealthily withdrawing in every direction into the woods, as at the breaking up of some nocturnal conventicle [assembly]. The very dew seemed to hang upon the trees later into the day than usual, as on the sides of mountains.

This small lake was of most value as a neighbor in the intervals of a gentle rain-storm in August, when, both air and water being perfectly still, but the sky overcast, mid-afternoon had all the serenity of evening, and the wood thrush sang around, and was heard from shore to shore. A lake like this is never smoother than at such a time; and the clear portion of the air above it being shallow and darkened by clouds, the water, full of light and reflections, becomes a lower heaven itself so much the more important. From a hill-top near by, where the wood had been recently cut off, there was a pleasing vista southward across the pond, through a wide indentation in the hills which form the shore there, where their opposite sides sloping toward each other suggested a stream flowing out in that direction through a wooded valley, but stream there was none. That way I looked between and over the near green hills to some distant and higher ones in the horizon, tinged with blue. . . .

We must learn to reawaken and keep ourselves awake, not by mechanical aids, but by an infinite expectation of the dawn, which does not forsake us in our soundest sleep. I know of no more encouraging fact than the unquestionable ability of man to elevate his life by a conscious endeavor. It is something to be able to paint a particular picture, or to carve a statue, and so to make a few objects beautiful; but it is far more glorious to carve and paint the very atmosphere and medium through which we look, which morally we can do. To affect the quality of the day, that is the highest of arts. Every man is tasked to make his life, even in its details, worthy of the contemplation of his most elevated and critical hour. If we refused, or rather used up, such paltry information as we get, the oracles would distinctly inform us how this might be done.

I went to the woods because I wished to live deliberately, to front only the essential facts of life, and see if I could not learn what it had to teach, and not, when I came to die, discover that I had not lived. I did not wish to live what was not life, living is so dear; nor did I wish to practise resignation, unless it was quite necessary. I wanted to live deep and suck out all the marrow of life, to live so sturdily and Spartan-like as to put to rout all that was not life, to cut a broad swath and shave close, to drive life into a corner, and reduce it to its lowest terms, and, if it proved to be mean, why then to get the whole and genuine meanness of it, and publish its meanness to the world; or if it were sublime, to know it by experience, and be able to give a true account of it in my next excursion. For most men, it appears to me, are in a strange uncertainty about it, whether it is of the devil or of God, and have *somewhat hastily* concluded that it is the chief end of man here to "glorify God and enjoy him forever."

Still we live meanly, like ants, though the fable tells us that we were long ago changed into men; like pygmies we fight with cranes; it is error upon error, and clout upon clout, and our best virtue has for its occasion a superfluous and evitable wretchedness. Our life is frittered away by detail. An honest man has hardly need to count more than his ten fingers, or in extreme cases he may add his ten toes, and lump the rest. Simplicity, simplicity, simplicity! I say, let your affairs be as two or three, and not a hundred or a thousand; instead of a million count half a dozen, and keep your accounts on your thumb-nail. In the midst of this chopping sea of civilized life, such are the clouds and storms and quicksands and thousand-and-one items to be allowed for, that a man has to live, if he would not founder and go to the bottom and not make his port at all, by dead reckoning, and he must be a great calculator indeed who succeeds. Simplify, simplify. Instead of three meals a day, if it be necessary eat but one; instead of a hundred dishes, five; and reduce other things in proportion. Our life is like a German Confederacy, made up of petty states, with its boundary forever fluctuating, so that even a German cannot tell you how it is bounded at any moment. The nation itself, with all its so-called internal improvements, which, by the way, are all external and superficial, is just such an unwieldy and overgrown establishment, cluttered with furniture and tripped up by its own traps, ruined by luxury and heedless expense, by want of calculation and a worthy aim, as the million households in the land; and the only cure for it, as for them, is in a rigid economy, a stern and more than Spartan simplicity of life and elevation of purpose. It lives too fast. Men think that it is essential that the *Nation* have commerce, and export ice, and talk through a telegraph, and ride thirty miles an hour, without a doubt, whether *they* do or not; but whether we should live like baboons or like men, is a little uncertain. If we do not get out sleepers [timber holding rails in place], and forge rails, and devote days and nights to the work, but go to tinkering upon our *lives* to improve *them*, who will build railroads? And if railroads are not built, how shall we get to heaven in season? But if we stay at home and mind our business, who will want railroads? We do not ride on the railroad; it rides upon us. Did you ever think what those sleepers are that underlie the railroad? Each one is a man, an Irishman, or a Yankee man. The rails are laid on them, and they are covered with sand, and the cars run smoothly over them. They are sound sleepers, I assure you. And every few years a new lot is laid down and run over; so that, if some have the pleasure of riding on a rail, others have the misfortune to be ridden upon. And when they run over a man that is walking in his sleep, a supernumerary sleeper in the wrong position, and wake him up, they suddenly stop the cars, and make a hue and cry about it, as if this were an exception. I am glad to know that it takes a gang of men for every five miles to keep the sleepers down and level in their beds as it is, for this is a sign that they may sometime get up again. . . .

Let us spend one day as deliberately as Nature, and not be thrown off the track by every nutshell and mosquito's wing that falls on the rails. Let us rise early and fast, or break fast, gently and without perturbation; let company come and let company go, let the bells ring and the children cry,—determined to make a day of it. Why should we knock under and go with the stream? Let us not be upset and overwhelmed in that terrible rapid and whirlpool called a dinner, situated in the meridian [midday] shallows. Weather this danger and you are safe, for the rest of the way is down hill. With unrelaxed nerves, with morning vigor, sail by it, looking another way, tied to the mast like Ulysses. If the engine whistles, let it whistle till it is hoarse for its pains. If the bell rings, why should we run? We will consider what kind of music they are like. Let us settle ourselves, and work and wedge our feet downward through the mud and slush of opinion, and prejudice, and tradition, and delusion, and appearance, that alluvion [flood] which covers the globe, through Paris and London, through New York and Boston and Concord, through Church and State, through poetry and philosophy and religion, till we come to a hard bottom and rocks in place, which we can call *reality*, and say, This is, and no mistake; and then begin, having a *point d'appui* [foundation], below freshet and frost and fire, a place where you might found a wall or a state, or set a lamp-post safely, or perhaps a gauge, not a Nilometer, but a Realometer, that future ages might know how deep a freshet of shams and appearances had gathered from time to time. If you stand right fronting and face to face to a fact, you will see the sun glimmer on both its surfaces, as if it were a cimeter [scimitar], and feel its sweet edge dividing you through the heart and marrow, and so you will happily conclude your mortal career. Be it life or death, we crave only reality. If we are really dying, let us hear the rattle in our throats and feel cold in the extremities; if we are alive, let us go about our business.

Time is but the stream I go a-fishing in. I drink at it; but while I drink I see the sandy bottom and detect how shallow it is. Its thin current slides away, but eternity remains. I would drink deeper; fish in the sky, whose bottom is pebbly with stars. I cannot count one. I know not the first letter of the alphabet. I have always been regretting that I was not as wise as the day I was born. The intellect is a cleaver; it discerns and rifts its way into the secret of things. I do not wish to be any more busy with my hands than is necessary. My head is hands and feet. I feel all my best faculties concentrated in it. My instinct tells me that my head is an organ for burrowing, as some creatures use their snout and fore paws, and with it I would mine and burrow my way through these hills. I think that the richest vein is somewhere hereabouts; so by the divining-rod and thin rising vapors I judge; and here I will begin to mine.

JOHN MUIR

12 | My First Summer in the Sierra (1868)

June 20. Some of the silly sheep got caught fast in a tangle of chaparral this morning, like flies in a spider's web, and had to be helped out. Carlo found them and tried to drive them from the trap by the easiest way. How far above sheep are intelligent dogs! No friend and helper can be more affectionate and constant than Carlo. The noble St. Bernard is an honor to his race.

The air is distinctly fragrant with balsam and resin and mint,— every breath of it a gift we may well thank God for. Who could ever guess that so rough a wilderness should yet be so fine, so full of good things. One seems to be in a majestic domed pavilion in which a grand play is being acted with scenery and music and incense,—all the furniture and action so interesting we are in no danger of being called on to endure one dull moment. God himself seems to be always doing his best here, working like a man in a glow of enthusiasm. . . .

June 23. Oh, these vast, calm, measureless mountain days, inciting at once to work and rest! Days in whose light everything seems equally divine, opening a thousand windows to show us God. Nevermore, however weary, should one faint by the way who gains the blessings of one mountain day; whatever his fate, long life, short life, stormy or calm, he is rich forever. . . .

July 8. Now away we go toward the top-most mountains. Many still, small voices, as well as the noon thunder, are calling, "Come higher." Farewell, blessed dell, woods, gardens, streams, birds, squirrels, lizards, and a thousand others. Farewell, farewell. . . .

From John Muir, *My First Summer in the Sierra* (Boston: Houghton Mifflin and Company, 1916), 59–61, 86, 115–17, 131–34.

July 15. Followed the Mono Trail up the eastern rim of the basin nearly to its summit, then turned off southward to a small shallow valley that extends to the edge of the Yosemite, which we reached about noon, and encamped. After luncheon I made haste to high ground, and from the top of the ridge on the west side of Indian Cañon gained the noblest view of the summit peaks I have ever yet enjoyed. Nearly all the upper basin of the Merced was displayed, with its sublime domes and cañons, dark upsweeping forests, and glorious array of white peaks deep in the sky, every feature glowing, radiating beauty that pours into our flesh and bones like heat rays from fire. Sunshine over all; no breath of wind to stir the brooding calm. Never before had I seen so glorious a landscape, so boundless an affluence of sublime mountain beauty. The most extravagant description I might give of this view to any one who has not seen similar landscapes with his own eyes would not so much as hint its grandeur and the spiritual glow that covered it. I shouted and gesticulated in a wild burst of ecstasy, much to the astonishment of St. Bernard Carlo, who came running up to me, manifesting in his intelligent eyes a puzzled concern that was very ludicrous, which had the effect of bringing me to my senses. A brown bear, too, it would seem, had been a spectator of the show I had made of myself, for I had gone but a few yards when I started one from a thicket of brush. He evidently considered me dangerous, for he ran away very fast, tumbling over the tops of the tangled manzanita bushes in his haste. Carlo drew back, with his ears depressed as if afraid, and kept looking me in the face, as if expecting me to pursue and shoot, for he had seen many a bear battle in his day.

Following the ridge, which made a gradual descent to the south, I came at length to the brow of that massive cliff that stands between Indian Cañon and Yosemite Falls, and here the far-famed valley came suddenly into view throughout almost its whole extent. The noble walls—sculptured into endless variety of domes and gables, spires and battlements and plain mural precipices—all a-tremble with the thunder tones of the falling water. The level bottom seemed to be dressed like a garden—sunny meadows here and there, and groves of pine and oak; the river of Mercy sweeping in majesty through the midst of them and flashing back the sunbeams. The great Tissiack, or Half-Dome, rising at the upper end of the valley to a height of nearly a mile, is nobly proportioned and life-like, the most impressive of all the rocks, holding the eye in devout admiration, calling it back again and again from falls or meadows, or even the mountains beyond,—marvelous cliffs, marvelous in sheer dizzy depth and sculpture, types of endurance. Thousands of years have they stood in the sky exposed to rain, snow, frost, earthquake and avalanche, yet they still wear the bloom of youth. . . .

Sketching on the North Dome. It commands views of nearly all the valley besides a few of the high mountains. I would fain draw everything in sight—rock, tree, and leaf. But little can I do beyond mere outlines,—marks with meanings like words, readable only to myself,—yet I sharpen my pencils and work on as if others might possibly be benefited. Whether these picture-sheets are to vanish like fallen leaves or go to friends like letters, matters not much; for little can they tell to those who have not themselves seen similar wildness, and like a language have learned it. No pain here, no dull empty hours, no fear of the past, no fear of the future. These blessed mountains are so compactly filled with God's beauty, no petty personal hope or experience has room to be. Drinking this champagne water is pure pleasure, so is breathing the living air, and every movement of limbs is pleasure, while the whole body seems to feel beauty when exposed to it as it feels the campfire or sunshine, entering not by the eyes alone, but equally through all one's flesh like radiant heat, making a passionate ecstatic pleasure-glow not explainable. One's body then seems homogeneous throughout, sound as a crystal.

Perched like a fly on this Yosemite dome, I gaze and sketch and bask, oftentimes settling down into dumb admiration without definite hope of ever learning much, yet with the longing, unresting effort that lies at the door of hope, humbly prostrate before the vast display of God's power, and eager to offer self-denial and renunciation with eternal toil to learn any lesson in the divine manuscript.

It is easier to feel than to realize, or in any way explain, Yosemite grandeur. The magnitudes of the rocks and trees and streams are so delicately harmonized they are mostly hidden. Sheer precipices three thousand feet high are fringed with tall trees growing close like grass on the brow of a lowland hill, and extending along the feet of these precipices is a ribbon of meadow a mile wide and seven or eight long, that seems like a strip a farmer might mow in less than a day. Waterfalls, five hundred to one or two thousand feet high, are so subordinated to the mighty cliffs over which they pour that they seem like wisps of smoke, gentle as floating clouds, though their voices fill the valley and make the rocks tremble. The mountains, too, along the eastern sky, and the domes in front of them, and the succession of smooth rounded waves between, swelling higher, higher, with dark woods in their hollows, serene in massive exuberant bulk and beauty, tend yet more to hide the grandeur of the Yosemite temple and make it appear as a subdued subordinate feature of the vast harmonious landscape. Thus every attempt to appreciate any one feature is beaten down by the overwhelming influence of all the others. And, as if this were not enough, lo! in the sky arises another mountain range with topography as rugged and substantial-looking as the one beneath it—snowy peaks and domes and shadowy Yosemite valleys—another version of the snowy Sierra, a new creation heralded by a thunder-storm. How fiercely, devoutly wild is Nature in the midst of her beauty-loving tenderness!—painting lilies, watering them, caressing them with gentle hand, going from flower to flower like a gardener while building rock mountains and cloud mountains full of lightning and rain. Gladly we run for shelter beneath an overhanging cliff and examine the reassuring ferns and mosses, gentle love tokens growing in cracks and chinks. Daisies, too, and ivesias, confiding wild children of light, too small to fear. To these one's heart goes home, and the voices of the storm become gentle. Now the sun breaks forth and fragrant steam arises. The birds are out singing on the edges of the groves. The west is flaming in gold and purple, ready for the ceremony of the sunset, and back I go to camp with my notes and pictures, the best of them printed in my mind as dreams. A fruitful day, without measured beginning or ending. A terrestrial eternity. A gift of good God.

13 | Spring at the Capital (1871)

I came to Washington to live in the fall of 1863, and, with the exception of a month each summer spent in the interior of New York, have lived here ever since.

I saw my first novelty in Natural History the day after my arrival. As I was walking near some woods north of the city, a grasshopper of prodigious size flew up from the ground and alighted in a tree. As I pursued him, he proved to be nearly as wild and as fleet of wing as a bird. I thought I had reached the capital of grasshopperdom, and that this was perhaps one of the chiefs or leaders, or perhaps the great High Cock O'lorum [braggart] himself, taking an airing in the fields. I have never yet been able to settle the question, as every fall I start up a few of these gigantic specimens, which perch on the trees. They are about three inches long, of a gray striped or spotted color, and have quite a reptile look.

The greatest novelty I found, however, was the superb autumn weather, the bright, strong, electric days, lasting well into November, and the general mildness of the entire winter. Though the mercury occasionally sinks to zero, yet the earth is never so seared and blighted by the cold but that in some sheltered nook or corner signs of vegetable life still remain, which on a little encouragement even asserts itself. I have found wild flowers here every month in the year; violets

From John Burroughs, "Spring at the Capital," *Wake-Robin* (first published 1871; reprint, Boston: Houghton, Mifflin and Company, 1894), 147–51, 155–57, 161–66, 175–76.

in December, a single houstonia in January (the little lump of earth upon which it stood was frozen hard), and a tiny, weed-like plant, with a flower almost microscopic in its smallness, growing along graveled walks and in old plowed fields in February. The liverwort sometimes comes out as early as the first week in March, and the little frogs begin to pipe doubtfully about the same time. Apricot-trees are usually in bloom on All-Fool's Day and the apple-trees on May Day. By August, mother hen will lead forth her third brood, and I had a March pullet that came off with a family of her own in September. Our calendar is made for this climate. March is a spring month. One is quite sure to see some marked and striking change during the first eight or ten days. This season (1868) is a backward one, and the memorable change did not come till the 10th.

Then the sun rose up from a bed of vapors, and seemed fairly to dissolve with tenderness and warmth. For an hour or two the air was perfectly motionless, and full of low, humming, awakening sounds. The naked trees had a rapt, expectant look. From some unreclaimed common near by came the first strain of the song sparrow; so homely, because so old and familiar, yet so inexpressibly pleasing. Presently a full chorus of voices arose, tender, musical, half suppressed, but full of genuine hilarity and joy. The bluebird warbled, the robin called, the snowbird chattered, the meadowlark uttered her strong but tender note. Over a deserted field a turkey buzzard hovered low, and alighted on a stake in the fence, standing a moment with outstretched, vibrating wings till he was sure of his hold. A soft, warm, brooding day. Roads becoming dry in many places, and looking so good after the mud and the snow. I walk up beyond the boundary and over Meridian Hill. To move along the drying road and feel the delicious warmth is enough. The cattle low long and loud, and look wistfully into the distance. I sympathize with them. Never a spring comes but I have an almost irresistible desire to depart. Some nomadic or migrating instinct or reminiscence stirs within me. I ache to be off.

As I pass along, the high-hole [flicker] calls in the distance precisely as I have heard him in the North. After a pause he repeats his summons. What can be more welcome to the ear than these early first sounds! They have such a margin of silence!

One need but pass the boundary of Washington city to be fairly in the country, and ten minutes' walk in the country brings one to real primitive woods. The town has not yet overflowed its limits like the great Northern commercial capitals, and Nature, wild and unkempt, comes up to its very threshold, and even in many places crosses it.

The woods, which I soon reach, are stark and still. The signs of returning life are so faint as to be almost imperceptible, but there is a fresh, earthy smell in the air, as if something had stirred here under the leaves. The crows caw above the wood, or walk about the brown fields. I look at the gray, silent trees long and long, but they show no sign. The catkins of some alders by a little pool have just swelled perceptibly; and, brushing away the dry leaves and débris on a sunny slope, I discover the liverwort just pushing up a fuzzy, tender sprout. But the waters have brought forth. The little frogs are musical. From every marsh and pool goes up their shrill but pleasing chorus. Peering into one of their haunts, a little body of semi-stagnant water, I discover masses of frogs' spawn covering the bottom. I take up great chunks of the cold, quivering jelly in my hands. In some places there are gallons of it. A youth who accompanies me wonders if it would not be good cooked, or if it could not be used as a substitute for eggs. It is a perfect jelly, of a slightly milky tinge, thickly imbedded with black spots about the size of a small bird's eye. When just deposited it is perfectly transparent. These hatch in eight or ten days, gradually absorb their gelatinous surroundings, and the tiny tadpoles issue forth.

In the city, even before the shop-windows have caught the inspiration, spring is heralded by the silver poplars which line all the streets and avenues. After a few mild, sunshiny March days, you suddenly perceive a change has come over the trees. Their tops have a less naked look. If the weather continues warm, a single day will work wonders. Presently the tree will be one vast plume of gray, downy tassels, while not the least speck of green foliage is visible. The first week in April these long mimic caterpillars lie all about the streets and fill the gutters. . . .

A glimpse of the birds usually found here in the latter part of winter may be had in the following extract, which I take from my diary under date of February 4th:—

"Made a long excursion through the woods and over the hills. Went directly north from the Capitol for about three miles. The ground bare and the day cold and sharp. In the suburbs, among the scattered Irish and negro shanties, came suddenly upon a flock of birds, feeding about like our northern snow buntings. Every now and then they uttered a piping, disconsolate note, as if they had a very sorry time of it. They proved to be shore larks, the first I had ever seen. They had the walk characteristic of all larks; were a little larger than the sparrow; had a black spot on the breast, with much white on the under parts of their bodies. As I approached them the nearer ones paused, and, half squatting, eyed me suspiciously. Presently, at a movement of my arm, away they went, flying exactly like the snow bunting, and showing nearly as much white." (I have since discovered that the shore lark is a regular visitant here in February and March, when large quantities of them are shot or trapped, and exposed for sale in the market. During a heavy snow I have seen numbers of them feeding upon the seeds of various weedy growths in a large market-garden well into town.) "Pressing on, the walk became exhilarating. Followed a little brook, the eastern branch of the Tiber, lined with bushes and a rank growth of green-brier. Sparrows started out here and there, and flew across the little bends and points. Among some pines just beyond the boundary, saw a number of American gold-finches, in their gray winter dress, pecking the pine-cones. A golden-crowned kinglet was there also, a little tuft of gray feathers, hopping about as restless as a spirit. Had the old pine-trees food delicate enough for him also? Farther on, in some low open woods, saw many sparrows,—the fox, white-throated, white-crowned, the Canada, the song, the swamp,—all herding together along the warm and sheltered borders. To my surprise, saw a chewink also, and the yellow-rumped warbler. The purple finch was there likewise, and the Carolina wren and brown creeper. In the higher, colder woods not a bird was to be seen. Returning, near sunset, across the eastern slope of a hill which overlooked the city, was delighted to see a number of grass finches or vesper sparrows,—birds which will be forever associated in my mind with my father's sheep pastures. They ran before me, now flitting a pace or two, now skulking in the low stubble, just as I had observed them when a boy."

A month later, March 4th, is this note:—

"After the second memorable inauguration of President Lincoln, took my first trip of the season. The afternoon was very clear and warm,—real vernal sunshine at last, though the wind roared like a lion over the woods. It seemed novel enough to find within two miles of the White House a simple woodsman chopping away as if no President was being inaugurated! Some puppies, snugly nestled in the cavity of an old hollow tree, he said, belonged to a wild dog. I imagine I saw the 'wild dog,' on the other side of Rock Creek, in a great state of grief and trepidation, running up and down, crying and yelping, and looking wistfully over the swollen flood, which the poor thing had not the courage to brave. This day, for the first time, I heard the song of the Canada sparrow, a soft, sweet note, almost running into a warble. Saw a small, black, velvety butterfly with a yellow border to its wings. Under a warm bank found two flowers of the houstonia in bloom. Saw frogs' spawn near Piny Branch, and heard the hyla." . . .

The national capital is situated in such a vast spread of wild, wooded, or semi-cultivated country, and is in itself so open and spacious, with its parks and large government reservations, that an unusual number of birds find their way into it in the course of the season. Rare warblers, as the black-poll, the yellow red-poll, and the bay-breasted, pausing in May on their northward journey, pursue their insect game in the very heart of the town.

I have heard the veery thrush in the trees near the White House; and one rainy April morning, about six o'clock, he came and blew his soft, mellow flute in a pear-tree in my garden. The tones had all the sweetness and wildness they have when heard in June in our deep northern forests. A day or two afterward, in the same tree, I heard for the first time the song of the ruby-crowned wren, or kinglet,—the same liquid bubble and cadence which characterize the wren-songs generally, but much finer and more delicate than the song of any other variety known to me; beginning in a fine, round, needle-like note, and rising into a full, sustained warble,— a strain, on the whole, remarkably exquisite and pleasing, the singer being all the while as busy as a bee, catching some kind of insect. It is certainly one of our most beautiful bird-songs, and Audubon's enthusiasm concerning its song, as he heard it in the wilds of Labrador, is not a bit extravagant. The song of the kinglet is the only characteristic that allies it to the wrens.

The Capitol grounds, with their fine large trees of many varieties, draw many kinds of birds. In the rear of the building the extensive grounds are peculiarly attractive, being a gentle slope, warm and protected, and quite thickly wooded. Here in early spring I go to hear the robins, catbirds, blackbirds, wrens, etc. In March the white-throated and white-crowned sparrows may be seen, hopping about on the flower-beds or peering slyly from the evergreens. The robin hops about freely upon the grass, notwithstanding the keeper's large-lettered warning, and at intervals, and especially at sunset, carols from the treetops his loud, hearty strain.

The kingbird and orchard starling remain the whole season, and breed in the treetops. The rich, copious song of the starling may be heard there all the forenoon. The song of some birds is like scarlet,—strong, intense, emphatic. This is the character of the orchard starlings, also of the tanagers and the various grosbeaks. On the other hand, the songs of other birds, as of certain of the thrushes, suggest the serene blue of the upper sky.

In February one may hear, in the Smithsonian grounds, the song of the fox sparrow. It is a strong, richly modulated whistle,—the finest sparrow note I have ever heard. . . .

The bobolink does not breed in the District, but usually pauses in his journey and feeds during the day in the grass-lands north of the city. When the season is backward, they tarry a week or ten days, singing freely and appearing quite at home. In large flocks they search over every inch of ground, and at intervals hover on the wing or alight in the treetops, all pouring forth their gladness at once, and filling the air with a multitudinous musical clamor. . . .

Outside of the city limits, the great point of interest to the rambler and lover of nature is the Rock Creek region. Rock Creek is a large, rough, rapid stream, which has its source in the interior of Maryland, and flows into the Potomac between Washington and Georgetown. Its course, for five or six miles out of Washington, is marked by great diversity of scenery. Flowing in a deep valley, which now and then becomes a wild gorge with overhanging rocks and high precipitous headlands, for the most part wooded; here reposing in long, dark reaches, there sweeping and hurrying around a sudden bend or over a rocky bed; receiving at short intervals small runs and spring rivulets, which open up vistas and outlooks to the right and left, of the most charming description,—Rock Creek has an abundance of all the elements that make up not only pleasing but wild and rugged scenery. There is, perhaps, not another city in the Union that has on its very threshold so much natural beauty and grandeur, such as men seek for in remote forests and mountains. A few touches of art would convert this whole region, extending from Georgetown to what is known as Crystal Springs, not more than two miles from the present State Department, into a park unequaled by anything in the world. There are passages between these two points as wild and savage, and apparently as remote from civilization, as anything one meets with in the mountain sources of the Hudson or the Delaware.

One of the tributaries to Rock Creek within this limit is called Piny Branch. It is a small, noisy brook, flowing through a valley of great natural beauty and picturesqueness, shaded nearly all the way by woods of oak, chestnut, and beech, and abounding in dark recesses and hidden retreats.

I must not forget to mention the many springs with which this whole region is supplied, each the centre of some wild nook, perhaps the head of a little valley one or two hundred yards long, through which one catches a glimpse, or hears the voice, of the main creek rushing along below.

My walks tend in this direction more frequently than in any other. Here the boys go, too, troops of them, of a Sunday, to bathe and prowl around, and indulge the semi-barbarous instincts that still lurk within them. Life, in all its forms, is most abundant near water. The rank vegetation nurtures the insects, and the insects draw the birds. The first week in March, on some southern slope where the sunshine lies warm and long, I usually find the hepatica in bloom, though with scarcely an inch of stalk. In the spring runs, the skunk cabbage pushes its pike up through the mould, the flower appearing first, as if Nature had made a mistake. . . .

Another favorite beat of mine is northeast of the city. Looking from the Capitol in this direction, scarcely more than a mile distant, you see a broad green hill-slope, falling very gently, and spreading into a large expanse of meadow-land. The summit, if so gentle a swell of greensward may be said to have a summit, is covered with a grove of large oaks; and, sweeping back out of sight like a mantle, the front line of a thick forest bounds the sides. This emerald landscape is seen from a number of points in the city. Looking along New York Avenue from Northern Liberty Market, the eye glances, as it were, from the red clay of the street, and alights upon this fresh scene in the distance. It is a standing invitation to the citizen to come forth and be refreshed. As I turn from some hot, hard street, how inviting it looks! I bathe my eyes in it as in a fountain. Sometimes troops of cattle are seen grazing upon it. In June the gathering of the hay may be witnessed. When the ground is covered with snow, numerous stacks, or clusters of stacks, are still left for the eye to contemplate.

The woods which clothe the east side of this hill, and sweep away to the east, are among the most charming to be found in the District. The main growth is oak and chestnut, with a thin sprinkling of laurel, azalea, and dogwood. It is the only locality in which I have found the dogtooth violet in bloom, and the best place I know of to gather arbutus. On one slope the ground is covered with moss, through which the arbutus trails its glories.

Emerging from these woods toward the city, one sees the white dome of the Capitol soaring over the green swell of earth immediately in front, and lifting its four thousand tons of iron gracefully and lightly into the air. Of all the sights in Washington, that which will survive longest in my memory is the vision of the great dome thus rising cloud-like above the hills.

MARY AUSTIN

14 The Land of Little Rain (1903)

East away from the Sierras, south from Panamint
and Amargosa, east and south many an uncounted
mile, is the Country of Lost Borders.

Ute, Paiute, Mojave, and Shoshone inhabit its frontiers, and as far
into the heart of it as a man dare go. Not the law, but the land sets the
limit. Desert is the name it wears upon the maps, but the Indian's is
the better word. Desert is a loose term to indicate land that supports
no man; whether the land can be bitted and broken to that purpose is
not proven. Void of life it never is, however dry the air and villainous
the soil.

This is the nature of that country. There are hills, rounded, blunt,
burned, squeezed up out of chaos, chrome and vermilion painted, aspiring to the snow-line. Between the hills lie high level-looking plains
full of intolerable sun glare, or narrow valleys drowned in a blue haze.
The hill surface is streaked with ash drift and black, unweathered lava
flows. After rains, water accumulates in the hollows of small closed
valleys, and, evaporating, leaves hard dry levels of pure desertness
that get the local name of dry lakes. Where the mountains are steep
and the rains heavy, the pool is never quite dry, but dark and bitter,
rimmed about with the efflorescence of alkaline deposits. A thin crust
of it lies along the marsh over the vegetating area, which has neither
beauty nor freshness. In the broad wastes open to the wind the sand
drifts in hummocks about the stubby shrubs, and between them the
soil shows saline traces. The sculpture of the hills here is more wind

From Mary Austin, *The Land of Little Rain* (Boston: Houghton, Mifflin and Company,
1903), 3–6, 8–10, 12–13, 16–17, 19–21.

than water work, though the quick storms do sometimes scar them past many a year's redeeming. In all the Western desert edges there are essays in miniature at the famed, terrible Grand Cañon, to which, if you keep on long enough in this country, you will come at last.

Since this is a hill country one expects to find springs, but not to depend upon them; for when found they are often brackish and unwholesome, or maddening, slow dribbles in a thirsty soil. Here you find the hot sink of Death Valley, or high rolling districts where the air has always a tang of frost. Here are the long heavy winds and breathless calms on the tilted mesas where dust devils dance, whirling up into a wide, pale sky. Here you have no rain when all the earth cries for it, or quick downpours called cloud-bursts for violence. A land of lost rivers, with little in it to love; yet a land that once visited must be come back to inevitably. If it were not so, there would be little told of it. . . .

There are many areas in the desert where drinkable water lies within a few feet of the surface, indicated by the mesquite and the bunch grass (*Sporobolus airoides*). It is this nearness of unimagined help that makes the tragedy of desert deaths. It is related that the final breakdown of that hapless party that gave Death Valley its forbidding name occurred in a locality where shallow wells would have saved them. But how were they to know that? Properly equipped it is possible to go safely across that ghastly sink, yet every year it takes its toll of death, and yet men find there sun-dried mummies, of whom no trace or recollection is preserved. To underestimate one's thirst, to pass a given landmark to the right or left, to find a dry spring where one looked for running water—there is no help for any of these things.

Along springs and sunken watercourses one is surprised to find such water-loving plants as grow widely in moist ground, but the true desert breeds its own kind, each in its particular habitat. The angle of the slope, the frontage of a hill, the structure of the soil determines the plant. South-looking hills are nearly bare, and the lower tree-line higher here by a thousand feet. Cañons running east and west will have one wall naked and one clothed. Around dry lakes and marshes the herbage preserves a set and orderly arrangement. Most species have well-defined areas of growth, the best index the voiceless land can give the traveler of his whereabouts.

If you have any doubt about it, know that the desert begins with the creosote. This immortal shrub spreads down into Death Valley and up to the lower timber-line, odorous and medicinal as you might guess from the name, wandlike, with shining fretted foliage. Its vivid green is grateful to the eye in a wilderness of gray and greenish white shrubs. In the spring it exudes a resinous gum which the Indians of those parts know how to use with pulverized rock for cementing arrow points to shafts. Trust Indians not to miss any virtues of the plant world! . . .

There is neither poverty of soil nor species to account for the sparseness of desert growth, but simply that each plant requires more room. So much earth must be preëmpted to extract so much moisture. The real struggle for existence, the real brain of the plant, is underground; above there is room for a rounded perfect growth. In Death Valley, reputed the very core of desolation, are nearly two hundred identified species. . . .

There is no special preponderance of self-fertilized or wind-fertilized plants, but everywhere the demand for and evidence of insect life. Now where there are seeds and insects there will be birds and small mammals, and where these are, will come the slinking, sharp-toothed kind that prey on them. Go as far as you dare in the heart of a lonely land, you cannot go so far that life and death are not before you. Painted lizards slip in and out of rock crevices, and pant on the white hot sands. Birds, hummingbirds even, nest in the cactus scrub; woodpeckers befriend the demoniac yuccas; out of the stark, treeless waste rings the music of the night-singing mockingbird. If it be summer and the sun well down, there will be a burrowing owl to call. Strange, furry, tricksy things dart across the open places, or sit motionless in the conning towers of the creosote. . . .

If one is inclined to wonder at first how so many dwellers came to be in the loneliest land that ever came out of God's hands, what they do there and why stay, one does not wonder so much after having lived there. None other than this long brown land lays such a hold on the affections. The rainbow hills, the tender bluish mists, the luminous radiance of the spring, have the lotus charm. They trick the sense of time, so that once inhabiting there you always mean to go away without quite realizing that you have not done it. Men who have lived there, miners and cattle-men, will tell you this, not so fluently, but emphatically, cursing the land and going back to it. For one thing there is the divinest, cleanest air to be breathed anywhere in God's world. Some day the world will understand that, and the little oases on the windy tops of hills will harbor for healing its ailing, house-weary broods. There is promise there of great wealth in ores and earths, which is no wealth by reason of being so far removed from water and workable conditions, but men are bewitched by it and tempted to try the impossible. . . .

The palpable sense of mystery in the desert air breeds fables, chiefly of lost treasure. Somewhere within its stark borders, if one believes reports, is a hill strewn with nuggets; one seamed with virgin silver; an old clayey water-bed where Indians scooped up earth to make cooking pots and shaped them reeking with grains of pure gold. Old miners drifting about the desert edges, weathered into the semblance of the tawny hills, will tell you tales like these convincingly. After a little sojourn in that land you will believe them on their own account. It is a question whether it is not better to be bitten by the little horned snake of the desert that goes sidewise and strikes without coiling, than by the tradition of a lost mine.

And yet—and yet—is it not perhaps to satisfy expectation that one falls into the tragic key in writing of desertness? The more you wish of it the more you get, and in the mean time lose much of pleasantness. In that country which begins at the foot of the east slope of the Sierras and spreads out by less and less lofty hill ranges toward the Great Basin, it is possible to live with great zest, to have red blood and delicate joys, to pass and repass about one's daily performance an area that would make an Atlantic seaboard State, and that with no peril, and, according to our way of thought, no particular difficulty. At any rate, it was not people who went into the desert merely to write it up who invented the fabled Hassaympa, of whose waters, if any drink, they can no more see fact as naked fact, but all radiant with the color of romance. I, who must have drunk of it in my twice seven years' wanderings, am assured that it is worth while.

For all the toll the desert takes of a man it gives compensations, deep breaths, deep sleep, and the communion of the stars. It comes upon one with new force in the pauses of the night that the Chaldeans were a desert-bred people. It is hard to escape the sense of mastery as the stars move in the wide clear heavens to risings and settings unobscured. They look large and near and palpitant; as if they moved on some stately service not needful to declare. Wheeling to their stations in the sky, they make the poor world-fret of no account. Of no account you who lie out there watching, nor the lean coyote that stands off in the scrub from you and howls and howls.

ANNIE DILLARD

15 The Present at Tinker Creek (1974)

I am sitting under a sycamore by Tinker Creek. It is early spring, the day after I patted the puppy. I have come to the creek—the backyard stretch of the creek—in the middle of the day, to feel the delicate gathering of heat, real sun's heat, in the air, and to watch new water come down the creek. Don't expect more than this, and a mental ramble. I'm in the market for some present tense; I'm on the lookout, shopping around, more so every year. It's a seller's market—do you think I won't sell all that I have to buy it? Thomas Merton wrote, in a light passage in one of his Gethsemane journals: "Suggested emendation in the Lord's Prayer: Take out 'Thy Kingdom come' and substitute 'Give us time!' " But time is the one thing we have been given, and we have been given to time. Time gives us a whirl. We keep waking from a dream we can't recall, looking around in surprise, and lapsing back, for years on end. All I want to do is stay awake, keep my head up, prop my eyes open, with toothpicks, with trees.

Before me the creek is seventeen feet wide, splashing over random sandstone outcroppings and scattered rocks. I'm lucky; the creek is loud here, because of the rocks, and wild. In the low water of summer and fall I can cross to the opposite bank by leaping from stone to stone. Upstream is a wall of light split into planks by smooth sandstone ledges that cross the creek evenly, like steps. Downstream the

From Annie Dillard, "The Present," *Pilgrim at Tinker Creek* (New York: Harper's Magazine Press, in association with Harper and Row, 1974), 85–89, 97–103. © 1974 by Annie Dillard. Reprinted by permission of HarperCollins Publishers.

live water before me stills, dies suddenly as if extinguished, and vanishes around a bend shaded summer and winter by overarching tulips, locusts, and Osage orange. Everywhere I look are creekside trees whose ascending boles against water and grass accent the vertical thrust of the land in this spot. The creek rests the eye, a haven, a breast; the two steep banks vault from the creek like wings. Not even the sycamore's crown can peek over the land in any direction.

My friend Rosanne Coggeshall, the poet, says that "sycamore" is the most intrinsically beautiful word in English. This sycamore is old; its lower bark is always dusty from years of floodwaters lapping up its trunk. Like many sycamores, too, it is quirky, given to flights and excursions. Its trunk lists over the creek at a dizzying angle, and from that trunk extends a long, skinny limb that spurts high over the opposite bank without branching. The creek reflects the speckled surface of this limb, pale even against the highest clouds, and that image pales whiter and thins as it crosses the creek, shatters in the riffles and melds together, quivering and mottled, like some enormous primeval reptile under the water.

I want to think about trees. Trees have a curious relationship to the subject of the present moment. There are many created things in the universe that outlive us, that outlive the sun, even, but I can't think about them. I live with trees. There are creatures under our feet, creatures that live over our heads, but trees live quite convincingly in the same filament of air we inhabit, and, in addition, they extend impressively in both directions, up and down, shearing rock and fanning air, doing their real business just out of reach. A blind man's idea of hugeness is a tree. They have their sturdy bodies and special skills; they garner fresh water; they abide. This sycamore above me, below me, by Tinker Creek, is a case in point; the sight of it crowds my brain with an assortment of diverting thoughts, all as present to me as these slivers of pressure from grass on my elbow's skin. I want to come at the subject of the present by showing how consciousness dashes and ambles around the labyrinthine tracks of the mind, returning again and again, however briefly, to the senses: "If there were but one erect and solid standing tree in the woods, all creatures would go to rub against it and make sure of their footing." But so long as I stay in my thoughts, my foot slides under trees; I fall, or I dance. . . .

These trees stir me. The past inserts a finger into a slit in the skin of the present, and pulls. I remember how sycamores grew—and presumably still grow—in the city, in Pittsburgh, even along the busiest streets. I used to spend hours in the backyard, thinking God knows what, and peeling the mottled bark of a sycamore, idly, littering the grass with dried lappets and strips, leaving the tree's trunk at eye level moist, thin-skinned and yellow—until someone would catch me at it from the kitchen window, and I would awake, and look at my work in astonishment, and think oh no, this time I've killed the sycamore for sure.

Here in Virginia the trees reach enormous proportions, especially in the lowlands on banksides. It is hard to understand how the same tree could thrive both choking along Pittsburgh's Penn Avenue and slogging knee-deep in Tinker Creek. Of course, come to think of it, I've done the same thing myself. Because a sycamore's primitive bark is not elastic but frangible, it sheds continuously as it grows; seen from a distance, a sycamore seems to grow in pallor and vulnerability as it grows in height; the bare uppermost branches are white against the sky. . . .

What else is going on right this minute while ground water creeps under my feet? The galaxy is careening in a slow, muffled widening. If a million solar systems are born every hour, then surely hundreds burst into being as I shift my weight to the other elbow. The sun's surface is now exploding; other stars implode and vanish, heavy and black, out of sight. Meteorites are arcing to earth invisibly all day long. On the planet the winds are blowing: the polar easterlies, the westerlies, the northeast and southeast trades. Somewhere, someone under full sail is becalmed, in the horse latitudes, in the doldrums; in the northland, a trapper is maddened, crazed, by the eerie scent of the chinook, the snow-eater, a wind that can melt two feet of snow in a day. The pampero blows, and the tramontane, and the Boro, sirocco, levanter, mistral. Lick a finger: feel the now.

Spring is seeping north, towards me and away from me, at sixteen miles a day. Caribou straggle across the tundra from the spruce-fir forests of the south, first the pregnant does, hurried, then the old and unmated does, then suddenly a massing of bucks, and finally the diseased and injured, one by one. Somewhere, people in airplanes are watching the sun set and peering down at clustered houselights, stricken. In the montana in Peru, on the rain-forested slopes of the Andes, a woman kneels in a dust clearing before a dark shelter of overlapping broadleaves; between her breasts hangs a cross of smooth sticks she peeled with her teeth and lashed with twistings of vine. Along estuary banks of tidal rivers all over the world, snails in black clusters like currants are gliding up and down the stems of reed and sedge, migrating every moment with the dip and swing of tides. Behind me, Tinker Mountain, and to my left, Dead Man Mountain, are eroding one thousandth of an inch a year.

The tomcat that used to wake me is dead; he was long since grist for an earthworm's casting, and is now the clear sap of a Pittsburgh sycamore, or the honeydew of aphids sucked from that sycamore's high twigs and sprayed in sticky drops on a stranger's car. A steer across the road stumbles into the creek to drink; he blinks; he laps; a floating leaf in the current catches against his hock and wrenches away. The giant water bug I saw is dead, long dead, and its moist gut and rigid casing are both, like the empty skin of the frog it sucked, dissolved, spread, still spreading right now, in the steer's capillaries, in the windblown smatter of clouds overhead, in the Sargasso Sea. The mockingbird that dropped furled from a roof . . . but this is no time to count my dead. That is nightwork. The dead are staring, underground, their sleeping heels in the air.

The sharks I saw are roving up and down the coast. If the sharks cease roving, if they still their twist and rest for a moment, they die. They need new water pushed into their gills; they need dance. Somewhere east of me, on another continent, it is sunset, and starlings in breathtaking bands are winding high in the sky to their evening roost. Under the water just around the bend downstream, the coot feels with its foot in the creek, rolling its round red eyes. In the house a spider slumbers at her wheel like a spinster curled in a corner all day long. The mantis egg cases are tied to the mock-orange hedge; within each case, within each egg, cells elongate, narrow, and split; cells bubble and curve inward, align, harden or hollow or stretch. The Polyphemus moth, its wings crushed to its back, crawls down the driveway, crawls down the driveway, crawls. . . . The snake whose skin I tossed away, whose homemade, personal skin is now tangled at the county dump— that snake in the woods by the quarry stirs now, quickens now, prodded under the leafmold by sunlight, by the probing root of May apple, the bud of bloodroot. And where are you now?

I stand. All the blood in my body crashes to my feet and instantly heaves to my head, so I blind and blush, as a tree blasts into leaf spouting water hurled up from roots. What happens to me? I stand before the sycamore dazed; I gaze at its giant trunk.

Big trees stir memories. You stand in their dimness, where the very light is blue, staring unfocused at the thickest part of the trunk as though it were a long, dim tunnel—: the Squirrel Hill tunnel. You're gone. The egg-shaped patch of light at the end of the blackened tunnel swells and looms; the sing of tire tread over brick reaches an ear-splitting crescendo; the light breaks over the hood, smack and full on your face. You have achieved the past. . . .

Live water heals memories. I look up the creek and here it comes, the future, being borne aloft as on a winding succession of laden trays. You may wake and look from the window and breathe the real air, and say, with satisfaction or with longing, "This is it." But if you look up the creek, if you look up the creek in any weather, your spirit fills, and you are saying, with an exulting rise of the lungs, "Here it comes!"

Here it comes. In the far distance I can see the concrete bridge where the road crosses the creek. Under that bridge and beyond it the water is flat and silent, blued by distance and stilled by depth. It is so much sky, a fallen shred caught in the cleft of banks. But it pours. The channel here is straight as an arrow; grace itself is an archer. Between the dangling wands of bankside willows, beneath the overarching limbs of tulip, walnut, and Osage orange, I see the creek pour down. It spills toward me streaming over a series of sandstone tiers, down, and down, and down. I feel as though I stand at the foot of an infinitely high staircase, down which some exuberant spirit is flinging tennis ball after tennis ball, eternally, and the one thing I want in the world is a tennis ball.

There must be something wrong with a creekside person who, all things being equal, chooses to face downstream. It's like fouling your own nest. For this and a leather couch they pay fifty dollars an hour? Tinker Creek doesn't back up, pushed up its own craw, from the Roanoke River; it flows down, easing, from the northern, unseen side of Tinker Mountain. "Gravity, to Copernicus, is the nostalgia of things to become spheres." This is a curious, tugged version of the great chain of being. Ease is the way of perfection, letting fall. But, as in the classic version of the great chain, the pure trickle that leaks from the unfathomable heart of Tinker Mountain, this Tinker Creek, widens, taking shape and cleaving banks, weighted with the live and intricate impurities of time, as it descends to me, to where I happen to find myself, in this intermediate spot, halfway between here and there. Look upstream. Just simply turn around; have you no will? The future is a spirit, or a distillation of *the* spirit, heading my way. It is north. The future is the light on the water; it comes, mediated, only on the skin of the real and present creek. My eyes can stand no brighter light than this; nor can they see without it, if only the undersides of leaves.

Trees are tough. They last, taproot and bark, and we soften at their feet. "For we are strangers before thee, and sojourners, as were all our fathers: our days on the earth are as a shadow, and there is none abiding." We can't take the lightning, the scourge of high places and rare airs. But we can take the light, the reflected light that shines up the valleys on creeks. Trees stir memories; live waters heal them. The creek is the mediator, benevolent, impartial, subsuming my shabbiest evils and dissolving them, transforming them into live moles, and shiners, and sycamore leaves. It is a place even my faithlessness hasn't offended; it still flashes for me, now and tomorrow, that intricate, innocent face. It waters an undeserving world, saturating cells with lodes of light. I stand by the creek over rock under trees.

It is sheer coincidence that my hunk of the creek is strewn with boulders. I never merited this grace, that when I face upstream I scent the virgin breath of mountains, I feel a spray of mist on my cheeks and lips, I hear a ceaseless splash and susurrus [whisper], a sound of water not merely poured smoothly down air to fill a steady pool, but tumbling live about, over, under, around, between, through an intricate speckling of rock. It is sheer coincidence that upstream from me the creek's bed is ridged in horizontal croppings of sandstone. I never merited this grace, that when I face upstream I see the light on the water careening towards me, inevitably, freely, down a graded series of terraces like the balanced winged platforms on an infinite, inexhaustible font. "Ho, if you are thirsty, come down to the water; ho, if you are hungry, come and sit and eat." This is the present, at last. I can pat the puppy any time I want. This is the now, this flickering, broken light, this air that the wind of the future presses down my throat, pumping me buoyant and giddy with praise.

My God, I look at the creek. It is the answer to Merton's prayer, "Give us time!" It never stops. If I seek the senses and skill of children, the information of a thousand books, the innocence of puppies, even the insights of my own city past, I do so only, solely, and entirely that I might look well at the creek. You don't run down the present, pursue it with baited hooks and nets. You wait for it, empty-handed, and you are filled. You'll have fish left over. The creek is the one great giver. It is, by definition, Christmas, the incarnation. This old rock planet gets the present for a present on its birthday every day.

Here is the word from a subatomic physicist: "Everything that has already happened is particles, everything in the future is waves." Let me twist his meaning. Here it comes. The particles are broken; the waves are translucent, laving, roiling with beauty like sharks. The present is the wave that explodes over my head, flinging the air with particles at the height of its breathless unroll; it is the live water and light that bears from undisclosed sources the freshest news, renewed and renewing, world without end.

III | Science, Nature, and the Emergence of an Ecological Ethic

O truth of the earth! O truth of things! I am determined to press
The whole way toward you,
Sound your voice! I scale mountains or dive in the sea after you.
                              —Walt Whitman, *Leaves of Grass*, 1855[1]

Born a rebellious child of the Industrial Revolution, the romantic nature aesthetic coexisted with the expansionist impulse of the nineteenth century. Because there was so much of it, infatuation with nature did not require Americans to do anything resembling conservation. Quite the contrary: the seeming infinity of the continent—so vast it had barely been realized—urged domination and use. When in 1841

103

George Catlin called for the establishment of a "nation's Park" complete with wild animals and Indians, he was easily ignored; the idea was tucked away for another thirty years.[2] In the romantic period, the aesthetic appreciation of nature did not translate easily to either an ecological recognition of its fragile complexity or to conservation policy. The physical advance of the republic easily absorbed both sentiment and science. Transforming earth into capital had long been a hyper-rational affair. Since the age of Descartes, Galileo, and Bacon, men of reason had placed science in the service of nature's development. The dominant world view conceived by the Scientific Revolution redefined the material universe as one of mechanical parts and resources to be probed, dissected, manipulated, and extracted by men for the material benefit of men.[3] The scientific, mechanistic paradigm supported the Industrial Revolution that began to radically transform the western world in the eighteenth century. It held virtually without dissent until the late 1700s, when ideas that would later be recognized as the seeds of ecology began to emerge.

Part III will sketch the development of both ecological and conservationist ethics in science. We begin with William Bartram, one of the early naturalists whose work aspired to a more holistic and metaphysical vision of nature's parts. Bartram represents that first wave of European and American natural historians who catalogued voluminous discoveries even as they worked against the dominant grain of science by reaffirming the mystery and vitalism of nature. They established the tone for the divergence of natural science from purely mechanistic thinking, a departure that would take several paths: one, a conservationist ethic, crystallized in the signal work of George Perkins Marsh in 1864, which led to the modern science of resource management for sustained yield. Second, Ellen Swallow Richards's formulation of human ecology bespeaks the central role of women scientists and urban reformers in recognizing and remedying a degraded urban industrial environment at the turn of the twentieth century. And although it would take longer and require the experience of ecological crises to get there, Aldo Leopold's "Land Ethic" and the writings of Rachel Carson (although the latter do not accompany this introduction) demonstrate the diversity and verve that scientific and philosophic ecology would embody in the second half of the twentieth century.

Beyond sketching the evolution of ecological thought and conservationist science, the selections in Part III should remind us that like a passage from meadow to forest, divisions in American nature writing are shaded. Essayists whose primary thrust is to describe the landscape have also often had something to say about the less apparent ecological relationships of its living parts. As we have seen, scientific fact often braced the aesthetic, spiritual impressions of naturalists such as John Burroughs and John Muir. Some of the greatest American nature writing is found at the nexus of heart and mind and soul and reason. It is there that some of the most influential work in both American science and nature writing is found.

————

The scientific reevaluation of nature in America begins in the Old World with the Swedish botanist, Carl von Linné, known as Linnaeus (1707–1778). Throughout a remarkable career of scientific travel and exploration, Linnaeus focused on the central idea that each species played a vital role in the overall maintenance of life. Understanding the natural world, Linnaeus deduced, required a categorical ordering of its parts, and so he created his own system of nature taxonomy, the *Systema Naturae*. Linnaeus's core truth—that nature operated according to an efficient, orderly logic of its own—further cultivated the theory of evolution that would crystallize in Charles Darwin's work decades later.[4] Beyond his arrangement of species, Linnaeus argued that the "oeconomy of nature" was both scientific and spiritual wonder. For nearly two centuries, science had reasoned that the universe consisted purely of physical matter; nature was what men could see and use, and nothing more. In service to commerce, nature had been shorn of its soul. Linnaeus offered a reconciliation between reason and faith, between the practical endeavors of men and the glories of nature. In doing so, the once-obscure botanist struck a chord of anxiety over rapid socioeconomic and environmental change. Linnaeus's stature in Europe and America grew after his death in 1778. People met to discuss his ideas, while botanical studies extended his efforts to fully understand the arrangement of nature's holy parts.[5]

Shortly thereafter, in 1789, naturalist Gilbert White published *The Natural History of Selborne*, which explored the landscape, wildlife, and seasonal changes of White's quiet English village. The book became one of the most popular in the history of the English language and helped to establish the natural history essay as a legitimate literary form. White's sense of place honored the beauty, divinity, and complexity of nature, yet it was also unequivocally practical in purpose: a good botanist, he urged, should make "two blades of grass [grow] where one alone was seen before."[6] What made White's work immensely popular was not his utilitarianism but, rather, the same theme that had propelled Linnaeus to folk hero stature: a desire to rediscover peace in nature. White found in the bucolic greensward of Selborne the sense of harmonic balance between humans and nature that seemed increasingly concealed and debased by the Industrial Revolution then taking hold in England.

————

Across the Atlantic in the same years, William Bartram was traveling and preparing to chronicle a much wilder American landscape. Bartram is that rare nature writer whose pedigree could have forecast his career. Linnaeus himself described William's father, John Bartram, as "the greatest natural botanist in the world."[7] In the elder Bartram's expansive botanical gardens near Philadelphia, young William studied the myriad species cultivated by his father. After joining him on several botanical adventures, in the spring of 1773 William Bartram commenced a four-year journey into the heart of the continent's southern wilderness. The result in 1791 was *Travels and other Writings* (Selection 16), a rich mix of botanical science, landscape narrative, and nature philosophy.

Travels stands as an early prototype of the more scientific strain of the American nature essay.[8] Bartram documented with exacting detail the physiography, flora, and fauna of the southern colonies. His exhaustive catalog of species impressed scientists from Philadelphia to London. With the expansive view of an eighteenth-century scientist, Bartram embraced a wide range of disciplines in his study, including Native American anthropology. Noting "very many magnificant [*sic*] monuments of the power and industry of the ancient inhabitants," Bartram gives lie to the Virgin Wilderness Myth. Even more remarkably for his time, he indicts "the invasion of the Europeans" as the source of rapid regional changes in biological diversity, specifically the decimation of the buffalo population.[9]

Bartram's work is permeated with currents of thought that in most circles in 1791 would have been deemed heresy. He audaciously suggests that animal life is equal to that of humans, departing sharply from the anthropocentrism of western culture. In one passage he compares the brilliantly devised inner workings of a timepiece or fine fabric to the genius of the animal mind that must lie behind its own outward beauty: "If then the visible . . . part of the animal creation . . .

is so beautiful, harmonious, and incomprehensible, what must be the intellectual system? that inexpressibly more essential principle, which secretly operates within?" Bartram acknowledges that his thinking falls outside "the general opinion of philosophers." With a biocentrism more evocative of the 1970s than the 1770s, he suggests that they just might be wrong.[10] Further, he reconciles his biocentric view with the Judeo-Christian belief in the divinity of nature. That nature is a Godly creation in no way suggests that humans occupy a privileged position in the scheme of life. Why, Bartram asks, would God necessarily position the reason of humans above the equally complex impulse that moves animals?

A brief editorial defense: of all the august, glorious scenes that Bartram paints throughout *Travels*, we find ourselves reading about bugs. Few nature writers have deemed insect life a fit subject for study, yet this narrative of the region's ephemera captures the essence of ecological thought in its embryonic period. Without explicitly proclaiming it, a close look at insect life foretells a discipline that eventually would discover the vitality of every species, the complexity of every habitat. If there is redemption for the "viscid scum" that keeps safe the ephemera's birthing larva, what part of nature can be without value? Moreover, the ephemera's significance seems grounded not in utilitarian merit (that is, they keep this ecosystem functional, which in turn means a productive fishery). Rather, their worth, like their easily overlooked beauty and intricacy, needs no defense. Finding tender tragedy in the sunset death of ephemera, Bartram rudely reminds us that our own demise means no more to the workings of nature.

Moreover, Bartram anticipates ecology's fundamentally ethical question: What is the human role and responsibility in the web of life? What were *we* "created merely for"? This "deep" biocentric impulse marked ecology from the outset as a potentially leveling force. It is precisely the field's democratic view of the universe—its capacity to reveal the sobering equity of species in the web of life—that rendered ecology such a radical current of thought. For this reason would twentieth-century ecologist Paul Sears label his field the "subversive science."[11] Bartram represents a turning point in scientific thinking about nature. Unlike Gilbert White, one blade of grass on a patch of hillside was enough for William Bartram. He lies somewhere between Linnaeus and Walt Whitman on the continuum of calculation and wonder that would become the abode of ecological study.

Environmental history, no less than history on the whole, is carried forward by the most unlikely of persons. Consider George Perkins Marsh, a native of the backwoods of Vermont who had tried, succeeded, and failed at numerous professions by the time he published *Man and Nature* (Selection 17) in 1864. Well bred and well schooled, he graduated at the head of his class at Dartmouth, which seemed to foretell early success. Yet Marsh was not prone to a single career track. Rather, he exemplified what Ralph Waldo Emerson had famously described as "the American Scholar": a man well engaged with nature, informed and inspired by books, and, most important, unwilling to forsake, simply for "his nerve and his nap, . . . any action in which he can partake."[12] Marsh's own view of a scholar's life was "not [that of] a recluse devoted to quiet literary research, but one who lives and acts in the busy whirl of the great world."[13] His résumé included lawyer, politician, government diplomat, sheep rancher, teacher, lumberman, woolen mill owner, newspaper editor, highway builder, marble quarry developer, real estate speculator, linguist-lecturer, and a stint as Vermont State Fish Commissioner. "If you live much longer," a friend once wrote to him, "you will be obliged to *invent* trades, for you will have exhausted the present category."[14] With his pioneering work of environmental history, Marsh would do just that.

Through his various careers, Marsh continually amassed evidence for the book that became *Man and Nature*. Alarmed by the deterioration of his own New England landscape, at a county agricultural fair in 1847 he warned fellow Vermont farmers that deforestation was already causing regional climate changes, severe flooding and erosion, and a deterioration in water quality.[15] The next year, Marsh began service as a foreign diplomat, a position he would hold for much of the time until his death in 1882. It allowed him to journey throughout the Middle East and Europe, where he studied the regions' deep and mostly tragic environmental history. The subject would not let him go, and soon Marsh proposed to botanist Asa Gray the outlines of a book that would document the history of exploited environments. He gathered further evidence and credibility when he served as Vermont's fish commissioner in 1857. Mincing few words in his official report to the Vermont legislature, Marsh declared the culprits in the decline of the state's fisheries to be entirely human: urban and industrial waste, fishing during spawning season, and soil erosion caused by excessive timbering. "Barren and pestilential wastes" like those found in areas of Europe awaited Vermont if it did not reverse its course.[16]

The once-deforested Vermont countryside has largely recovered since the midnineteenth century when George Perkins Marsh decried its exploitation. Photograph by Mary Ellen Magoc.

Though best remembered for his indictment of human ecological impact, Marsh's nature sensibility was in fact ambiguous, laden with both nature romanticism and traditional teleology. Early in his life he had come to see the birds and trees of his surrounding forest as "persons, not things." Some men, he offered, "would find it hard to make out as good a claim to *personality* as a respectable oak can establish."[17] Maudlin sentimentalist, however, he was not. "The great question," he wrote in 1860 for the *Christian Examiner*—"whether man is of nature or above her"—was for him rhetorical. Marsh reassured his audience that science challenged not the biblical command to subdue the earth, but the execution of that holy mission. "Wherever [man] fails to make himself her master," Marsh assured his readers, "he can but be her slave."[18] With "exalted parentage," humanity could not possibly be "of her." Men are endowed with reason and so remained above and apart from nature.

That virtue, however, entailed greater responsibility and wisdom than the species had demonstrated either in New England or the Old

World. Such became the essential message of *Man and Nature*. Let the sorry environmental history of fallen European and Middle Eastern civilizations be a lesson to Americans, urged Marsh: heedless, wasteful transmogrification of the land has invariably preceded the decline of great civilizations. Only wiser stewardship of natural resources would prevent a similar fate from befalling Americans and maintain the future capacity of the land to produce. He tempered his critique with a wholly American remedy. Largely eschewing public ownership, Marsh believed that out of their "enlightened self interest," his fellow citizens must individually begin to restore and manage the forests for their own long-term prosperity. He did urge the creation of one large American forest reserve. Thirteen years after Henry David Thoreau ended his famous "word for Nature" lecture by declaring the absurdity that "in Wildness is the preservation of the world,"[19] Marsh explained to the transcendentally challenged the practical basis of that idea. He believed that such a place would appeal to the romantic "lover of nature" as well as fulfill more "economical" needs of forest management and watershed protection. Based on recent European practice, forest conservation would regulate stream flow over a wide region, protect farmers from drought, and stabilize declining wildlife populations.[20]

Both critical and comprehensive, Marsh's magnum opus embraced the universe of everything he had absorbed in his travels and prior lives as a farmer and failed entrepreneur. His editor, Charles Scribner, was not impressed with the manuscript, however, and suggested to the author that he abandon it and write something "in the department of English languages and literature of which you are the acknowledged head."[21] Marsh himself predicted self-effacingly that *Man and Nature* "will have no value for scientific men." Scientists, he asserted, will "condemn it as trash, which very likely it is, but it may interest some people who are willing to look upon nature with unlearned eyes."[22]

Indeed, scientists and lay persons alike embraced the book. Marsh at once strengthened the nature preservation arguments made by cultural aesthetes and helped to shape the emerging field of scientific forest management. Toward the goal of watershed management, forest conservation came to pass in 1883 when the New York legislature set aside the Adirondack Forest Reserve as "forever wild."[23] Well into the next century, moreover, American and European ecologists, foresters, and land stewards generally would regard *Man and Nature* as the pivotal work in the early cultivation of modern land management.[24]

Apart from its practical impact in the field of conservation there was in *Man and Nature* something deeper. Arguing that nature's fragile complexity lay beyond human understanding, Marsh captured the relentlessly questioning heart of modern ecological thought. In an age of burgeoning scientific confidence and explosive physical development, his declaration that "we can never know" the extent of the ecological impact on human activity and, further, that certain aspects of nature were beyond human intelligence, was unsettling.[25] One cannot imagine too many Americans in 1864 warming to the occasionally grave tone of this book. Beyond promoting watershed protection, Marsh challenged the cultural underpinnings of human environmental impact in the modern era: material consumption and the delusion of human ownership of the earth. Surely news for most in our time as well, Marsh declares the earth "for usufruct alone."[26] While the conservation philosophy Marsh outlined has flourished, Americans still struggle to comprehend that more challenging message.

The years after the publication of *Man and Nature* saw growing concern over deforestation and the necessity of watershed protection, in the Adirondacks and elsewhere. In 1891 the Forest Organic Act was passed, establishing the nation's first Forest Reserves (later changed to National Forests). Among those who aspired to manage those forests was a young Marsh disciple, Gifford Pinchot. After studying scientific methods of timber management in Europe, Pinchot returned to the United States and became a leading proponent of managing American forests in the same way—for long-term "sustained yield." The subsequent 1897 Forest Management Act made clear that philosophy and the overriding purpose of the National Forests: "to furnish a continuous supply of timber for the use and necessities of citizens of the United States."[27] To ensure a continuous supply of expert personnel to do the job, Pinchot family money helped to establish the nation's first school of forestry at Yale University. Its essential philosophy was that if smartly managed, timber could be extracted forever, much like corn. (The transfer of the National Forest Reserves to the U.S. Department of Agriculture during President Theodore Roosevelt's administration symbolized the approach.) This seemed all the more urgent in light of the 1890 census declaration that the nation had reached "the end" of the frontier, and resource exhaustibility became a source of mounting anxiety.

Something other than an ecological impulse, then, defines the first generation of professional public land managers. Belonging very much to the Progressive Era of reform, Pinchot's "wise use" school sought to restrain the evils of greed and waste that reformers believed had exhausted so much of the nation's forests, consequently resulting in damage to seasonal water flow and quality in various watersheds. Progressive conservationists concluded that timber and mineral companies, along with cattle and agricultural interests, had plundered for their own short-term self-interest vast stretches of the resources of the West—a region that was vital to the economic growth of the nation. What was needed now was prudent foresight and modern scientific expertise that could bring managed efficiency to the extraction and consumption of the region's timber, water, mineral, and agricultural resources. Well-trained government experts would channel—restraining only when necessary—the force of individual private gain for the long-term larger public good.[28]

Restraint came quickly and boldly, as the Roosevelt administration withdrew 53 million acres from the public domain to create twenty-three new national forests. Additional millions were placed off limits to mining and electric power development. Competitive bidding and permitting now regulated timber cutting and cattle grazing on the expanded public domain. Charged by big businessmen with imposing a socialistic regime, conservationists in fact shaped a future that would be defined in the decades to come largely by a close association of expert government managers and large, organized (and presumptively efficient) timber, cattle, and agricultural interests. Progressive conservationists aimed not to prohibit but to regulate and manage private use of greatly expanded government lands. Under President Theodore Roosevelt, Pinchot served as the first head of the United States Forest Service. In his tenure there, he vigorously implemented scientific wise use in the national forests by determining what could be cut and when, depending upon the varying regenerative growth rates of forests in particular regions of the country.[29] Pinchot's management approach—to provide indefinitely "the greatest good for the greatest number of people"—became the guiding principle for managing the nation's other public lands for most of the twentieth century, though not without contention.

It was during the Pinchot era that a chasm opened up between the conflicting impulses of conservation and preservation. Roosevelt himself sat astride this tension. He had long been a firm believer in the national parks as places where Americans could discover the "strenuous life" of the outdoors and make contact with the grandeur of the western frontier heritage. He established five new national parks, fifty-three wildlife refuges, and sixteen new national monuments (the latter system established through the National Antiquities Act of 1906). Parks, refuges, and monuments were afforded greater levels of protection than the forests. Most conservationists, however, had little use for setting land aside merely for its aesthetic or cultural value. The utilitarian-versus-contemplative struggle over the highest purpose of public land was symbolized by the disaffection of Pinchot and wilderness enthusiast John Muir. Although initially supportive of resource-centered conservation, by 1897 Muir had seen what that could mean: domesticated sheep invited to graze in large numbers in the national forests like herds of "hoofed locusts," he complained.[30] He grew increasingly disenchanted with the "wise-use" policy in the national forests, fearful of its long-term implications and repulsed by its utilitarian assumptions. The philosophical divide widened in 1913 when the U.S. Congress, after a protracted battle, voted to allow the damming of Hetch-Hetchy Valley, located within California's Yosemite National Park. The "greatest good" here would be served by impoundment, not "sentimentalism," as dam proponents dismissed the opposition. A landmark Progressive Era achievement, Hetch-Hetchy was for preservationists a bitter defeat never to be forgotten; it became a rallying cry in their battle decades later to stop the damming of rivers in the Southwest.[31]

Concurrent with the emergence of public lands conservation was the development of the urban ecological science to meet the growing public health crisis triggered by America's industrialization. The problems of urban industrial environment mounted in the late nineteenth century: open sewers carrying human waste, streets fouled with tons of horse manure, and the air filled with the smoky, noisy "nuisances" of industrialism. Most infamous were the Chicago slaughterhouses, where conditions seemed subhuman for the workers inside for families living in nearby Packingtown, and did not promise especially good health to those who consumed their products. Upton Sinclair made this state of affairs powerfully clear in his fictional account, *The Jungle* (1906), which aroused the indignation of the middle class and led to the passage of reform legislation.

Women led the movement to reform the worst environmental abuses of urban America. Variously titled "municipal housekeeping" and "sanitary science," these activities were generally viewed by both men and women as acceptable extensions of traditional female roles.

It seemed "natural" to most authoritative voices of the day that women, long assigned during Victorian America to be the nurturing caretakers of the family and stewards of the home environment, take up the charge of cleansing the domestic environment immediately beyond the home. From New York to Chicago and in dozens of other cities, women and women's organizations led the movement to reform the ways that cities treated their waste, regulated slaughterhouses and food markets, paid their refuse workers, and dealt generally with the living and working conditions of the urban, industrial environment.[32]

"Public health" and "efficiency" were watchwords of the Progressive Era and its conservationist impulse in particular. These goals grew not only from tangible effects of industrialization but also from the general anxiety in *fin de siècle* America that urban life was enervating the nation's moral and physical vitality. Capitalists concerned with productivity, middle-class people anxious about class conflict and the general degradation of the industrial and increasingly "foreign" urban scene, and lower-class immigrant workers themselves whose lives were at risk shared at least parts of the growing consensus to improve living and working conditions. These principles guided the sanitary sciences of municipal and domestic housekeeping, as Ellen Swallow Richards outlines in the introduction to her 1907 book, *Sanitation in Daily Life* (Selection 18). The first woman graduate of the Massachusetts Institute of Technology, Richards also offered the first formative definition of "ecology" in America (a word first coined by a German biologist in 1873). She applies it to an unlikely urban, human environment, far from the green, generally uninhabited forests of Pinchot and Muir. Beyond a reinforcement of progressive themes of health and efficiency, Richards focuses attention on the underlying environmental causes of what reformers were convinced was the diminished physical and mental capacities of the cities' working poor. Amid explosive industrialization, the teeming disorder and quickening pace of urban life, and the enlargement of society at all levels, Richards argues for two important ideas: the sanctity of "the individual"; and, despite unprecedented private accumulations of corporate wealth, a "common environment" in the cities to which all were bound. More profound is the cardinal ecological principle that "what touches my neighbor, touches me."

Interestingly, women's focus on the industrial environment not only represented a new strain of ecological thinking but also foreshadowed a general divide that prevailed throughout most of the twentieth century: between ecologists concerned with Nature Out There (forests, parks, and the like); and those more focused on protection of the human industrialized environment, led by women scientists and activists such as Richards, Alice Hamilton, Rachel Carson, and Lois Gibbs (a discussion that resumes in Part IV).

———

History has an uncanny habit of turning on a dime. Decades pass as old paradigms get prodded, new ideas are cultivated, and culture prepares unwittingly for the next tectonic shift in thought. And then some event of magnitude triggers a convulsion; what seemed radical becomes the gist of mainstream discussion, inviting new directions in thought, behavior, and, in the modern age, government policy. This seems especially true with respect to the history of science.[33] For the maturation of ecology as a respectable discipline, the Dust Bowl proved to be such a watershed event. As historian Donald Worster has argued, the 1930s Dust Bowl inspired a "more inclusive, coordinated, and ecological perspective" in the field of conservation.[34] It is hard to overstate the force of this environmental disaster. Millions of people living as far away as Washington, DC, were choked by dust that once had been the soil of the Great Plains.

Most people blamed nature—drought and wind—for the Dust Bowl. But the Great Plains Committee, a government-sponsored scientific investigator of its causes, concluded that ill-conceived human activity was at least equally to blame. The committee relied largely upon the seminal ecological ideas of Frederic Clements, who decades earlier had formulated the concept of ecological succession. Plant communities in any particular region, Clements had argued, evolve from a simple, unstable state with few plants and animals to a more mature, highly complex, stable, and balanced condition of "climax." Ecologists on the committee argued that a richly complex, climax ecosystem of tall grasslands prairie had evolved over the course of millennia, only to be recklessly broken, rapidly overplowed, and simplistically managed by modern Americans.[35] Between 1925 and 1930 alone, 5,260,000 acres of the southern Great Plains—an area seven times the size of the state of Rhode Island—had been plowed under for the production of wheat. Having disturbed the innate logic of the landscape, men were now reaping the results. The economic climax of large, mechanized, monocropped farms had overrun the natural climax state of Great Plains prairie vegetation to produce the misery of the Dust Bowl.[36] The underlying question raised by the committee was more troubling: Should the limits of nature (Americans have yet to accept such a notion) or the march of moderns be the final determinant of the best use of land?

In the midst of this and less grave calamities, an increasing number of resource managers began calling for a more holistic understanding of the land, in the Great Plains and elsewhere. As Worster notes, amid the zeitgeist of the Great Depression, with the economic system that produced the Dust Bowl having crumbled, a major reevaluation of the human-environmental relationship was possible.[37] From the Gilded Age through the 1920s, an every-man-for-himself ethos had been capitalizing the landscape, shaping the culture, and, the era of progressive reform notwithstanding, dominating the politics of modern America. And now, fully unleashed, industrial capitalism had proven capable of bringing distress to the economies of both men and nature.

In this atmosphere, pregnant with bold ecological thought and a broader challenge to institutional authority, came new thinking about the role of predators in maintaining the ecological balance. For three hundred years, Americans—as individuals and, since the late nineteenth century, as public land managers—had engaged in a systematic extermination of countless numbers of wolves, coyotes, mountain lions, and other predators. The slaughter of predators derived from both deeply rooted mythic fear and from the need to protect cattle, which in the West had displaced a leading predator food source, the buffalo. Predator extermination also increased the numbers of ungulate species (elk and the like) favored by sportsmen. Centuries-old myths about wolves seemed unshakable, but change was coming. In 1929, Olaus Murie, a wildlife biologist for the Bureau of the Biological Survey (BBS), sharply criticized his agency's predator-control program. The bureau buried Murie's report and prevented him from speaking at a wildlife conference.[38] Murie's boss, Stanley Young, senior biologist for the BBS, acknowledged some admiration for the ferocity of wolves but concluded that they were "killers" and had "no place in modern civilization."[39] Still, an increasing number of biologists and wildlife managers grew anxious, and some were sharply critical of systematic predator control. In the mid-1920s the policy of shooting, trapping, and poisoning wolves and other predators resulted in one of the great disasters in American environmental history. On the Kaibab Plateau of northern Arizona, tenacious extermination of their predators drove the deer population from 4,000 in 1906 to nearly 100,000 by 1924. But neither the land nor men's desires for venison and trophies could sustain such numbers: the deer increase was largely eliminated in the following year by starvation and hunting. What had been hailed as a great achievement now shook confidence in the prevailing production-centered approach to land management.[40]

Change would come slowly, however, as evidenced by the publication in 1933 of Aldo Leopold's *Game Management*, which shrugged off the Kaibab disaster. Trained in the Yale (Pinchot-initiated) School of Forestry, Leopold applied the same wise-use principle of "harvest" to the management of wildlife, likening game managers to modern farmers who "[produced] a crop by controlling the . . . factors which hold down the natural increase, or productivity, of the seed stock."[41]

Yet even as *Game Management* was becoming the manual for his profession, its author's ideas were undergoing profound change. Leopold's tale of personal transformation on the issue of predator control rings with the force of religious conversion. Recounted in *A Sand County Almanac* (Selection 19), Leopold's revelation began while he was serving dutifully as a predator manager in the Southwest. The "fierce green fire" of the wolf's eyes that is at the center of this essay told him something intuitively about the rights of nature and the responsibility of being human. Leopold's epiphany with the dying wolf inspired a succession of major life changes: he abandoned government service, became inaugural chair of the Game Management program at the University of Wisconsin, helped form the Wilderness Society, and went to live in a broken-down shack on an ill-managed Wisconsin farm that he would nurse back to a wild and healthy state. It was there, on that restored prairie homestead, that he died of a heart attack in 1948 while helping his neighbors fight a brushfire.[42]

The following year, *A Sand County Almanac* was published and recognized almost immediately as a literary classic that would help forge the next generation of ecological thought. The book's opening section is a seasonal chronicle of life on his Wisconsin farm, during which Leopold, much in the same vein as William Bartram, finds beauty and integrity in the overlooked minutiae of the landscape. Although, for example, the very uncharismatic draba "plucks no heartstrings," the tiny plant plays an important role in the workings and the restoration of the landscape. As Kenneth Brower has noted, Leopold imbued his writing with a subtle animism, referring to plants as "creatures" and to certain trees as "he."[43] *And Sketches Here and There* follows, rambling with the author from place to place in his life as a land and wildlife manager. In the book's center pages, Leopold distills the wolf tale as the crystallizing moment of his metamorphosis toward a personal conservation ethic. The desires of sportsmen and land managers to encourage more deer, he reflects, had not accounted for the vitality and integrity of wolves and mountains. We can easily enough deconstruct the scientific source of human environmental impact in the Great Plains and elsewhere, Leopold suggests, but ultimately real ecological truth is metaphysical: the wisdom of wolves and mountains may well be superior to the destructive bumblings of men.

With the steady reason and passion of a good lawyer's closing argument, "The Land Ethic" resoundingly punctuates *A Sand County Almanac*. The central theme of this masterpiece of American nature writing challenges the prevailing Marsh-Pinchot axiom that economic self-interest was sufficient motivation for sound conservation. Leopold laments the fact that land management was still defined by the same limiting forces of human economy that had shaped the modern world. But there was hope: the "social conscience" that resulted from the maturation of industrial capitalism and led to its fundamental reform in the 1930s, Leopold argues, should now carry over to our treatment of the land. Americans must see the health of the environment as an essential good, like schools and roads. With great foresight, Leopold anticipates the chief obstacles inherent in public solutions to privately generated environmental problems: they would always have to be cost effective, paying their way in the system. Moreover, he observes, governmental remedies would be too simplistic and sweeping for infinitely complex and diverse environments.

Leopold argues instead for a universal but individually applied land ethic, grounded in the consideration of noneconomic values. Only an independently held sense of environmental obligation could succeed in a culture that held sacrosanct the rights—and, he would remind his readers, the responsibilities—of the individual. But while Leopold invokes America's social ethic as the model for a new land principle, suggesting that it was derived from a sense of moral obligation, he eschews for conservation the governmental enforced oversight that became vital to various elements essential to the improvement of social welfare (the right to organize unions, for example). Since Reconstruction, modest regulation designed primarily for the stability of capitalism had been tenaciously fought and often manipulated by and for big business.

Leopold's idealism allows him to hope for more with regard to a land ethic. The emphasis on individual action is part of what makes

A Sand County Almanac an American classic. The publication of the book came during an age of blinding faith in governmental authority, yet in his call for an independently held "love, respect, and admiration for land," there is the astute recognition that government is never enough. To extend Leopold's thesis: just as self-serving economics and racism often dictate how far Americans are willing to go in achieving social justice, so too does the cost-benefit perspective rein in environmental regulation. Like our treatment of one another, love and respect for the environment cannot be legislated. The sole criterion for thinking and acting on the land should be ecologically ethical: Does it "preserve the integrity, stability, and beauty of the biotic community"? And it must come from within.

The central problem, of course—and Leopold astutely recognized it—is that we are no longer of that community. Even in the 1940s, to Leopold's eye, modern, urban Americans had "outgrown" the land. By century's end, most of them would have neither the experience nor the memory of direct stewardship of nature. At the same time, elements of contemporary environmental policy came to reflect Leopold's "Land Ethic"—the growing emphasis on "ecosystem management," for example.[44] And, taking Leopold pure, "Deep Ecologists" in the 1970s began to adopt and extend his biocentric thinking.[45] Both phenomena, however, have been propelled by the sobering truth that Americans are more estranged from the natural world than ever. And while our infatuation with the image of nature has grown correspondingly, the hard question, as Leopold put it, is whether or not we can look the real thing directly in the eye.

———

Although the reader will find no accompanying excerpt, any discussion of the emergence of ecology in the twentieth century must include the life and work of Rachel Carson. Growing up in the industrial river valley north of Pittsburgh where Carson spent her childhood, I always found it curious that just five miles up the Allegheny River from Carson's home in the borough of Springdale lay the community of Natrona.[46] Born in 1850, Natrona was a company town belonging to Pennsylvania Salt, which for over a century manufactured a wide range of alkali-based products from lye soap to military explosives and later, chemical defoliants and pesticides, including DDT. Years later, residents joked darkly that they "never had a mosquito problem" in Natrona.[47] Within decades they faced a problem of another sort: up the steep hillside from the weathered brick remains of Penn Salt sat

ALSCO Park. The repository for Penn Salt's toxic waste for decades, by the 1980s ALSCO Park ranked high on the national list of toxic "Superfund" sites. Even as Penn Salt's glory years were ending in 1959, valley native Rachel Carson was busy writing *Silent Spring*, a passionate denunciation of the indiscriminate use and dangers of chemical pesticides in modern life. Penn Salt was not the subject of her book, nor is there evidence that Carson knew of the place. Without question, however, the fouled river and air of the region and the starkly contrasting bucolic farmstead where she grew up clearly imprinted her sensibility.[48]

Carson left Springdale by age 21, eventually receiving graduate training in marine biology at Johns Hopkins University. In 1936 she began working for the United States Bureau of Fisheries (later the Fish and Wildlife Service). Her first years at the Marine Biological Laboratory in Woods Hole, Massachusetts, resulted in the 1937 publication of *Under the Sea Wind*, and in 1951, *The Sea Around Us*. Recognized immediately as the most significant study by anyone of the world's oceans, *The Sea Around Us* achieved critical acclaim and an international audience. By 1962, *The Sea Around Us* had sold well over one million copies in more than a dozen languages. Its success prompted a reissue of *Under the Sea Wind*, making Carson the first author ever to have two books on the bestseller list concurrently. After her next work, *The Edge of the Sea*, Carson left government service, built a cottage on the coast of Maine, and led a writer's life.[49]

Beginning with *The Sea Around Us*, Carson established a prose style that succeeded on both scientific and literary grounds. Systematic without being technical, she wrote eloquent, interdisciplinary science. *The Sea Around Us* early demonstrated Carson's ability to translate science, some of it highly technical, with vigor and grace.[50] Like the pre-*Sand County* Aldo Leopold, the first edition of *The Sea Around Us* reflects Carson's belief in the veracity of both science and government. The challenge of science, as she saw it then, was to achieve a fuller understanding of the interconnectedness of planetary life that began in the depths of the seas and apply it to human progress.[51] Her thinking then seems economically centered and reflective of the unbridled, unblinking faith that Americans had in science and technology during the early postwar era. She notes, for example, the rewards and "long list of other uses" for a wide array of marine resources. Revealing the confident, arrogant intelligence of 1951 America, Carson notes blithely the "hazards" of offshore oil drilling "that must be faced and overcome."[52] She is sanguine about the human capacity to harness science in the interest of progress.

Appearing a decade later, the second edition of *The Sea Around Us* bore a new preface that cast the seas in a foreboding light and signaled the writer's increasing ambivalence toward science and technology. Carson applauds the achievements of the previous decade in oceanic exploration, but she concludes with a sustained and admittedly "ominous" passage about the dangers of dumping barrels of radioactive waste into the depths of the ocean. Certified as safe by scientific and governmental authority, the practice had accelerated during the 1950s escalation of the Cold War between the United States and the Soviet Union. In the first fifteen years of that struggle, Americans felt but largely suppressed a fear of all things nuclear. But after the discovery in 1959 of the lethal radioactive element, Strontium 90, in cow's milk, even mainstream publications such as the *Saturday Evening Post* produced alarming reports. Public sentiment for a ban on atmospheric and oceanic atomic testing was on the rise as the second edition of *The Sea Around Us* came out.[53] Carson confirms nuclear waste as a "lethal substance" and, even more unsettling, expresses no confidence in the Atomic Energy Commission to regulate its disposal.

This was no longer, then, just a nice book about the ocean. Contrary to her earlier "naive belief," Carson now recognizes that the seas are not "inviolate, beyond man's ability to change and to despoil." Moreover, she suggests, since all life ultimately originated there, the fate of the sea and that of the land are linked. These pages foreshadowed the temper and argumental thrust of the larger work that Carson then had in progress. The subject matter would shift away from oceans, but the fundamental message remained: the environment was more complex and fragile than humans had ever imagined. Human actions, she concludes soberingly, now posed a grave threat "to life itself."[54]

In 1957, Carson was intending to write a book about the broad subject of ecology when a series of events focused her more narrowly upon the insidious harm caused by the broad and indiscriminate use of chemical pesticides. She, like her colleagues, had been reading scattered reports about injurious aerial spraying. What moved Carson to act was a letter written by Olga Owens Huckins, a friend and Boston journalist, to the *Boston Herald* in which Huckins detailed the killing effects of aerial pesticide spraying at her bird sanctuary in Duxbury, Massachusetts. A heavy death toll of birds followed the 1957 spraying of a fatal mixture of DDT and fuel oil in a state-sanctioned mosquito-eradication program. Huckins sent a copy of the letter to Carson, along with a note requesting her assistance in stopping the state's planned expansion of aerial spraying. Was there anyone she knew in Washington, Huckins asked, who could prevent this?[55]

Carson responded as a writer might: by seeking someone to address the subject with a magazine article. But neither she nor her literary agent could find a publication willing to print such an exposé. On the contrary, Carson learned that *Reader's Digest* was preparing a laudatory piece on pesticides centered on the particular benefits of the gypsy moth "control program." Curious timing, since also at that moment a group of citizens of Long Island, New York, were in court trying to stop state and federal officials from spraying DDT as part of the gypsy moth-extermination strategy. Carson asked the distinguished E. B. White, on the staff of *The New Yorker* and an occasional nature writer himself, to "take up [his] own pen against this nonsense—though that is far too mild a word!" Recognizing that she had the credibility and recognition necessary for such a piece, White suggested that Carson write the article herself.[56]

After months of hesitation, Carson began writing not just the article, but a book on the broad subject of pesticide use. She had planned to finish *Silent Spring* by the end of the summer of 1958; it took nearly four years longer than its author had budgeted, ultimately consuming the balance of her life.[57] In addition to the cancer that she had begun to battle, Carson's rigorous fieldwork and interdisciplinary approach made the work stretch on. The more Carson learned, the more she realized how little was known about the effects of chemicals in the environment. Data from around the country revealed a path of damaged environments caused by the reckless use of chemical pesticides. Anticipating a fierce storm of rebuke from those whose profits and careers would be challenged by the book, Carson determined to ground it firmly in good science—to give it an "unshakable foundation."[58] She therefore gathered and synthesized data from professionals in various disciplines—scientists who had not shared their information with one another—as well as local citizens' groups.[59] Carson hoped to assimilate and translate this mountain of disparate data for average citizens, "to simplify without error."[60] This approach fundamentally challenged the old paradigm that had both compartmentalized nature and left it in the hands of well-trained experts.

That goal was bold enough. In the book, Carson further declared that the economic and political forces that had fathered the rapid expansion of the synthetic chemical industry after World War II simply had too much to lose in examining honestly the evidence of harmful side effects. Governmental agencies charged with regulating the production and use of pesticides could not be trusted to safeguard the public interest. Moreover, she suggested, chemical corporations were jeopardizing the credibility of supposedly independent research on pesticide use at academic institutions.[61] Biological pest control alternatives existed, she said, but these had been sold short in research funding because of the power of big business and self-serving science.

Intending to paint the worst possible scenario of continued chemical abuse, Carson offered in the book's opening chapter, ominously titled, "A Fable for Tomorrow," a portrait of a once-lovely place—a "town in the heart of America"—which now bore the grim countenance of "strange stillness." Where once teemed life, the "shadow of death" prevailed. The cause, evoking the nuclear fears of the age, was a "white granular powder" that had "fallen like snow" on the land. Like the best science fiction films of the time, Carson renders this dark prelude just fantastically enough to be fiction.

What follows in succeeding chapters are layers of evidence from around the country that the "Fable" in fact represented America's future if the present course were not reversed. Previously a celebrant of science and technology, Carson now argues that profit and an ingrained cultural propensity to control nature had rendered science and technology potential monsters. Simplistic technological solutions do not serve well the complexity of nature, argues Carson. Like an atom bomb whose destruction was total and indiscriminate, aerial DDT does not differentiate between a gypsy moth and a cow. The "violent crossfire" of chemical pesticides and insecticides had unwittingly wrought serious damage to the chain of life. Just how unwitting was it by 1962? Increasing numbers of industry and government professionals knew of the evidence, Carson suggests, but had slunk behind a wall of silence to protect their own interests. She castigates the conspiracy of "half-truths" that was everywhere meeting the public's protest of pesticide use.

Predictably, the publication of *Silent Spring* met a swift and angrily indignant reaction from the chemical industry and their allies in government and academe. Just after *The New Yorker* published excerpts of the book, one chemical corporation urged Houghton Mifflin to reconsider its decision to publish *Silent Spring*, arguing that Carson made "inaccurate and disparaging statements" about two of the chemicals that the company produced. The National Agricultural Chemicals Association spent $250,000 in a massive public relations campaign to denounce the book and cast aspersions on its writer. In their view, Carson offered a gullible public "a reckless misinterpretation of scientific facts." The book, suggested an industry brochure, was "more poisonous than the pesticides she condemns."[62] F. A. Soraci, director of the New Jersey Department of Agriculture, dismissed Carson as a spokesperson for the "vociferous, misinformed group of nature-balancing, organic-gardening, bird-loving, unreasonable citizenry" that his agency was increasingly confronting in its pesticide control program.[63] There is nothing to gain by slogging through some of the less elevated allegations made about Carson's personal life from her opponents. Some were brazenly misogynist. Those who were intellectually or financially invested in the "Better Living through Chemistry" paradigm of the postwar era could not accept Carson's indictment. Monsanto published "The Desolate Year," a serious parody of the book which described the misery Americans would find in a world without petrochemicals. The potential impact of *Silent Spring* moved Carson's opponents to label her a nature fanatic, a hysterical woman, and, worst of all in 1962, a Communist.[64]

Contrasting the industry's offensive were letters of support from other scientists, laudatory editorials in major newspapers, a groundswell of initiatives on the state level to restrict pesticide use, and calls for federal action. Anthropologist and essayist Loren Eisley declared it a "devastating, heavily documented, relentless attack upon human carelessness, greed, and responsibility"; ecologist William Vogt predicted that *Silent Spring*'s impact on environmental policy would parallel what Sinclair's *The Jungle* had done for health and safety in the food and drug industries at the turn of the century.[65] That prophecy proved correct. Weeks after publication, President John F. Kennedy was referring to the influence of "Miss Carson's book" at the executive level. Before her death in 1963, Carson testified before congressional committees established to investigate the health effects of chemical pesticides. A decade of government inquiry and increasing public pressure led to the banning of DDT and the federal control of pesticides in the early 1970s.[66]

Like a thunderbolt, Carson's book struck at the heart of postwar optimism and signaled the birth of the modern environmental movement that would concern itself increasingly with issues of public health. *Silent Spring* is a work of immediate and enduring power, remaining influential and bitterly contested decades after its publication.[67] The book that Rachel Carson never intended to write wounded the self-assured faith that men had in themselves and their world and would cast a long shadow on the doings of that technocratic society. *Silent Spring* culminated the centuries-long evolution of a scientifically based ethic that at last had begun to confront the environmental problems of modern America.

NOTES

1. Walt Whitman, "Great Are the Myths," in *Leaves of Grass*, ed. and with Introduction by Malcolm Cowley (New York: Viking Penguin, 1959, originally published 1855), 144.
2. George Catlin, *North American Indians; Letters and Notes on the Manners, Customs, and Condition of the North American Indians: Written during eight years' travel amongst the wildest tribes of Indians in North America in 1832, 33, 34, 35, 36, 37, 38, and 39* (Minneapolis: Ross and Haines, 1965; originally published 1841), 294–95.
3. Carolyn Merchant, *The Death of Nature: Women, Ecology, and the Scientific Revolution* (San Francisco: Harper and Row, 1980).
4. Donald Worster, *Nature's Economy: A History of Ecological Ideas* (New York: Cambridge University Press, 1977), 31–32.
5. Ibid., 33.
6. Ibid., 5, 9, quoting Gilbert White, *The Natural History of Selborne* (1789).
7. Robert Ellman, *First in the Field: America's Pioneering Naturalists* (New York: Van Nostrand Reinhold, 1977), 26, quoted by Michael Branch, "Indexing American Possibilities: The Natural History Writing of Bartram, Wilson, and Audubon," in Cheryll Glotfelty and Harold Fromm, eds., *The Ecocriticism Reader: Landmarks in Literary Ecology* (Athens: University of Georgia Press, 1996), 286.
8. Branch, "Indexing American Possibilities," 287.
9. William Bartram, *Travels and other Writings. . . Travels Through North and South Carolina, Georgia, East and West Florida. Travels in Georgia and Florida, 1773–1774: A Report to Dr. John Fothergill. Miscellaneous Writings* (Philadelphia: James and Johnson, 1791), 56, 61.
10. Ibid., 19.
11. The phrase belongs to ecologist Paul Sears, "Ecology—A Subversive Subject," *BioScience* 14 (July 1964): 11–13, quoted by Worster, *Nature's Economy*, 23.
12. Ralph Waldo Emerson, "The American Scholar," 1837, quoted from *American Poetry and Prose*, Norman Foerster and Robert Morss Lovett, eds. (New York: Houghton Mifflin Company, 1934), 534–44.
13. George Perkins Marsh, *Human Knowledge: A Discourse Delivered before the Massachusetts Alpha of the Phi Beta Kappa Society, at Cambridge, August 26, 1847* (Boston, 1847), 4, quoted by David Lowenthal, ed. and Introduction to George Perkins Marsh, *Man and Nature: or Physical Geography as Modified by Human Action* (Cambridge, MA: Harvard University Press, 1965, 1973; reprinted from Boston 1864 original text), xxvi.

14. James M. Gilliss to Marsh, September 15, 1857, Marsh Collection, University of Vermont (hereafter UVM), quoted by Lowenthal, Introduction to *Man and Nature*, xvi.

15. *Address Delivered before the Agricultural Society of Rutland County, September 30, 1847* (Rutland, Vermont, 1848), 18, quoted by Lowenthal, ed., *Man and Nature*, xvii.

16. Marsh to Gray, May 9, 1849, UVM, and Marsh, *Report, on the Artificial Propagation of Fish, Made under the Authority of the Legislature of Vermont* (Burlington, VT, 1857), 20n, both quoted by Lowenthal, ed., *Man and Nature*, xviii.

17. Marsh to Charles Eliot Norton, May 24, 1871, Norton Papers, Harvard University Library, quoted by Lowenthal, ed., *Man and Nature*, xi.

18. Marsh, "The Study of nature," *Christian Examiner* 68 (1860): 34, quoted by Lowenthal, ed., *Man and Nature*, xxv.

19. Henry David Thoreau, "Walking," in *Excursions: The Writings of Henry David Thoreau*, Riverside edition, 11 vols. (Boston, 1893), 275, quoted by Roderick Nash, *Wilderness and the American Mind*, 3d ed. (New Haven: Yale University Press, 1982), 84.

20. Marsh, *Man and Nature* (1973 edition), 228, 235, 328–29.

21. Charles Scribner to Marsh, December 1, 1863, UVM, quoted by Lowenthal, ed., *Man and Nature* (1973 ed.), x.

22. Marsh to Charles Eliot Norton, October 17, 1863, UVM, quoted by Lowenthal, ed., *Man and Nature*, xi.

23. Phillip G. Terrie, *Forever Wild: Environmental Aesthetics and the Adirondack Forest Preserve* (Philadelphia: Temple University Press, 1985).

24. Gifford Pinchot proclaimed the book "epoch-making" in Gifford Pinchot, *Breaking New Ground* (New York: Harcourt Brace, 1947), xvi–xvii; Nash, *Wilderness and the American Mind*, 105, cites the following examples of Marsh's early influence on forest conservation: I. A. Lapham et al., *Report of the Disastrous Effects of the Destruction of Forest Trees* (Madison, WI, 1867); "Forest Preservation," *New York Times*, May 30, 1872; "Spare the Trees," *Appleton's Journal* 1 (1876): 470–73; and Felix Oswald, "The Preservation of Forests," *North American Review* 129 (1879): 35–46. See also Stewart L. Udall, *The Quiet Crisis* (New York: Holt, Rinehart, and Winston, 1963), 82; and Worster, *Nature's Economy*, 269.

25. Marsh, *Man and Nature* (1973 edition), 91–92.

26. "Usufruct" denotes the "legal use and enjoyment of the fruits . . . of *something belonging to another*" (emphasis mine). Merriam Webster's *New Collegiate Dictionary* (Springfield, MA: Merriam and Co., 1974), 1289.

27. United States *Statutes at Large*, 30, p. 35, quoted by Nash, *Wilderness and the American Mind*, 137.

28. See Samuel P. Hays's landmark work, *Conservation and the Gospel of Efficiency: The Progressive Conservation Movement, 1890–1920* (Cambridge, MA: Harvard University Press, 1959).

29. John Ise, *The United States Forest Policy* (New Haven, CT: Yale University Press, 1920), 108–20.

30. Linnie Marsh Wolfe, *Son of the Wilderness: The Life of John Muir* (New York, 1945), 275–76, and Lawrence Rakestraw, "Sheep Grazing in the Cascade Range: John Minto vs. John Muir," *Pacific Historical Review* 27 (1958): 371–82, quoted by Nash, *Wilderness and the American Mind*, 138.

31. See Nash, *Wilderness and the American Mind*, 161–81. On the wilderness cult, see ibid., 141–60; and Peter J. Schmitt, *Back to Nature: The Arcadian Myth in Urban America*, with Foreword by John R. Stilgoe (Baltimore: Johns Hopkins University Press, 1990), 106–14, 125–40, and 167–71. On the Colorado dam wars, see Russell Martin, *A Story That Stands Like a Dam* (New York: Holt, 1989).

32. See Suellen M. Hoy, " 'Municipal Housekeeping': The Role of Women in Improving Urban Sanitation Practices, 1880–1917," in Martin Melosi, ed., *Pollution and Reform in American Cities, 1870–1930* (Austin: University of Texas Press, 1980).

33. Thomas Kuhn, *The Structure of Scientific Revolutions* (Chicago: University of Chicago Press, 1962).

34. Worster, *Nature's Economy*, 232–35.

35. Ibid., 205–40. Among others, Worster cites Frederic E. Clements, *The Development and Structure of Vegetation* (Lincoln, NE, 1904); *The Dynamics of Vegetation: Selections from the Writings of F. E. Clements*, ed. B. W. Allred and E. S. Clements (New York, 1949); and Frederic Clements with Ralph Chaney, *Environment and Life in the Great Plains* (New York, 1939). See also Paul Sears, *Deserts on the March* (Norman, OK: University of Oklahoma Press, 1935).

36. Worster, *Nature's Economy*, 205–57.

37. Ibid., 237.

38. Worster, *Nature's Economy*, 279, citing Olaus Murie, "Memorandum to Mr. Reddington," August 20, 1929 (carbon copy in Olaus Murie Papers, Denver Public Library).

39. Stanley Young to Arthur Carhart, November 24, 1930, in Stanley P. Young Papers, Denver Public Library, Conservation Center, quoted by Worster, *Nature's Economy*, 277–78.

40. Worster, *Nature's Economy*, 270–73.

41. Aldo Leopold, *Game Management* (New York, 1933), quoted by Worster, *Nature's Economy*, 272.

42. See Susan Flader's excellent biography, *Thinking Like a Mountain: Aldo Leopold and the Evolution of an Ecological Attitude Toward Deer, Wolves, and Forests* (Columbia: University of Missouri Press, 1974); also Robert Finch, Introduction to Leopold's classic, *A Sand County Almanac: And Sketches Here and There* (New York: Oxford University Press, 1987 reprint; first published by Oxford in 1949).

43. Kenneth Brower, "Leopold's Gift," *Sierra* 86, no. 1 (January/February 2001): 35–36.

44. Ecosystem management, although it has entered the legitimate vernacular of conservation policy, is in practice often not what it suggests. For example, see Chris Magoc, *Yellowstone: The Creation and Selling of an American Landscape, 1870–1903* (Albuquerque: University of New Mexico Press, 1999), chapter 7.

45. See, for example, Bill Devall and George Sessions, *Deep Ecology: Living As If Nature Mattered* (Salt Lake City: Gibbs M. Smith, 1985).

46. Springdale is located in the Allegheny-Kiskiminetas Valley near Pittsburgh's industrial core. One can hardly doubt that like any environment, the picturesque Allegheny River and industrial landscape of southwestern Pennsylvania bore heavily on Carson's nature sensibility.

47. To Natronans, the Penn Salt plant was both life and death, although in those days one thought less of the latter. The actual quote comes from an

interview by the author with Lou Chernan, Natrona historian, in 1993; recorded under the auspices of the Steel Industry Heritage Corporation, tape and index in SIHC's Homestead, Pennsylvania, Steel Heritage Archives and in the Allegheny-Kiski Valley Historical Society Archives, Tarentum, Pennsylvania.

48. Linda Lear, *Rachel Carson: Witness for Nature* (New York: Holt and Company, 1997), 1–55.
49. H. Patricia Hynes, *The Recurring Silent Spring* (New York: Pergamon Press, 1989), 30.
50. *The National Cyclopedia of American Biography* (New York: James T. White, 1960), Current Volume (1953–1959) 1:131–32.
51. Vera L. Norwood, "Heroines of Nature: Four Women Respond to the American Landscape," in Glotfeltz and Fromm, eds., *The Ecocriticism Reader*, 335.
52. Rachel L. Carson, *The Sea Around Us* (New York: Oxford University Press, 1951), 188–201.
53. Paul Boyer, *American Thought and Culture at the Dawn of the Atomic Age* (New York: Pantheon Books, 1985), 352–53; Spencer Weart, *Nuclear Fear: A History of Images* (Cambridge, MA: Harvard University Press, 1985), 325. Boyer cites Steven M. Spencer, "Fallout: The Silent Killer," *Saturday Evening Post* (August 29, 1959): 26, 89; (September 5, 1959): 86. See also Robert A. Divine, *Blowing on the Wind: The Nuclear Test Ban Debate, 1954–1960* (New York: Oxford University Press, 1978).
54. Carson, *The Sea Around Us*, revised edition (New York: Oxford University Press, 1961), preface.
55. Lear, *Carson: Witness for Nature*, 314–15; Frank Graham, Jr., *Since Silent Spring* (New York: Houghton Mifflin, 1970), 16–17; Hynes, *Recurring Silent Spring*, 31.
56. Quoted in Graham, *Since Silent Spring*, 18–19, from Rachel Carson Papers, Yale University Library.
57. Ibid., 20.
58. Hynes, *Recurring Silent Spring*, 32.
59. Lear, *Carson: Witness for Nature*, 339–95.
60. Paul Brooks, *The House of Life: Rachel Carson at Work* (Boston: Houghton Mifflin, 1972), 270.
61. Rachel Carson, *Silent Spring*, Foreword by Paul Brooks (Boston: Houghton Mifflin, 1987 edition, originally published in 1962), 228–29.
62. George C. Decker, "Pros and Cons of Pests, Pest Control and Pesticides," *World Review of Pest Control* (Spring 1962): 6–18; idem, "How to Answer Rachel Carson," *County Agent and Vo-Ag Teacher* (November 1962), quoted by Lear, *Carson: Witness for Nature*, 428–32.
63. F. A. Soraci, in *Conservation News* (1962), cited by Graham, *Since Silent Spring*, 55–56.
64. Lear, *Carson: Witness for Nature*, 428–29.
65. Hynes, *Recurring Silent Spring*, 39, quoting Graham, *Since Silent Spring*, 76; P. Sterling, *Sea and Earth: The Life of Rachel Carson* (New York: Dell, 1970), 153.
66. Samuel P. Hays, *Beauty, Health and Permanence: Environmental Politics in the United States, 1955–1985* (New York: Cambridge University Press, 1987), 174–75; Hynes, *Since Silent Spring*, 43–45.
67. See, for example, *After Silent Spring: The Unsolved Problems of Pesticide Use in the United States* (Washington, DC: Natural Resources De-

fense Council, 1993). Former vice president Al Gore noted the profound influence of Carson's book on his mother and on the development of his own environmental ethic. See *Earth in the Balance: Ecology and the Human Spirit* (New York: Penguin Plume Books, 1992), 3. One study, William Ashworth's *The Carson Factor* (New York: Hawthorn Books, 1979), focused on the impact of Carson's book on a disaster in Oregon resulting from predator extermination. On the continued attack on Carson's ideas, see, for example, Richard Neuhaus, *In Defense of People* (New York: Macmillan, 1971); and Ronald Bailey, *Eco-Scam: The False Prophets of Ecological Catastrophe* (New York: St. Martin's Press, 1993).

WILLIAM BARTRAM

16 | The Animal Creation and the Importance of Ephemera (1791)

The animal creation also excites our admiration, and equally manifests the almighty power, wisdom, and beneficence of the Supreme Creator and Sovereign Lord of the universe; some in their vast size and strength, as the mammoth, the elephant, the whale, the lion, and alligator; others in agility; others in their beauty and elegance of colour, plumage, and rapidity of flight, having the faculty of moving and living in the air; others for their immediate and indispensable use and convenience to man, in furnishing means for our clothing and sustenance, and administering to our help in the toils and labours of life: how wonderful is the mechanism of these finely formed self-moving beings, how complicated their system, yet what unerring uniformity prevails through every tribe and particular species! The effect we see and contemplate, the cause is invisible, incomprehensible; how can it be otherwise? when we cannot see the end or origin of a nerve or vein, while the divisibility of matter or fluid, is infinite. We admire the mechanism of a watch, and the fabric of a piece of brocade, as being the production of art; these merit our admiration, and must excite our esteem for the ingenious artist or modifier; but nature is the work of God omnipotent; and an

From William Bartram, *Travels and other Writings . . . Travels Through North and South Carolina, Georgia, East and West Florida. Travels in Georgia and Florida, 1773–1774: A Report to Dr. John Fothergill. Miscellaneous Writings* (Philadelphia: James and Johnson, 1791), xxiii–xxv, 36–39, 80–83.

elephant, nay even this world, is comparatively but a very minute part of his works. If then the visible, the mechanical part of the animal creation, the mere material part, is so admirably beautiful, harmonious, and incomprehensible, what must be the intellectual system? that inexpressibly more essential principle, which secretly operates within? that which animates the inimitable machines, which gives them motion, impowers them to act, speak, and perform, this must be divine and immortal?

I am sensible that the general opinion of philosophers, has distinguished the moral system of the brute creature from that of mankind, by an epithet which implies a mere mechanical impulse, which leads and impels them to necessary actions, without any premeditated design or contrivance; this we term instinct, which faculty we suppose to be inferior to reason in man.

The parental and filial affections seem to be as ardent, their sensibility and attachment as active and faithful, as those observed in human nature. . . .

Leaving the pleasant town of Wrightsborough [Georgia] we continued eight or nine miles through a fertile plain and high forest, to the north branch of Little River, being the largest of the two, crossing which, we entered an extensive fertile plain, bordering on the river, and shaded by trees of vast growth, which at once spoke its fertility. Continuing some time through these shady groves, the scene opens, and discloses to view the most magnificent forest I had ever seen. We rose gradually a sloping bank of twenty or thirty feet elevation, and immediately entered this sublime forest. The ground is perfectly a level green plain, thinly planted by nature with the most stately forest trees, such as the gigantic black oak* (q. tinctoria), liriodendron, juglans nigra, platanus, juglans exaltata, fagus sylvatica, ulmus sylvatica, liquidambar styraciflua, whose mighty trunks, seemingly of an equal height, appeared like superb columns. To keep within the bounds of truth and reality, in describing the magnitude and grandeur of these trees, would, I fear, fail of credibility; yet, I think I can assert, that many of the black oaks measured eight, nine, ten, and eleven feet in diameter five feet above the ground, as we measured several that were above thirty feet in girt, and from hence they ascend perfectly straight, with a gradual taper, forty or fifty feet to the limbs; but, below five or

---

*Gigantic black oak. Querc. tinctoria; the bark of this species of oak is found to afford a valuable yellow dye. This tree is known by the name of black oak in Pennsylvania, New-Jersey, New-York, and New-England.

six feet, these trunks would measure a third more in circumference, on account of the projecting jambs, or supports, which are more or less, according to the number of horizontal roots that they arise from: the tulip tree, liquidambar, and beech, were equally stately.

Not far distant from the terrace, or eminence, overlooking the low grounds of the river, many very magnificent monuments of the power and industry of the ancient inhabitants of these lands are visible. I observed a stupendous conical pyramid, or artificial mount of earth, vast tetragon terraces, and a large sunken area, of a cubical form, encompassed with banks of earth; and certain traces of a larger Indian town, the work of a powerful nation, whose period of grandeur perhaps long preceded the discovery of this continent.

After about seven miles progress through this forest of gigantic black oaks, we enter on territories which exhibit more varied scenes: the land rises almost insensibly by gentle ascents, exhibiting desert plains, high forests, gravelly and stony ridges, ever in sight of rapid rivulets; the soil, as already described. We then passed over large rich savannas, or natural meadows, wide spreading cane swamps, and frequently old Indian settlements, now deserted and overgrown with forests. These are always on or near the banks of rivers, or great swamps, the artificial mounts and terraces elevating them above the surrounding groves. I observed in the ancient cultivated fields, 1. diospyros, 2. gleditsia triacanthos, 3. prunus chicasaw, 4. callicarpa, 5. morus rubra, 6. juglans exaltata, 7. juglans nigra, which inform us, that these trees were cultivated by the ancients, on account of their fruit, as being wholesome and nourishing food. Though these are natives of the forest*, yet they thrive better, and are more fruitful, in cultivated plantations, and the fruit is in great estimation with the present generation of Indians, particularly juglans exaltata, commonly called shell-barked hiccory. The Creeks store up the last in their towns. I have seen above an hundred bushels of these nuts belonging to one family. They pound them to pieces, and then cast them into boiling water, which, after passing through fine strainers, preserves the most oily part of the liquid: this they call by a name which signifies hiccory milk; it is as sweet and rich as fresh cream, and is an ingredient in most of their cookery, especially hominy and corn cakes.

*The Chicasaw plumb I think must be excepted, for though certainly a native of America, yet I never saw it wild in the forests, but always in old deserted Indian plantations: I suppose it to have been brought from the S. W. beyond the Mississippi, by the Chicasaws.

After four days moderate and pleasant travelling, we arrived in the evening at the Buffalo Lick. This extraordinary place occupies several acres of ground, at the foot of the S. E. promontory of the Great Ridge, which, as before observed, divides the rivers Savanna and Alatamaha. A large cane swamp and meadows, forming an immense plain, lie S. E. from it; in this swamp I believe the head branches of the great Ogeeche river take their rise. The place called the Lick contains three or four acres, is nearly level, and lies between the head of the cane swamp and the ascent of the Ridge. The earth, from the superficies to an unknown depth, is an almost white or cinereous [ashy] coloured tenacious fattish clay, which all kinds of cattle lick into great caves, pursuing the delicious vein. It is the common opinion of the inhabitants, that this clay is impregnated with saline vapours, arising from fossile salts deep in the earth; but I could discover nothing saline in its taste, but I imagined an insipid sweetness. Horned cattle, horses, and deer, are immoderately fond of it, insomuch, that their excrement, which almost totally covers the earth to some distance round this place, appears to be perfect clay; which, when dried by the sun and air, is almost as hard as brick. . . .

Leaving Picolata [Florida], I continued to ascend the river. I observed this day, during my progress up the river, incredible numbers of small flying insects, of the genus termed by naturalists Ephemera, continually emerging from the shallow water near shore, some of them immediately taking their flight to the land, whilst myriads crept up the grass and herbage, where remaining for a short time, as they acquired sufficient strength, they took their flight also, following their kindred to the main land. This resurrection from the deep, if I may so express it, commences early in the morning, and ceases after the sun is up. At evening they are seen in clouds of innumerable millions, swarming and wantoning in the still air, gradually drawing near the river. They descend upon its surface, and there quickly end their day, after committing their eggs to the deep; which being for a little while tossed about, enveloped in a viscid scum, are hatched, and the little Larva descend into their secure and dark habitation, in the oozy bed beneath, where they remain, gradually increasing in size, until the returning spring: they then change to a Nymph, when the genial heat brings them, as it were, into existence, and they again arise into the world. This fly seems to be delicious food for birds, frogs, and fish. In the morning, when they arise, and in the evening, when they return, the tumult is great indeed, and the surface of the water along shore broken into bubbles, or spirted into the air, by the contending aquatic tribes; and such is the avidity of the fish and frogs, that they spring into the air after this delicious prey.

Early in the evening, after a pleasant day's voyage, I made a convenient and safe harbour, in a little lagoon, under an elevated bank, on the West shore of the river; where I shall entreat the reader's patience, whilst we behold the closing scene of the short-lived Ephemera, and communicate to each other the reflections which so singular an exhibition might rationally suggest to an inquisitive mind. Our place of observation is happily situated under the protecting shade of majestic Live Oaks, glorious Magnolias, and the fragrant Orange, open to the view of the great river and still waters of the lagoon just before us.

At the cool eve's approach, the sweet enchanting melody of the feathered songsters gradually ceases, and they betake themselves to their leafy coverts for security and repose.

Solemnly and slowly move onward, to the river's shore, the rustling clouds of the Ephemera. How awful the procession! innumerable millions of winged beings, voluntarily verging on to destruction, to the brink of the grave, where they behold bands of their enemies with wide open jaws, ready to receive them. But as if insensible of their danger, gay and tranquil each meets his beloved mate in the still air, inimitably bedecked in their new nuptial robes. What eye can trace them, in their varied wanton amorous chaces, bounding and fluttering on the odoriferous air! With what peace, love, and joy, do they end the last moments of their existence!

I think we may assert, without any fear of exaggeration, that there are annually of these beautiful winged beings, which rise into existence, and for a few moments take a transient view of the glory of the Creator's works, a number greater than the whole race of mankind that have ever existed since the creation; and that, only from the shores of this river. How many then must have been produced since the creation, when we consider the number of large rivers in America, in comparison with which, this river is but a brook or rivulet.

The importance of the existence of these beautiful and delicately formed little creatures, whose frame and organization are equally wonderful, more delicate, and perhaps as complicated as those of the most perfect human being, is well worth a few moments contemplation; I mean particularly when they appear in the fly state. And if we consider the very short period of that stage of existence, which we may reasonably suppose to be the only space of their life that admits of pleasure and enjoyment, what a lesson doth it not afford us of the vanity of our own pursuits!

Their whole existence in this world is but one complete year: and at least three hundred and sixty days of that time they are in the form of an ugly grub, buried in mud, eighteen inches under water, and in this condition scarcely locomotive, as each Larva or grub has but its own narrow solitary cell, from which it never travels or moves, but in a perpendicular progression of a few inches, up and down, from the bottom to the surface of the mud, in order to intercept the passing atoms for its food, and get a momentary respiration of fresh air; and even here it must be perpetually on its guard, in order to escape the troops of fish and shrimps watching to catch it, and from whom it has no escape, but by instantly retreating back into its cell. One would be apt almost to imagine them created merely for the food of fish and other animals. . . .

17 The Destructiveness of Man (1864)

Man has too long forgotten that the earth was given to him for usufruct alone, not for consumption, still less for profligate waste. Nature has provided against the absolute destruction of any of her elementary matter, the raw material of her works; the thunderbolt and the tornado, the most convulsive throes of even the volcano and the earthquake, being only phenomena of decomposition and recomposition. But she has left it within the power of man irreparably to derange the combinations of inorganic matter and of organic life, which through the night of aeons she had been proportioning and balancing, to prepare the earth for his habitation, when, in the fulness of time, his Creator should call him forth to enter into its possession.

Apart from the hostile influence of man, the organic and the inorganic world are, as I have remarked, bound together by such mutual relations and adaptations as secure, if not the absolute permanence and equilibrium of both, a long continuance of the established conditions of each at any given time and place, or at least, a very slow and gradual succession of changes in those conditions. But man is everywhere a disturbing agent. Wherever he plants his foot, the harmonies of nature are turned to discords. The proportions and accommodations which insured the stability of existing arrangements are overthrown. Indigenous vegetable and animal species are extirpated, and supplanted by others of foreign origin, spontaneous production is for-

From George Perkins Marsh, "The Destructiveness of Man," *Man and Nature; or, Physical Geography as Modified by Human Action* (New York: Charles Scribner, 1864), 35–41.

bidden or restricted, and the face of the earth is either laid bare or covered with a new and reluctant growth of vegetable forms, and with alien tribes of animal life. These intentional changes and substitutions constitute, indeed, great revolutions; but vast as is their magnitude and importance, they are, as we shall see, insignificant in comparison with the contingent and unsought results which have flowed from them.

The fact that, of all organic beings, man alone is to be regarded as essentially a destructive power, and that he wields energies to resist which, nature—that nature whom all material life and all inorganic substance obey—is wholly impotent, tends to prove that, though living in physical nature, he is not of her, that he is of more exalted parentage, and belongs to a higher order of existences than those born of her womb and submissive to her dictates.

There are, indeed, brute destroyers, beasts and birds and insects of prey—all animal life feeds upon, and, of course, destroys other life,— but this destruction is balanced by compensations. It is, in fact, the very means by which the existence of one tribe of animals or of vegetables is secured against being smothered by the encroachments of another; and the reproductive powers of species, which serve as the food of others, are always proportioned to the demand they are destined to supply. Man pursues his victims with reckless destructiveness: and, while the sacrifice of life by the lower animals is limited by the cravings of appetite, he unsparingly persecutes, even to extirpation, thousands of organic forms which he cannot consume.[1]

The earth was not, in its natural condition, completely adapted to the use of man, but only to the sustenance of wild animals and wild vegetation. These live, multiply their kind in just proportion, and attain their perfect measure of strength and beauty, without producing or requiring any change in the natural arrangements of surface, or in each other's spontaneous tendencies, except such mutual repression of excessive increase as may prevent the extirpation of one species by the encroachments of another. In short, without man, lower animal and spontaneous vegetable life would have been constant in type, distribution, and proportion, and the physical geography of the earth would have remained undisturbed for indefinite periods, and been subject to revolution only from possible, unknown cosmical causes, or from geological action.

But man, the domestic animals that serve him, the field and garden plants the products of which supply him with food and clothing,

cannot subsist and rise to the full development of their higher properties, unless brute and unconscious nature be effectually combated,
and, in a great degree, vanquished by human art. Hence, a certain
measure of transformation of terrestrial surface, of suppression of natural, and stimulation of artificially modified productivity becomes necessary. This measure man has unfortunately exceeded. He has felled
the forests whose network of fibrous roots bound the mould to the
rocky skeleton of the earth; but had he allowed here and there a belt of
woodland to reproduce itself by spontaneous propagation, most of the
mischiefs which his reckless destruction of the natural protection of
the soil has occasioned would have been averted. He has broken up
the mountain reservoirs, the percolation of whose waters through unseen channels supplied the fountains that refreshed his cattle and fer-
tilized his fields; but he has neglected to maintain the cisterns and the
canals of irrigation which a wise antiquity had constructed to neutral-
ize the consequences of its own imprudence. While he has torn the
thin glebe [rich soil] which confined the light earth of extensive plains,
and has destroyed the fringe of semi-aquatic plants which skirted the
coast and checked the drifting of the sea sand, he has failed to prevent
the spreading of the dunes by clothing them with artificially propa-
gated vegetation. He has ruthlessly warred on all the tribes of animated nature whose spoil he could convert to his own uses, and he
has not protected the birds which prey on the insects most destructive
to his own harvests.

Purely untutored humanity, it is true, interferes comparatively little
with the arrangements of nature,[2] and the destructive agency of man
becomes more and more energetic and unsparing as he advances in
civilization, until the impoverishment, with which his exhaustion of
the natural resources of the soil is threatening him, at last awakens
him to the necessity of preserving what is left, if not of restoring what
has been wantonly wasted. The wandering savage grows no cultivated
vegetable, fells no forest, and extirpates no useful plant, no noxious
weed. If his skill in the chase enables him to entrap numbers of the
animals on which he feeds, he compensates this loss by destroying
also the lion, the tiger, the wolf, the otter, the seal, and the eagle, thus
indirectly protecting the feebler quadrupeds and fish and fowls, which
would otherwise become the booty of beasts and birds of prey. But
with stationary life, or rather with the pastoral state, man at once commences an almost indiscriminate warfare upon all the forms of animal
and vegetable existence around him, and as he advances in civiliza-

tion, he gradually eradicates or transforms every spontaneous product of the soil he occupies.[3]

NOTES

1. The terrible destructiveness of man is remarkably exemplified in the chase of large mammalia and birds for single products, attended with the entire waste of enormous quantities of flesh, and of other parts of the animal, which are capable of valuable uses. The wild cattle of South America are slaughtered by millions for their hides and horns; the buffalo of North America for his skin or his tongue; the elephant, the walrus, and the narwhal for their tusks; the cetacea, and some other marine animals, for their oil and whalebone; the ostrich and other large birds, for their plumage. Within a few years, sheep have been killed in New England by whole flocks, for their pelts and suet alone, the flesh being thrown away; and it is even said that the bodies of the same quadrupeds have been used in Australia as fuel for limekilns. What a vast amount of human nutriment, of bone, and of other animal products valuable in the arts, is thus recklessly squandered! In nearly all these cases, the part which constitutes the motive for this wholesale destruction, and is alone saved, is essentially of insignificant value as compared with what is thrown away. The horns and hide of an ox are not economically worth a tenth part as much as the entire carcass.

   One of the greatest benefits to be expected from the improvements of civilization is, that increased facilities of communication will render it possible to transport to places of consumption much valuable material that is now wasted because the price at the nearest market will not pay freight. The cattle slaughtered in South America for their hides would feed millions of the starving population of the Old World, if their flesh could be economically preserved and transported across the ocean.

   We are beginning to learn a better economy in dealing with the inorganic world. The utilization—or, as the Germans more happily call it, the Verwerthung, the *beworthing*—of waste from metallurgical, chemical, and manufacturing establishments, is among the most important results of the application of science to industrial purposes. The incidental products from the laboratories of manufacturing chemists often become more valuable than those for the preparation of which they were erected. The slags from silver refineries, and even from smelting houses of the coarser metals, have not unfrequently yielded to a second operator a better return than the first had derived from dealing with the natural ore; and the saving of lead carried off in the smoke of furnaces has, of itself, given a large profit on the capital invested in the works. A few years ago, an officer of an American mint was charged with embezzling gold committed to him for coinage. He insisted, in his defence, that much of the metal was volatilized and lost in refining and melting, and upon scraping the chimneys of the melting furnaces and the roofs of the adjacent houses, gold enough was found in the soot to account for no small part of the deficiency.

2. It is an interesting and not hitherto sufficiently noticed fact, that the domestication of the organic world, so far as it has yet been achieved, belongs, not indeed to the savage state, but to the earliest dawn of

civilization, the conquest of inorganic nature almost as exclusively to the most advanced stages of artificial culture. It is familiarly known to all who have occupied themselves with the psychology and habits of the ruder races, and of persons with imperfectly developed intellects in civilized life, that although these humble tribes and individuals sacrifice, without scruple, the lives of the lower animals to the gratification of their appetites and the supply of their other physical wants, yet they nevertheless seem to cherish with brutes, and even with vegetable life, sympathies which are much more feebly felt by civilized men. The popular traditions of the simpler peoples recognize a certain community of nature between man, brute animals, and even plants; and this serves to explain why the apologue or fable, which ascribes the power of speech and the faculty of reason to birds, quadrupeds, insects, flowers, and trees, is one of the earliest forms of literary composition.

In almost every wild tribe, some particular quadruped or bird, though persecuted as a destroyer of more domestic beasts, or hunted for food, is regarded with peculiar respect, one might almost say, affection. Some of the North American aboriginal nations celebrate a propitiatory feast to the manes of the intended victim before they commence a bear hunt; and the Norwegian peasantry have not only retained an old proverb which ascribes to the same animal "*ti Mænds Styrke og tolv Mænds Vid*," ten men's strength and twelve men's cunning; but they still pay to him something of the reverence with which ancient superstition invested him. The student of Icelandic literature will find in the saga of *Finnbogi hinn rami* a curious illustration of this feeling, in an account of a dialogue between a Norwegian bear and an Icelandic champion—dumb show on the part of Bruin, and chivalric words on that of Finnbogi—followed by a duel, in which the latter, who had thrown away his arms and armor in order that the combatants might meet on equal terms, was victorious. John Hay Drummond-Hay's very interesting work [*Journal of an Expedition to the Court of Morocco*] contains many amusing notices of a similar feeling entertained by the Moors toward the redoubtable enemy of their flocks—the lion.

This sympathy helps us to understand how it is that most if not all the domestic animals—if indeed they ever existed in a wild state—were appropriated, reclaimed, and trained before men had been gathered into organized and fixed communities, that almost every known esculent plant had acquired substantially its present artificial character, and that the properties of nearly all vegetable drugs and poisons were known at the remotest period to which historical records reach. Did nature bestow upon primitive man some instinct akin to that by which she teaches the brute to select the nutritious and to reject the noxious vegetables indiscriminately mixed in forest and pasture?

This instinct, it must be admitted, is far from infallible, and, as has been hundreds of times remarked by naturalists, it is in many cases not an original faculty but an acquired and transmitted habit. It is a fact familiar to persons engaged in sheep husbandry in New England—and I have seen it confirmed by personal observation—that sheep bred where the common laurel, as it is called, *Kalmia angustifolia*, abounds, almost always avoid browsing upon the leaves of that plant, while those brought from districts where laurel is unknown, and turned into pastures where it grows, very often feed upon it and are poisoned by it. A curious acquired and hereditary instinct, of a different character, may not improperly be noticed here. I refer to that by which horses bred in provinces where quicksands are common avoid their dangers or extricate themselves from them. See Nicolas Théodore Brémontier, "Mémoire sur les dunes . . . entre Bayonne et la pointe de Grave" (1790), reprinted in *Annales des Ponts et Chaussées*, 5 (1833), 155–157.

It is commonly said in New England, and I believe with reason, that the crows of this generation are wiser than their ancestors. Scarecrows which were effectual fifty years ago are no longer respected by the plunderers of the cornfield, and new terrors must from time to time be invented for its protection.

Civilization has added little to the number of vegetable or animal species grown in our fields or bred in our folds, while, on the contrary, the subjugation of the inorganic forces, and the consequent extension of man's sway over, not the annual products of the earth only, but her substance and her springs of action, is almost entirely the work of highly refined and cultivated ages. The employment of the elasticity of wood and of horn, as a projectile power in the bow, is nearly universal among the rudest savages. The application of compressed air to the same purpose, in the blowpipe, is more restricted, and the use of the mechanical powers, the inclined plane, the wheel and axle, and even the wedge and lever, seems almost unknown except to civilized man. I have myself seen European peasants to whom one of the simplest applications of this latter power was a revelation.

3. The difference between the relations of savage life, and of incipient civilization, to nature, is well seen in that part of the valley of the Mississippi which was once occupied by the mound builders and afterward by the far less developed Indian tribes. When the tillers of the fields which must have been cultivated to sustain the large population that once inhabited those regions perished or were driven out, the soil fell back to the normal forest state, and the savages who succeeded the more advanced race interfered very little, if at all, with the ordinary course of spontaneous nature.

18 Human Ecology and the Habits of Sanitation in the Modern Urban Environment (1907)

Sanitary science teaches that mode of life which promotes health and efficiency.

The individual is one of a community influencing and influenced by the common environment.

Human ecology is the study of the surroundings of human beings in the effects they produce on the lives of men. The features of the environment are natural, as climate, and artificial, produced by human activity, as noise, dust, poisonous vapors, vitiated air, dirty water, and unclean food.

The study of this environment is in two chief lines:

First, what is often called municipal housekeeping—the co-operation of the citizens in securing clean streets, the suppression of nuisances, abundant water supply, market inspection, etc.

Second, family housekeeping. The healthful home demands a management of the house which shall promote vigorous life and prevent the physical deterioration so evident under modern conditions.

From Ellen Swallow Richards, "The Habits of Sanitation in Daily Life," *Sanitation in Daily Life* (Boston: Whitcomb and Barrows, 1907), v–viii.

The close interrelation of these two parts of sanitation should be borne in mind. Even if a man has been so blessed as to be born into favorable conditions, he must nevertheless face the problem of retaining health and strength under the strain of modern progress and civilization. Formerly a man's occupation in the fields and woods kept him in health, but now he must ordinarily give what strength he has to his occupation, and rely upon other sources from which to secure a healthy body.[1] It is possible to understand the effect that is produced by unfavorable environment, if we compare the difference in physical stature between the Scotch agricultural worker and the inhabitant of certain manufacturing towns in England. There is an average of five inches in height and thirty-one pounds in weight in favor of the Scotchman. H. G. Wells, in speaking of the responsibility for man's physical efficiency, compares the city dweller in crowded streets and tenements with the man living in the freer, more open country, and makes the difference from three and one-half to five inches in stature and from twenty to thirty pounds in weight in favor of the country dweller.[2] The former belongs to the physically unfit for the struggle of life.

A casual observer visiting the poorer parts of one of our large cities must necessarily be impressed with the stunted appearance of the children on the streets.

Since physical strength and power have always been desired by men; and since, in these modern days, women wish to be not far behind their brothers in endurance, the facts just given should furnish food for serious thought as to the means of acquiring a body physically fit, capable of securing the greatest capacity for work and for play—for life.

Is this physical fitness and consequent mental power so good a thing, so desirable, that the pupils in our schools and colleges are ready to give their attention to habits of right living when the methods of acquiring these habits are presented to them? Is it worth their while? Let the habits be once acquired, then the attention may be turned in other directions. It has been said, "Sow a habit and reap a character." This is true of the physical and mental as of the moral. Habits become fixed. It is necessary, then, that they be good habits. Right habits of living are the foundations of health of body and mind.

To secure and maintain a safe environment there must be inculcated *habits* of using the material things in daily life in such a way as to promote and not to diminish health. Avoid spitting in the streets, avoid throwing refuse on the sidewalk, avoid dust and bad air in the house and sleeping room, etc.

It is, however, of the greatest importance that every one should acquire such habits of *belief* in the importance of this material environment as shall lead him to insist upon sanitary regulations, and to see that they are carried out.

What touches my neighbor, touches me. For my sake, and for his, the city inspector and the city garbage cart visit us, and I keep my premises in such a condition as I expect him to strive for.

The first law of sanitation requires quick removal and destruction of all wastes—of things done with.

The second law enjoins such use of the air, water, and food necessary to life that the person may be in a state of health and efficiency.

This right use depends so largely upon habit that a great portion of sanitary teaching must be given to inculcating right and safe ways in daily life.

NOTES

1. D. A. Sargent, "Health, Strength, and Power."
2. "Mankind in the Making."

ALDO LEOPOLD

19 Land-Use Ethics and Economic Self-Interest (1949)

Thinking Like a Mountain

A deep chesty bawl echoes from rimrock to rim-rock, rolls down the mountain, and fades into the far blackness of the night. It is an outburst of wild defiant sorrow, and of contempt for all the adversities of the world.

Every living thing (and perhaps many a dead one as well) pays heed to that call. To the deer it is a reminder of the way of all flesh, to the pine a forecast of midnight scuffles and of blood upon the snow, to the coyote a promise of gleanings to come, to the cowman a threat of red ink at the bank, to the hunter a challenge of fang against bullet. Yet behind these obvious and immediate hopes and fears there lies a deeper meaning, known only to the mountain itself. Only the mountain has lived long enough to listen objectively to the howl of a wolf.

Those unable to decipher the hidden meaning know nevertheless that it is there, for it is felt in all wolf country, and distinguishes that country from all other land. It tingles in the spine of all who hear wolves by night, or who scan their tracks by day. Even without sight or sound of a wolf, it is implicit in a hundred small events: the midnight whinny of a pack horse, the rattle of rolling rocks, the bound of a fleeing deer,

From Aldo Leopold, *A Sand County Almanac: And Sketches Here and There.* © 1949, 1977 by Oxford University Press, 129–30, 207–10, 213–14, 223–25. Reprinted by permission of Oxford University Press.

the way shadows lie under the spruces. Only the ineducable tyro [novice] can fail to sense the presence or absence of wolves, or the fact that mountains have a secret opinion about them.

My own conviction on this score dates from the day I saw a wolf die. We were eating lunch on a high rimrock, at the foot of which a turbulent river elbowed its way. We saw what we thought was a doe fording the torrent, her breast awash in white water. When she climbed the bank toward us and shook out her tail, we realized our error: it was a wolf. A half-dozen others, evidently grown pups, sprang from the willows and all joined in a welcoming mêlée of wagging tails and playful maulings. What was literally a pile of wolves writhed and tumbled in the center of an open flat at the foot of our rimrock.

In those days we had never heard of passing up a chance to kill a wolf. In a second we were pumping lead into the pack, but with more excitement than accuracy: how to aim a steep downhill shot is always confusing. When our rifles were empty, the old wolf was down, and a pup was dragging a leg into impassable slide-rocks.

We reached the old wolf in time to watch a fierce green fire dying in her eyes. I realized then, and have known ever since, that there was something new to me in those eyes—something known only to her and to the mountain. I was young then, and full of trigger-itch; I thought that because fewer wolves meant more deer, that no wolves would mean hunters' paradise. But after seeing the green fire die, I sensed that neither the wolf nor the mountain agreed with such a view. . . .

The Ecological Conscience

Conservation is a state of harmony between men and land. Despite nearly a century of propaganda, conservation still proceeds at a snail's pace; progress still consists largely of letterhead pieties and convention oratory. On the back forty we still slip two steps backward for each forward stride.

The usual answer to this dilemma is "more conservation education." No one will debate this, but is it certain that only the *volume* of education needs stepping up? Is something lacking in the *content* as well?

It is difficult to give a fair summary of its content in brief form, but, as I understand it, the content is substantially this: obey the law, vote right, join some organizations, and practice what conservation is profitable on your own land; the government will do the rest.

Is not this formula too easy to accomplish anything worth-while? It defines no right or wrong, assigns no obligation, calls for no sacrifice, implies no change in the current philosophy of values. In respect of land-use, it urges only enlightened self-interest. Just how far will such education take us? An example will perhaps yield a partial answer.

By 1930 it had become clear to all except the ecologically blind that southwestern Wisconsin's topsoil was slipping seaward. In 1933 the farmers were told that if they would adopt certain remedial practices for five years, the public would donate CCC [Civilian Conservation Corps] labor to install them, plus the necessary machinery and materials. The offer was widely accepted, but the practices were widely forgotten when the five-year contract period was up. The farmers continued only those practices that yielded an immediate and visible economic gain for themselves.

This led to the idea that maybe farmers would learn more quickly if they themselves wrote the rules. Accordingly the Wisconsin Legislature in 1937 passed the Soil Conservation District Law. This said to farmers, in effect: *We, the public, will furnish you free technical service and loan you specialized machinery, if you will write your own rules for land-use. Each county may write its own rules, and these will have the force of law.* Nearly all the counties promptly organized to accept the proffered help, but after a decade of operation, *no county has yet written a single rule.* There has been visible progress in such practices as strip-cropping, pasture renovation, and soil liming, but none in fencing woodlots against grazing, and none in excluding plow and cow from steep slopes. The farmers, in short, have selected those remedial practices which were profitable anyhow, and ignored those which were profitable to the community, but not clearly profitable to themselves.

When one asks why no rules have been written, one is told that the community is not yet ready to support them; education must precede rules. But the education actually in progress makes no mention of obligations to land over and above those dictated by self-interest. The net result is that we have more education but less soil, fewer healthy woods, and as many floods as in 1937.

The puzzling aspect of such situations is that the existence of obligations over and above self-interest is taken for granted in such rural community enterprises as the betterment of roads, schools, churches, and baseball teams. Their existence is not taken for granted, nor as yet seriously discussed, in bettering the behavior of the water that falls on the land, or in the preserving of the beauty of diversity of the farm landscape. Land-use ethics are still governed wholly by economic self-interest, just as social ethics were a century ago.

To sum up: we asked the farmer to do what he conveniently could to save his soil, and he has done just that, and only that. The farmer who clears the woods off a 75 per cent slope, turns his cows into the clearing, and dumps its rainfall, rocks, and soil into the community creek, is still (if otherwise decent) a respected member of society. If he puts lime on his fields and plants his crops on contour, he is still entitled to all the privileges and emoluments of his Soil Conservation District. The District is a beautiful piece of social machinery, but it is coughing along on two cylinders because we have been too timid, and too anxious for quick success, to tell the farmer the true magnitude of his obligations. Obligations have no meaning without conscience, and the problem we face is the extension of the social conscience from people to land.

No important change in ethics was ever accomplished without an internal change in our intellectual emphasis, loyalties, affections, and convictions. The proof that conservation has not yet touched these foundations of conduct lies in the fact that philosophy and religion have not yet heard of it. In our attempt to make conservation easy, we have made it trivial. . . .

There is a clear tendency in American conservation to relegate to government all necessary jobs that private landowners fail to perform. Government ownership, operation, subsidy, or regulation is now widely prevalent in forestry, range management, soil and watershed management, park and wilderness conservation, fisheries management, and migratory bird management, with more to come. Most of this growth in governmental conservation is proper and logical, some of it is inevitable. That I imply no disapproval of it is implicit in the fact that I have spent most of my life working for it. Nevertheless the question arises: What is the ultimate magnitude of the enterprise? Will the tax base carry its eventual ramifications? At what point will governmental conservation, like the mastodon, become handicapped by its own dimensions? The answer, if there is any, seems to be in a land ethic, or some other force which assigns more obligation to the private landowner.

Industrial landowners and users, especially lumbermen and stockmen, are inclined to wail long and loudly about the extension of government ownership and regulation to land, but (with notable exceptions) they show little disposition to develop the only visible alternative: the voluntary practice of conservation on their own lands.

When the private landowner is asked to perform some unprofitable act for the good of the community, he today assents only with outstretched palm. If the act costs him cash this is fair and proper, but when it costs only forethought, open-mindedness, or time, the issue is at least debatable. The overwhelming growth of land-use subsidies in recent years must be ascribed, in large part, to the government's own agencies for conservation education: the land bureaus, the agricultural colleges, and the extension services. As far as I can detect, no ethical obligation toward land is taught in these institutions.

To sum up: a system of conservation based solely on economic self-interest is hopelessly lopsided. It tends to ignore, and thus eventually to eliminate, many elements in the land community that lack commercial value, but that are (as far as we know) essential to its healthy functioning. It assumes, falsely, I think, that the economic parts of the biotic clock will function without the uneconomic parts. It tends to relegate to government many functions eventually too large, too complex, or too widely dispersed to be performed by government.

An ethical obligation on the part of the private owner is the only visible remedy for these situations. . . .

The Outlook

It is inconceivable to me that an ethical relation to land can exist without love, respect, and admiration for land, and a high regard for its value. By value, I of course mean something far broader than mere economic value; I mean value in the philosophical sense.

Perhaps the most serious obstacle impeding the evolution of a land ethic is the fact that our educational and economic system is headed away from, rather than toward, an intense consciousness of land. Your true modern is separated from the land by many middlemen, and by innumerable physical gadgets. He has no vital relation to it; to him it is the space between cities on which crops grow. Turn him loose for a day on the land, and if the spot does not happen to be a golf links or a "scenic" area, he is bored stiff. If crops could be raised by hydroponics instead of farming, it would suit him very well. Synthetic substitutes for wood, leather, wool, and other natural land products suit him better than the originals. In short, land is something he has "outgrown."

Almost equally serious as an obstacle to a land ethic is the attitude of the farmer for whom the land is still an adversary, or a taskmaster that keeps him in slavery. Theoretically, the mechanization of farming ought to cut the farmer's chains, but whether it really does is debatable.

One of the requisites for an ecological comprehension of land is an understanding of ecology, and this is by no means co-extensive with "education"; in fact, much higher education seems deliberately to avoid ecological concepts. An understanding of ecology does not necessarily originate in courses bearing ecological labels; it is quite as likely to be labeled geography, botany, agronomy, history, or economics. This is as it should be, but whatever the label, ecological training is scarce.

The case for a land ethic would appear hopeless but for the minority which is in obvious revolt against these "modern" trends.

The "key-log" which must be moved to release the evolutionary process for an ethic is simply this: quit thinking about decent land-use as solely an economic problem. Examine each question in terms of what is ethically and esthetically right, as well as what is economically expedient. A thing is right when it tends to preserve the integrity, stability, and beauty of the biotic community. It is wrong when it tends otherwise.

IV Power and Place
The Meeting of Social and Environmental History

> What we call Man's power over Nature turns out to be a power exercised by some men over other men with Nature as its instrument.
>
> —C. S. Lewis[1]

I had the good fortune to grow up in the Allegheny foothills of western Pennsylvania. My brothers and cousins and I lived near enough to Pittsburgh to see Roberto Clemente throw a baseball, yet far enough away to know our way around the woods. After my dad began unearthing arrowheads in the furrows of his garden, I remember imagining that Indians had once roamed the same primeval hollow where we built our shack. It turned out that the Shawnee were the last of various tribes to inhabit the Bull Creek Valley and its surrounding hills. They had called the valley Cowanwanik, "place of the bull buffalo."[2] The revelation that for centuries the great North American bison had wandered through the same fertile hollow where I spent my childhood was nothing short of astonishing. The bison, like the Shawnee, were drawn to the Allegheny-Kiskiminetas Valley for its biological bounty.

The Europeans followed—first to cultivate the land, then to profit from what lay beneath it. Here in this valley the world's first oil wells were drilled (by William A. "Uncle Billy" Smith, who would perform the same task more famously at Titusville in 1859), the first successful plate glass factory (Pittsburgh Plate Glass, or PPG) was established, the aluminum industry (Aluminum Company of America, or ALCOA) was born, and the industrial "workers' paradise" of Vandergrift was designed by the landscape architectural firm of Frederick Law Olmsted.[3] Like the Greater Pittsburgh area, the Alle-Kiski Valley embodies the grand epic of American industrial capitalism. Indeed, part of the valley lies on the "Path of Progress," one of the sanguine touris-

Designed by the landscape architectural firm of Frederick Law Olmsted, Vandergrift, Pennsylvania, featured winding streets with wide front lawns, plenty of trees, and modern infrastructure. Progressive industrialist George McMurtry intended to ameliorate the harsh effects of an industrial landscape, and the town was hailed by muckraking journalist Ida Tarbell as a "workers' paradise." (The town was strictly for McMurtry's skilled workforce; unskilled workers were excluded.) *Courtesy Allegheny-Kiski Valley Historical Society, Tarentum, Pennsylvania*

tic sobriquets affixed to southwestern Pennsylvania in the 1990s by promoters and preservationists.[4] Our partial, positivistic American memory has written here thus far a classic story of economic progress. The layered and interwoven history of social, cultural, and environmental change in this place has yet to be fully explored.

That story would begin, not with the ambition and brilliance of the industrial titans who capitalized nature here, but with the lifeways of the Shawnee. It would continue with the organic world view brought to the region by early German farmers and later the industrialists' immigrant laborers: their reliance on gardening and food preservation, the deeply ingrained refusal to waste anything, and the rhythm of the seasons by which they lived. A social-environmental history of the region would lead through ethnic neighborhoods well defined by class, race, contour of land, and proximity to the industrial sites that were established in the last third of the nineteenth century. It would reveal the dark side of industrialism: "boney piles" of coal waste, highly toxic orange and red "mountains," and tailings ponds that were used by children as playgrounds; higher rates of multiple sclerosis and cancers in particular neighborhoods; union organizers fighting and dying for decent living and working conditions; my own beloved hillside giving way to four lanes of pavement that both quickened the trip to Pittsburgh and fractured our community; the tunneling and damming of the Allegheny, the latter reducing communal recreational use of the river; and the abandonment of small-town main streets in favor of cul-de-sac suburbs and strip malls.

These local headlines help to introduce the idea that all human history bears environmental dimensions, although only recently have they come to be examined. Seeking to connect the story of people with that of their environments, this fresh trail of historical inquiry opened in the 1960s with a number of questions: How do human societies transform their own social, economic, and political relationships as they take from the earth what they need and desire? How have the cravings of various social and economic classes for power, wealth, or, more modestly, the "American way of life," produced profound change and often paths of environmental wreckage across the landscape? How do the environmental values and life ways of traditional cultures survive (or not) in the face of external economic and political pressures? And who decides when and where and which nature should be protected, and what do issues of race and class have to do with that determination? In short, environmental historians have centered increasingly on the essential "struggle over who would control the natural world and to what ends," as Theodore Steinberg put it in his study of the industrial incorporation of New England water.[5]

These are the matters raised in Part IV, at the intersection of environmental and social history. Coming from and incorporating various disciplines—history, anthropology, ecology, and political science—this work, not surprisingly, has gone in many directions. But the central upshot threading its way through it all has been the discovery of the enormous impact that the structures of social, economic, and political power have had upon the fate of nature in America.

———

Long before Rachel Carson there was Alice Hamilton, whose achievement as America's "first great urban/industrial environmentalist" has only recently been recognized by historians and environmentalists. In the brief excerpt included here (Selection 20), Robert Gottlieb recounts Hamilton's dogged perseverance in the face of extraordinary odds on the issue of industrial occupational hazards faced by millions of workers in the first decades of the twentieth century. During the years when John Muir was doing battle with Gifford Pinchot over the Hetch-Hetchy Valley, Progressive reformer Alice Hamilton concerned herself with phossy jaw and lead poisoning suffered by lower-class immigrant workers. In the 1920s and 1930s, while Stephen Mather and Horace Albright urged refinement and expansion of the national park system, and as Robert Marshall, Benton MacKaye, and Aldo Leopold carried on Muir's legacy by formally establishing the wilderness movement, Hamilton and her colleagues were investigating the causes of industrial disease in the cities.

It was hard to recognize then, but these distinct movements signified two contrasting environments—or two *natures*—worthy of protection. They foretold what by the 1960s would be a stark divide between mainstream environmentalism—focused on the picturesque, the sublime, and the distinctly natural places—and grassroots efforts that emanated from the industrial workplace and the communities where people lived in increasingly toxic environments. The former grew out of the romantic nature aesthetic that promised pristine nature as the antidotal refuge from the evils of modern industrial life. As Jennifer Price has argued, it situated nature "Out There."[6] The latter movement, led by middle-class women such as Alice Hamilton, Ellen Swallow Richards (Selection 18), and Chicago's "Garbage Lady" Mary McDowell and Hull House Settlement House founder Jane Addams, sought to remedy those evils.

The fight to protect spectacular and natural places gathered momentum in midcentury over the same issue where it had first surfaced: dam building in the West. Throughout the first half of the twentieth century, John Wesley Powell's call to a lower density, communally based development of the arid West had been systematically ignored. Established in 1902, the federal Bureau of Reclamation, along with the Army Corps of Engineers, worked closely with western political and business leaders in constructing scores of dams throughout the West to control flooding, provide irrigation for intensive agricultural operations, and generate electric power to the burgeoning cities of the Southwest. The Sierra Club, the nation's largest nature organization ("environmental" had yet to enter the lexicon), supported those projects. But when the Bureau of Reclamation in the 1940s proposed a series of dams on the Colorado River and its tributaries—two of which were to be inside the bounds of Dinosaur National Monument—the organization battled hard, as it had at Hetch-Hetchy, to defend what were National Park Service lands from incursion.[7]

The multifaceted campaign to stop the dams inside the Echo Park and Split Mountain areas of Dinosaur National Monument required acquainting Americans with a place heretofore unknown. Historian and novelist Bernard De Voto wrote an article with the inflamatory title, "Shall We Let Them Ruin Our National Parks?" which appeared in such staid and mainstream magazines as *Reader's Digest* and *Saturday Evening Post*. In the years after World War II, more Americans than ever vacationed west—"See the U.S.A. in Your Chevrolet," one advertising slogan urged. Tourists began arriving in droves in the desert southwest, seeing for themselves the canyons about to be flooded. When they returned home, many of them read De Voto's article and wrote letters to their congressmen; mail ran 80 to 1 in opposition to the project. The public opinion campaign, coupled with some theatrics on the part of David Brower, the head of the Sierra Club, had a dramatic effect on congressional debate. In his testimony before Congress, part of which is excerpted here (Selection 21), Brower took to showing a still-montage film entitled *Two Yosemites*, which illustrated vividly what had happened to Hetch-Hetchy Valley when it was flooded decades earlier. Then Brower and the Sierra Club collaborated with author Wallace Stegner to produce a lavishly illustrated coffee-table book, *This Is Dinosaur*. These efforts combined to escalate opposition to the project; and in the spring of 1956, Congress passed the bill authorizing construction of the Colorado River Storage Project without the Dinosaur dams. Wilderness preservationists had achieved the first significant victory of the modern environmental era.[8]

The hydro struggle would continue through the 1960s. As a tradeoff to save Dinosaur, the Sierra Club had supported another proposed dam farther down the Colorado at Glen Canyon, a place that very few Americans had ever seen. Brower soon painfully regretted that decision and tried in vain to have the Sierra Club recant its support. The organization did oppose, with even more colorful tenacity than the Dinosaur campaign, a dam that would have flooded part of Grand Canyon National Park. The Grand Canyon! the Club repeated incredulously in its ultimately successful campaign to stop the project. "SHOULD WE ALSO FLOOD THE SISTINE CHAPEL SO THAT TOURISTS MAY GET NEARER THE CEILING?" the Sierra Club asked rhetorically in a full-page incendiary ad in the *New York Times*.[9]

In the 1960s the efforts of the Sierra Club were instrumental in stopping the further damming of the Colorado River, which would have partially flooded the Grand Canyon. Photograph by Chris Magoc.

The environmental victories at Dinosaur and Grand Canyon were not unblemished: the tradeoff of Glen Canyon Dam created Lake Powell, which had long-term negative effects on the health of the Colorado River and the ecosystems through which it flows. Moreover, dam building and land "reclamation" (the assumption being that arid "empty" lands were automatically in need of "reclaiming") continued apace throughout the West, usually under a lower profile without the opposition of mainstream environmental organizations. And it should not surprise us that Native and Hispanic Americans of the Southwest, who had learned centuries before to live with the scarcity of water in the region, were systematically locked out of the debate over water policy.

"Iron triangle politics" shaped the course of economic development in the region, which was inextricably tied to dam building. The iron triangle of western water served well the tripartite interests of a business elite, politicians, and government agencies. The interests of Indian tribes were well represented neither in Congress nor in the courts.[10]

Similarly, the Hispanic population, reduced to a disenfranchised and impoverished underclass in the nineteenth and early twentieth centuries, were largely shut out of the process that determined the course of water development. An inspired fight in the 1970s against a condominium project near Taos, New Mexico, came to symbolize the broader struggle of Hispanic people against outside Anglo developers throughout the Southwest.[11] Indeed, Donald Worster has chronicled the tale of western water as emblematic of the larger story of power in the West and of American society. Much about what C. Wright Mills in 1956 called *The Power Elite* as well as Americans' "managerial relationship" to the environment can be discovered in the story of "the hydraulic society" of the West, says Worster.[12]

Who in the society has the capacity to exercise power to restore or protect a particular place? And on whose behalf? Those are the central questions raised by the stories of Alice Hamilton and western water. Middle-class reformers such as Hamilton spoke for the ethnic, urban underclass. In part because labor unions were still fighting for the most basic rights of collective bargaining and industrial democracy, no large organization emerged that might have drawn attention to the health and safety issues of workers' lives, nor to the increasingly deteriorating condition of urban-suburban America. Until the 1970s, no major environmental organization spoke for *that* nature. The debate over western water development was shaped by white, middle-class environmentalists who, while increasingly effective, represented eastern-dwelling outdoor enthusiasts and vacationers. In the heady years of the postwar boom, mainstream environmentalism would continue to show little or no interest in the underclasses of people who lived in either the nation's dwindling rural spaces or in an increasingly befouled urban America.[13]

Alan Taylor has summarized the three shared, "mutually reinforcing" characteristics of social-environmental history: "a preoccupation with the common and the previously inconspicuous, the empirical examination of new sources, and an engaged political sympathy for the less powerful and most exploited."[14] Those traits are nicely exhibited in Harry M. Caudill's 1962 polemic, *Night Comes to the Cumberlands* (Selection 22). In the foreword, Stewart L. Udall calls the book "a tragic tale of the abuse and mismanagement of a resource heritage, and the human erosion that is always the concomitant of shortsighted exploitation."[15] Ever since George Perkins Marsh, it had become axiomatic that thoughtless exploitation of land led incidentally to human suffering. To Udall, the book is "a story of land failure and the failure of men"[16]—*failure* suggesting that what happened in this region was an accident of some kind, that no one meant to do any harm in the Appalachians. This view now seems hopelessly naive. Consider that the stock reports and balance sheets of the mining, steel, and timber corporations who executed what Caudill calls the "rape of the Appalachians" would certainly show anything but failure for their decades of work in the region. Udall held great expectations for Caudill's book, hoping that its political impact would compare to great works of American fiction such as Sinclair's *The Jungle*, John Steinbeck's *The Grapes of Wrath*, and James Agee's *Let Us Now Praise Famous Men*. To be sure, these works of fiction contained great truths that struck the raw nerve of America. Likewise, Caudill's book is a harsh indictment of the notion, increasingly under siege in the early 1960s, that all was right with American civilization.

Nor were conditions then "on the Cumberland Plateau an anachronism, a remnant of an ugly chapter of [American] history," as Udall offers. The mining and other laws that defined corporations as persons and gave them carte blanche to exploit the environment and trample the rights of individual Americans certainly derived, as Caudill says, from "a laissez-faire century." But the conditions that often resulted from laissez-faire economics were very much of the twentieth. As Caudill published *Night Comes to the Cumberlands* in 1962, social activist Michael Harrington put forth *The Other America: Poverty in the United States*. Harrington's damning, classic portrait of exploitive poverty throughout the United States (very much including the Appalachians) helped launch President Lyndon B. Johnson's War on Poverty.[17]

As President John F. Kennedy's secretary of the interior, Stewart Udall may have thought it prudent to temper his praise for Caudill's polemic. His was writing to be careful of. Caudill makes no pretense about "objective" history (if indeed there is such a thing). Fierce and passionately eloquent, *Night Comes to the Cumberlands* represented the first of a string of works in which Caudill revealed to Americans the physical and social devastation occurring in the Appalachian region.[18] In his introduction, the author describes the "curse of coal" that came to define the modern history of the Cumberland hills. It also served as the unifying theme of his book: "When men begin to wrest it from the earth it leaves a legacy of foul streams, hideous slag heaps and polluted air. It peoples this transformed land with blind and crippled men and with widows and orphans. It is an extractive industry which takes all away and restores nothing."[19]

Caudill bore the credentials to write such things. With family roots in the Cumberland mountains extending to 1792—as deep into history as white men go in the region—coupled with years of practicing law "in mountain courthouses" and a six-year tenure in the Kentucky House of Representatives, he knew well the place of which he wrote. "What I have written is drawn from experience—from seeing, hearing and working with mountaineers," he says plainly at the outset. It is "a land with few books and pens [where] many tales are transmitted from father and mother to son and daughter."

In establishing his deep attachment to the region, Caudill not only gives "evidence that [his] narrative is not founded on hasty first impressions," but he also suggests the rationale for writing the book. If change was to come in the Appalachians, it would ultimately come from the pressure of federal government intervention. But as the civil rights movement was then proving, the initial force for change would have to emerge from within the region. Environmental and social justice in these mountains, he suggests, would do more than improve basic living conditions. In this Kennedyesque appeal, Caudill argues that there was something in this for the nation collectively: a salving of the American conscience perhaps, but something more pragmatic. The plight of "the mountaineer," Caudill argued, bespeaks a condition of "idleness and waste [that is] antipathetic to progress and growth." The southern Appalachian region should not, he implored, "remain an anchor dragging behind the rest of America."[20] Progress here meant progress for the whole country. Caudill's book was written very much in the spirit of the early 1960s, when anything seemed possible. Just as Dr. Martin Luther King, Jr., stirred the nation with his Dream that summer of 1963, in the same way Harry Caudill's jeremiad hoped for the day when the words of "America the Beautiful" would ring true once again on the Cumberland Plateau. That song seemed to Caudill a cruel irony on the day when the singing of it in an eighth-grade class inspired him to write *Night Comes to the Cumberlands*.

The excerpt included here comes from deep in Caudill's book, following a full chronicle of the Cumberland Plateau people: how they got there and made from a raw wilderness a subsistence home for themselves, how they survived national crises of wars and depression, how they struggled to organize their own unions, and how they (most regrettably, he says) came to depend on a steady diet of government- and union-sponsored "Welfarism" in the 1930s and 1940s. The land and its condition lies at the center of the narrative throughout. Caudill writes that the mountain people generally cut trees for subsistence and enough lumber or firewood to sell on the market to ease their perennially cash-strapped plight. In the 1870s newly established corporations began buying and speculating wildly in eastern Kentucky timber. Mountaineers had neither a full understanding of the outside market value of their resources nor the desire for the material luxuries that the money being dangled in front of them could buy.

In the first decades of the twentieth century, countless protracted legal disputes ensued over land titles. Mountain people with few friends in high places stood little chance on such questions.[21] Kentucky's highest court and politicians at all levels were complicitous in the horrific transmogrification of the land that resulted from the "quick and easy enrichment" of the coal companies. Sold to corporations for a dollar an acre, "mining rights," which for mountain people had meant the privilege of taking pick and shovel to the side of a hill, now entailed denuding the surface of the land by strip mining and augering the coal from below. Caudill describes the excruciating pain of having witnessed community after community literally stripped of their traditional means of survival.

The shocking conditions revealed by Harry Caudill helped to incite the War on Poverty and brought about modest change in the Appalachians. Moreover, readers were put on notice that these sorts of social-environmental disasters were very much a part of contemporary America. Indeed, that sobering reminder continues to be one measure of the book's significance. Finally and more profoundly, *Night Comes to the Cumberlands* was one of the first narratives to argue that, as Udall put it, "conservation of the land is the conservation of human life."[22] That lesson would be painfully learned time and again in places far from the Cumberland Plateau.

———

The timeline of U.S. environmental experience is marked with pivotal events that serve to crystallize and make popular ideas long in germination; the 1864 publication of Marsh's *Man and Nature* comes to mind. Some episodes represent the spirit of their time: the Hetch-Hetchy Dam punctuated the victory of utilitarian thinking in conservation policy at the turn of the century. Other moments come like a flash in the night. From out of nowhere they rivet the nation's attention and lead to an awakened national consciousness, and often to policy changes. The disturbing and related tales of Love Canal, New York, and Warren County, North Carolina, would lead such a list.

Before the years 1978–1980, Americans only knew of the quiet suburban community of Love Canal if they passed through or around it on their way to nearby Niagara Falls. Nor were they very familiar with such phrases as "hazardous waste," "toxic dump site," or "not in my backyard!" That changed dramatically in these years, particularly as events climaxed in the summer of 1980 with the evacuation of hundreds of families from Love Canal after years of protest from residents who discovered that they had been living on top of a former chemical dump site. The national news media converged on Love Canal to record the relocation of hundreds of residents from the community. What was once a typical American suburb—green, lovely, and safe—had been transformed into a national symbol of growing environmental anxiety.[23] Its benign name now hung upon it with cruel irony.

How this came to pass we learn through the firsthand account of Lois Gibbs (Selection 23), one of the central figures of the Love Canal story. Like Harry Caudill, Lois Gibbs speaks with a candidly biased and passionate voice. This personal chronicle of Love Canal comes from a woman whose reasonable expectation of a safe and healthy community for her children has been betrayed. It is inspired by the outrage of her long encounter with face-saving, double-talking government officials and by the exhilarating self-discovery she found by making history.

Like a good Frank Capra film, the story begins innocently enough—a twenty-seven-year-old white, middle-class housewife and mother of two children lives with her family in a nice three-bedroom house in a quiet residential neighborhood. The Gibbs family and their neighbors lived the American Dream—except that it turned out to have been situated atop the toxic residue of modern America. Underneath this suburban paradise, William T. Love in 1892 had begun to dig a seven-mile-long canal that he later abandoned when its financial backing failed. Its purpose was to connect the upper and lower Niagara River in a power-generating project. From 1920 until 1953 the Love Canal served as a dumping trench for hundreds of tons of municipal garbage and forty-three million pounds of chemical waste generated by the Hooker Chemical Company. That waste included highly toxic benzene and dioxin. The New York State Health Commissioner would later call dioxin "the most toxic substance ever synthesized by man." It is the same stuff that made Agent Orange a deadly defoliant of South Vietnam's forests, incidentally poisoning Vietnamese peasants and American soldiers. More than two hundred tons of Trichlorophenol containing dioxin were buried in Love Canal.[24]

The nearby Hooker Chemical Corporation deposited most of the chemical waste, with the U.S. Army then contributing chemical byproducts of their own. After filling in the canal and covering it with dirt, Hooker sold the site at public auction in 1953 for one dollar to the Niagara Falls Board of Education. The deed of sale contained a clause holding Hooker blameless for any physical harm or death due to the buried wastes. A half-century later, that red flag would never get by the guarded sensibilities of a school solicitor. In the 1950s, however, Americans were bullish on progress and confident in the reassurance of experts; home construction began immediately. By 1955 an elementary school with a large playground had been built.[25]

By the time Lois Gibbs's children started attending the 99th Street School in the mid-1970s, residents had already been complaining of odors and health problems for nearly two decades. The complaints grew louder and more frequent until June 1978, when they finally reached the local newspaper. Gibbs read a series of articles that summer and began to connect the information in that exposé to her son's multiplying health problems—asthma, headaches, and nausea. She also had been hearing horror stories from her neighbors about miscarriages, stillbirths, and birth defects. In the next two years, Gibbs made herself into a tenacious organizer, lobbyist, spokesperson, and negotiator as well as an amateur expert in law, politics, engineering, epidemiology, and toxicology. Her leadership of the Love Canal Homeowners' Association took her to Albany, the White House, and national television.

Gibbs's story culminated in 1980 when President Jimmy Carter signed a bill ordering the evacuation of the last of the nine hundred Love Canal families from their homes. Her involvement with the issue of toxic hazardous waste had only begun. Gibbs went on to found the National Citizens' Clearinghouse for Hazardous Waste, which continues to provide support to hundreds of communities across the country confronted with similar hazardous waste threats. (It is now the Center for Health, Environment, and Justice.)[26]

The nightmare of Love Canal carried national impact. Followed immediately by a series of similar disasters from Warren County, North Carolina, to Elizabeth, New Jersey, Love Canal spurred Congress to complete action on a bill authorizing the cleanup of hazardous waste sites across the country. Administered by the U.S. Environmental Protection Agency, the Emergency Response, Compensation, and Liability Act of 1980—otherwise known as Superfund—bears the burden of remedial action at hundreds of priority hazardous waste sites around the nation.[27] The cost is borne in part by American taxpayers—as it should be, perhaps, for as beneficiaries of the old Du Pont slogan, "Better Living through Chemistry," Americans should help shoulder the poisonous, buried burden of its manufacture.

The kind of trust in authorities with which the residents of Love Canal begin this story now seems like a quaint reminder of another age. These ordinary middle-class Americans, Lois Gibbs tells us, did not seek this struggle and were anything but politically rebellious, yet they suddenly found themselves literally fighting for their lives. They challenged a power structure that was faced with a problem of monstrously unprecedented proportions. We hear in Gibbs's voice the angry indignation that fueled the struggle of Love Canal residents. By August 1979 they had had more than a year of fruitless meetings, broken promises, and denials of responsibility. In Gibbs's story, even as remedial construction on the site that summer exacerbates the health problems of residents and forces them into a motel, the governmental stonewalling continues. From Gibbs's vantage point, this is a good-versus-evil struggle: citizens holding dead branches and sick children confront cold-hearted bureaucrats who coolly minimize the risks of deathly poisons in their backyards. The technocratic language of "parts per billion" meets the sharp tongue of an outraged, ordinary American.

Along with the near disaster at the Three Mile Island nuclear power plant near Harrisburg in March 1979, Love Canal helped to shatter the myth born in the 1940s and 1950s that scientific and government experts were to be trusted at all times and at all costs on matters of science, technology, and environmental health. The breakdown of faith in experts extended more broadly, of course—the endless disaster in Vietnam, the Watergate break-in, CIA revelations, continuing suspicions about the Kennedy assassination, the oil crisis. Trust in public officials generally was plummeting by the time of Love Canal. It is amazing, ironic, and inspiring, then, that Lois Gibbs could emerge from this struggle with duplicitous bureaucrats not only not cynical but stronger than ever in her commitment to democracy.

———

Beyond Love Canal, scores of less infamous but well-poisoned landscapes would change the face of American environmentalism, which had always been largely white and middle and upper-middle class. As we have seen, the genesis of environmentalism lies in the cultural currency that nineteenth-century elites invested in nature's most visually striking locales. But on more than a few occasions, delineating new administrative boundaries in nature for the recreational pleasure of the genteel meant the cessation of rights of local and indigenous peoples. Throughout the West, for example, Native American tribes were displaced in order to establish national parks and forests. Progressive reformers spoke disparagingly of the wasteful and filthy hunting and living habits of immigrants and roughneck westerners who had to be eliminated in order to restore or protect species and environments. Privileged in background as they were, and faced with the resource-depleting juggernaut of industrial modernity, early conservationists and preservationists had neither the resources nor any genuine interest in objecting to the insidious and worsening health effects of industrialization on workers, the urban and rural poor, and their communities. Horrific testimony to that was the Gauley Bridge disaster of 1931 in West Virginia, which killed nearly five hundred miners of silicosis, the vast majority of them African-American.[28] Few noticed, certainly not conservationists of the era.

It would take the compounding and cascading effects of the postwar boom economy on workers' health and safety, coupled with the activist spirit of the 1960s, to render human exposure to toxic contaminants as an "environmental" issue. Environmental issues intertwined with, indeed, became matters of labor rights and social justice. In the 1960s, Cesar Chavez organized migrant farm workers in California whose health was afflicted by having to work with and live within an environment permeated by the same pesticides that Rachel Carson had written about. Coal miners in West Virginia suffered from black lung, uranium miners in the Rocky Mountain Southwest from high rates of certain cancers. This was not *nature*. Yet, increasingly, issues centered on public health and occupational safety became harder for mainstream environmentalism to ignore. In 1973 the Oil, Chemical, and Atomic Workers waged the first strike ever on occupational health issues with nominal but unprecedented support from environmental groups. Grassroots community organizations (such as the one that received national attention at Love Canal) increasingly spoke of an American right to live and work in a safe and healthy community. As Robert Gottlieb has shown, the direct challenge to regional and state power structures by local groups also prodded national mainstream organizations to implicitly adopt a broader definition of nature and, accordingly, to deploy resources to environments now deemed worthy of protection.[29]

One important manifestation of the new attention given to the human environment was what became known as the environmental justice movement. Eileen Maura McGurty's essay (Selection 24) recalls one of the important episodes in the birth of that phenomenon. She tells the story of an incident in hazardous waste contamination and landfill siting that climaxed around the same time as Love Canal. What happened in Warren County, North Carolina, from 1978 to 1982, McGurty says, not only helped to ensure passage of the national Superfund Act but was also the pivotal event that linked the cause of environmentalism to that of racial and social justice. She provides the historical context of these crusades, revealing how the civil rights and poor people's movements of the 1960s were indifferent at best to the heady excitement that climaxed with the first Earth Day in 1970. The environmental movement, as defined by the Sierra Club and other mainline organizations, held little or no relevance for African Americans. Indeed, most Black Power activists of the time (and many anti-Vietnam War activists) viewed the increasing focus on ecology as a distraction or worse for African Americans, a deliberate effort to sabotage economic development efforts in distressed urban communities. "Ecology" seemed to elevate the problems of the nonhuman world over African Americans' still-unresolved issues.[30] For their part, the environmental community saw the inequities of America and the horror of war in Southeast Asia as a world apart from concerns over endangered species and polluted beaches.[31] And with President Johnson's Great Society already withering, it became clearer to all constituencies that environmental and social problems would be dividing a shrinking share of federal dollars.

The events of Warren County a decade later helped to bring about a difficult but potentially powerful synergy between the two causes. As McGurty outlines, the locating of a chemical waste landfill in a rural and largely poor African-American region of North Carolina in

1982 made environmental history not because citizens won the day. They did not. Warren County became a milestone when what would now be a frighteningly ordinary "not in my backyard" landfill-siting incident was charged with the racial politics of the South. With dynamic leadership from experienced veterans of the civil rights movement—recently reinvigorated by the extension of the Voting Rights Act and a voter registration campaign—the traditional bureaucratic protests against the project suddenly took on the tenor of a civil rights crusade. Local white opponents of the landfill followed the lead of black activists, participating in colorful and militant, even dangerous activities in a futile attempt to stop the transferal of waste to their region.

The far-reaching legacy that emerged from Warren County was, on the one hand, a wake-up call to national environmental organizations of the moral imperative of taking on the issue of local environmental quality in working-class and poor neighborhoods.[32] On the other hand, as McGurty suggests, the Warren County episode offered sobering confirmation for leaders of both civil rights and environmental organizations of the "inextricable links," as Tom Bradley once put it, between socioeconomic and environmental conditions. History takes a long time: as McGurty points out, the chasm between these movements did not end in Warren County. But a whole new vehicle for social change was born in that fall of 1982. The environmental justice movement, with multiracial leadership and two decades of subsequent organizing battles, has continued to evolve and mature.[33] This union preceded by a few years the budding reconciliation of environmentalists with the religious community that began in the 1990s.

Social-environmental historians have come to wrestle over one of the central questions raised by the eco-justice movement: Is it race or class that is the stronger determinant of poor environmental quality in the United States?[34] Is it because people are of color or of less economic and political means that their lands, communities, and resources are poisoned, exploited, or expropriated by others? The question has drawn increasing interest from scholars, although no clear consensus has emerged. One must not discount race in any form of injustice in America, and the evidence that people of color suffer far more than their share of environmental degradation is overwhelming.[35] But those people of color who are victimized by toxic environments also generally happen to be poor. And poor people as a class—black, white, brown, yellow, and red— suffer environmental wrongs more frequently and more severely than those of greater means (who happen to be overwhelmingly white). Unlike the garden variety of racism, environmental racism is rarely, if ever, articulated. Few corporate executives or government officials of white-hooded mind are careless enough to record their views on such matters.

Case histories are less than unequivocal. Environmental historian Andrew Hurley has revealed that in one instance in the city of St. Louis, forces other than race worked to bring environmental hazards to the minority community of Wellston.[36] Hurley found that deindustrialization, shifting demographics, and the changing real estate market were the key factors in leaving a chemically poisoned former industrial site. Although race must certainly have been a factor within the force of migration in and out of the community, practically speaking, injustice comes after the fact of toxic contamination in the terribly deliberate pace of cleanup of a now-minority community. Likewise, Theodore Steinberg suggests in an article on the touristic development of south Florida that it was those with the means—financial and political—who literally shaped the environment and drove the environmental decision making of that region. The creation of a beachfront resort in a hurricane-prone locale disproportionately benefited an elite few, indirectly destroyed the lives of thousands of poor people (both black and white), and eventually was subsidized by millions of middle-class Americans.[37] Environmental historian Karl Jacoby has written about the fierce class warfare that broke out in the Adirondack Mountains over resource use at the turn of the twentieth century. When the state of New York established the Adirondack Forest Reserve in 1883, Jacoby writes, it did so with an alliance of genteel sportsmen concerned about the supply of big game, and industrialists worried about keeping the wheels of industry downstate well supplied with upstate water. Neither party was concerned about the rural white subsistence farmers and trappers who had for generations been responsible stewards of the land.[38] The mountain people reacted with anger to what they perceived to be an onerous infringement of their traditional rights to live from the land. Prior to state control, local custom and taboo had kept resource use in check throughout the Adirondacks. Clearly there are fault lines of both race and class.

More transparent are the planetary dimensions to this historic pattern of environmental injustice. In the 1980s indigenous peoples of the world's tropical rainforests began contending not only with loggers and cattle growers whose headquarters and profits are centered in the industrialized world, but also with Western environmentalists who, at least initially, were insensitive to preserving ancient human uses of the rainforest. Well intentioned though they may be, rainforest conservationists may have been guilty of a kind of imperialism of their own. The new twist on the old-fashioned imperialism is illustrated in a 1989 newspaper cartoon in which a gas-hogging, global-warming, fat-ended American car rolls up to an Amazonian rainforest where an indigenous man stands ready to take down a tree. From the car shouts a rich Yankee in a loud shirt and shades, "Yo! Amigo! We need that tree to protect us from the greenhouse effect!"[39] Nations of the primarily southern, less-developed half of the world seek equity in environmental matters that since about 1990 have been viewed increasingly by world leaders as global in nature: reducing the greenhouse effect (and thus carbon dioxide emissions), caring for the oceans, not siting toxic waste across borders, preserving and conserving forests, maintaining biologically diverse ecosystems, controlling population growth . . . the list goes dreadfully on. So, no doubt, will the verbal struggle between the haves and have-nots over environmental equity. Coincidentally or not, the latter are largely people of color. Americans, cursed by the Myth of Endless Abundance, find themselves in a hard bargaining position; it is tough to preach frugality and efficiency when one holds 6 percent of the world's population while consuming 35 percent of its resources and generating nearly half of its garbage.

The contemporary global picture is linked to the large and growing body of social-environmental history. All of these tales begin, in some sense, with the premise that environmental degradation does not just happen. It is not inevitable, and it is not equally distributed. The consumerist, capitalist economy that took hold of the planet in the second half of the twentieth century spreads neither its tidings nor its deadly by-products equitably. A disproportionate few have reaped a disproportionate profit and heaped a disproportionate share of the environmental burden upon those at the bottom. Meanwhile, as America Dot Com leaches its way around the globe, discovering the social and environmental consequences of that surreal phenomenon is one of the challenges for the next generation of historians.

NOTES

1. C. S. Lewis, *The Abolition of Man* (New York, 1947), quoted by numerous social and environmental historians, as Alan Taylor points out in "Unnatural Inequalities: Social and Environmental Histories," *Environmental History* 1, no. 4 (October 1996): 16. Taylor cites several appearances of the Lewis quote, including in Donald Worster, *Rivers of Empire:*

Water, Aridity, and the Growth of the American West (New York: Pantheon, 1985), 50.

2. Chris J. Magoc, writer and producer, *Tarentum: A History in the Making* (Tarentum: Allegheny-Kiski Valley Historical Society and Video Marketplace Productions, 1996), 92-minute video cassette.

3. In 1859, Smith went fifty miles north to Titusville to make Colonel Edwin Drake famous, though not wealthy, in the new oil industry. My own knowledge of this comes from exhibit texts at the Allegheny-Kiski Valley Heritage Museum, Tarentum, Pennsylvania, and Drake Well Museum, Titusville, Pennsylvania. The most comprehensive attempt to date to pull the industrial history of the Alle-Kiski Valley together was in a special two-part edition of the *Valley News Dispatch* (Tarentum, PA: Gannett, February 1996).

4. "Path of Progress" is the name used by the Southwestern Pennsylvania Heritage Preservation Commission, referring to the region from Vandergrift and New Kensington east to Johnstown and Altoona. It is a federally designated Heritage Area, as is "Rivers of Steel," overlapping part of the Path of Progress but centered in Pittsburgh.

5. Theodore Steinberg, *Nature Incorporated: Industrialization and the Waters of New England* (New York: Cambridge University Press, 1991), 102.

6. Jennifer Price, *Flight Maps: Adventures with Nature in Modern America* (New York: Basic Books, 1999). This is a central theme throughout Price's work.

7. Worster, *Rivers of Empire*, 206–11, 275.

8. Russell Martin, *A Story That Stands Like a Dam: Glen Canyon and the Struggle for the Soul of the West* (New York: Holt and Company, 1989), 53–66.

9. Ibid., 64–66, 254–57, and 271–75; Michael Cohen, *The History of the Sierra Club*, 160–80, 255–64, and 291–99.

10. Daniel McCool, *Command of the Waters: Iron Triangles, Federal Water Development, and Indian Water* (Berkeley: University of California Press, 1987).

11. Sylvia Rodriguez, "Land, Water, and Ethnic Identity in Taos," in Charles L. Briggs and John R. Van Ness, eds., *Land, Water, and Culture: New Perspectives on Hispanic Land Grants*, New Mexico Land Grant Series (Albuquerque: University of New Mexico Press, 1987).

12. Worster, *Rivers of Empire*, 7.

13. The best work on this subject is undoubtedly Robert Gottlieb, *Forcing the Spring: The Transformation of the American Environmental Movement* (Washington, DC: Island Press, 1993).

14. Taylor, "Unnatural Inequalities," 8.

15. Harry M. Caudill, *Night Comes to the Cumberlands: A Biography of a Depressed Area*, with Foreword by Stewart L. Udall (Boston: Little, Brown and Company, 1962). Quote is Udall's, vii.

16. Udall in Caudill, *Night Comes*, vii.

17. Michael Harrington, *The Other America: Poverty in the United States* (New York: Penguin Books, 1981, reprint from 1962). On the impact of Harrington's book, see, for example, Todd Gitlin, *The Sixties: Years of Hope, Days of Rage* (New York: Bantam, 1987), 131.

18. See also Harry M. Caudill, *The Watches of the Night* (Boston: Little, Brown and Company, 1976); *My Land Is Dying* (New York: E. P. Dutton

and Company, 1971); and "Are Capitalism and the Conservation of a Decent Environment Compatible?" in Harold W. Helfrich, Jr., *Agenda for Survival* (New Haven: Yale University Press, 1971).

19. Caudill, *Night Comes*, x.
20. Ibid., xii–xiii.
21. Ibid., 61–69.
22. Udall in Caudill, *Night Comes*, vii.
23. For an excellent discussion of the media coverage and resulting national impact of the Love Canal disaster, see Andrew Szasz, *Ecopopulism: Toxic Waste and the Movement for Environmental Justice* (Minneapolis: University of Minnesota Press, 1994).
24. Lois Marie Gibbs, *Love Canal: My Story*, with Murray Levine (Albany: State University of New York Press, 1982), 3.
25. Ibid., 3–9.
26. Lois Gibbs, "Love Canal Survivor Can't Escape Dioxin Pollution," letter to *USA Today*, July 27, 1998. Gibbs is also the author of *Dying from Dioxin: A Citizen's Guide to Reclaiming Our Health and Rebuilding Democracy* (1995), and a revised edition of the Love Canal story, *Love Canal: The Story Continues* (1998).
27. Samuel P. Hays, *Beauty, Health and Permanence: Environmental Politics in the United States, 1955–1985* (New York: Cambridge University Press, 1987), 200–206.
28. Gottlieb, *Forcing the Spring*, 236–40, 275.
29. Ibid., chapters 5–8.
30. A more recent and particularly strident perspective is Edmund A. Peterson, "It's Only Another Name for Genocide," *Pittsburgh Post-Gazette*, May 5, 1993.
31. For one expression of this view, see Richard Neuhaus, *In Defense of People: Ecology and the Seduction of Radicalism* (New York: Macmillan, 1971).
32. For a recent survey of the eco-justice movement, including grassroots efforts to inspire national organizations to take action on behalf of poor and minority communities, see James Schwab et al., *Deeper Shades of Green: The Rise of Blue Collar and Minority Environmentalism in America* (San Francisco: Sierra Club Books, 1994).
33. Other good histories of the evolution of eco-justice include James Noel Smith, ed., *Environmental Quality and Social Justice in Urban America* (Washington, DC: The Conservation Foundation, 1974); Robert D. Bullard, ed., *Confronting Environmental Racism: Voices from the Grassroots* (Boston: South End Press, 1993), and Bullard's *Unequal Protection: Environmental Justice and Communities of Color* (San Francisco: Sierra Club Books, 1994); and Robert Gottlieb, *Forcing the Spring*. Also relevant is U.S. Environmental Protection Agency, *Environmental Equity: Reducing Risks for All Communities*, vol. 1, EPA 230-R-92-008 (Washington, DC: Government Printing Office, 1992). Although not specifically focused on issues of race and class, the following are wide-ranging surveys of citizens' attempts to win environmental justice through the legal and political system: Thomas More Hoban and Richard Oliver Brooks, *Green Justice: The Environment and the Courts* (Boulder, CO: Westview Press, 1987); and Lynton K. Caldwell, Lynton R. Hayes, and Isabel M. MacWhirter, *Citizens and the Environment: Case Studies in Popular Action* (Bloomington: Indiana University Press, 1976). See also Nonny

De LaPena and Susan Davis, "The Greens are White (And Minorities Want In)," *Newsweek* (October 15, 1990): 34.

34. Representative of this body of work is Andrew Hurley, *Environmental Inequalities: Class, Race, and Industrial Pollution in Gary, Indiana, 1945–1980* (Chapel Hill: University of North Carolina Press, 1995).

35. See, for example, Jane Key, "Fighting Toxic Racism," *San Francisco Examiner*, April 7, 1991.

36. Andrew Hurley, "Fiasco at Wagner Electric: Environmental Justice and Urban Geography in St. Louis," *Environmental History* 2, no. 4 (October 1997): 460–81.

37. Theodore Steinberg, "Do-It-Yourself Deathscape: The Unnatural History of Natural Disaster in South Florida," *Environmental History* 2, no. 4 (October 1997): 414–38.

38. Karl Jacoby, "Class and Environmental History: Lessons from the War in the Adirondacks," *Environmental History* 2, no. 3 (July 1997): 324–42.

39. Cartoon by Scott Willis of the *San Jose Mercury News*, reprinted in Jonathan Piel et al., *Managing Planet Earth: Readings from Scientific American* (New York: W. H. Freeman, 1990), 129. The book elsewhere touches on these issues of north-versus-south development and environmental cleanup, 61–72, 92.

ROBERT GOTTLIEB

20 Alice Hamilton Explores the Dangerous Trades

A tenacious reformer, a compassionate advocate, a cautious and careful researcher, Alice Hamilton was this country's first great urban/industrial environmentalist. Born in 1869 in New York City and raised in Fort Wayne, Indiana, Hamilton decided to study medicine, one of the few disciplines available to this first generation of women able to enter the universities and embark on a professional career. "I chose medicine," Hamilton would later say in her autobiography, *Exploring the Dangerous Trades*, ". . . because as a doctor I could go anywhere I pleased—to far-off lands or to city slums— and be quite sure that I could be of use anywhere."[1]

Even prior to entering medical school at the University of Michigan, Hamilton thought of combining her interest in medicine and science with humanitarian service and social reform. She found the ideal outlet when she moved into the Hull House settlement in Chicago while accepting a position as professor of pathology at the Woman's Medical School of Northwestern University. During the 1890s and through the first decade of the new century, Hull House became an extraordinary meeting ground for reformers, humanitarians, and urban activists of all kinds. For Hamilton, as her biographer Barbara Sicherman noted, Hull House "was an ideal place from which to observe the connections between environment and disease." She began a whirlwind of activity, organizing a well-baby clinic, looking into the

From Robert Gottlieb, *Forcing the Spring: The Transformation of the American Environmental Movement* (Washington, DC: Island Press, 1993), 47–51. © 1993 by Robert Gottlieb. Reprinted by permission of Island Press.

cocaine traffic endemic in the neighborhood and the city, taking part in efforts to improve the quality of health care for the poor, and investigating a serious typhoid epidemic. The typhoid epidemic was particularly instructive, since Hamilton's investigation eventually helped reveal that a sewage outflow (an episode covered up by the Board of Health) bore a direct relationship to the outbreak of the disease in certain neighborhood wards. It became Hamilton's first experience with how the issues of health, the environment, and politics intersected.[2]

Hull House also became a staging ground for Hamilton's growing interest in the little understood and poorly treated area of industrial disease. At the settlement house, Hamilton heard countless stories about "industrial poisoning": carbon monoxide in the steel mills, pneumonia and rheumatism in the stockyards, "phossy jaw" from white phosphorus used in match factories. Though industrial medicine had become an accepted discipline in Europe, its detractors in the United States suggested, as Hamilton wryly noted, that "here was a subject tainted with Socialism or with feminine sentimentality for the poor."[3] Through her exploration of industrial poisons, Hamilton was able to combine her passion for reform and her desire to pursue a real world-based science.

During the first decade of the new century, there had been few investigations of occupational health and even fewer reforms of industrial practices in the United States, though occupational hazards were present in a wide range of industries. In 1908, Hamilton's interest in the subject was stimulated by an encounter at Hull House with John Andrews, the executive secretary of the American Association for Labor Legislation (AALL). Andrews had investigated more than 150 cases of phossy jaw, a debilitating and disfiguring disease prevalent in American match factories. Jane Addams of Hull House had been familiar with phossy jaw, having attended during the 1880s a mass meeting in London where several people had shown their scars and deformities. Until 1908, little had been done even to explore the problem in this country, since the American medical establishment argued that American factories were cleaner and less susceptible to occupational hazards. Andrews's report, however, not only documented the problem but pointed to a reasonably inexpensive substitute for white phosphorus and helped set in motion a high-profile campaign around the issue. It eventually led to the passage in 1912 of legislation that effectively eliminated all white phosphorus use through taxes and regulatory requirements.[4]

The success regarding phossy jaw, Hamilton later noted, proved to be an exception rather than the rule in investigating and addressing occupational hazards. Already initiating her own investigations of specific hazardous industries. Hamilton was appointed to the Illinois Commission on Occupational Diseases in December 1908 by Illinois reform governor Charles S. Deneen. Hamilton (the only female participant) and the commission's eight other members issued a report that identified a number of industries potentially exposing their workers to serious hazards and concluded that a far broader and lengthier study was needed. After some delay, the Illinois Legislature provided funding for a nine-month survey, with Hamilton as its medical investigator. Hamilton was discouraged by the difficulties in gathering information at the factory level, where "the foremen deny everything and the men will not talk and they live in all parts of the city and employ any number of physicians," but nevertheless agreed to participate in what would be the first investigation of its kind in the country.[5]

One of the key aspects of the survey was the investigation of the lead industries. Lead was a widely recognized industrial poison, known to be responsible for convulsions, abdominal pain, paralysis, temporary blindness, extreme pallor, loss of weight and appetite, indigestion, constipation, and numerous other problems. Hamilton sought to identify which industries used lead and the kinds of health problems associated with them. In pursuing her research among the lead companies, Hamilton frequently encountered the belief (a kind of ideological rationale for inaction) that worker unwillingness to do things such as "wash hands or scrub nails" was the primary cause for occupational lead poisoning and its occurrence was therefore "inevitable." Hamilton also quickly came to realize that lead hazards and health impacts were underreported by workers, who concealed their illnesses out of fear of losing their jobs.[6]

Though Hamilton was faced with a lack of documentation and information, few resources, company resistance, and workers' fears, her investigations, first with the Illinois survey and subsequently with the Bureau of Labor within the U.S. Department of Commerce, demonstrated an extraordinary resourcefulness and persistence as she pursued her "shoe-leather epidemiology." Her search for data led her to undertake numerous interviews, home visits, and discussions with physicians and apothecaries, undertakers, charity workers, visiting nurses, and countless others. It required long hours and uncertain information, but it was a duty, she felt, "to the producer, not to the product." Hamilton recognized that her compassion as a woman for the victims of the dangerous trades gave her certain advantages in soliciting information through more informal settings. "It seemed natural and right that a woman should put the care of the producing workman ahead of the value of the thing he was producing," Hamilton remarked. "In a man it would have been [seen as] sentimentality or radicalism."[7]

During the next several decades, Hamilton became the premier investigator of occupational hazards in the United States. Her research and advocacy ranged over a number of industries and toxic substances. Her insights and investigative techniques broke new ground in the areas of worker and community health and anticipated later interest in the occupational and environmental problems associated with such substances as heavy metals, solvents, and petroleum-based products. Forty years prior to the major environmental debates about the uses of science and technology and the nature of risk, Hamilton was already warning that workers were being used as "laboratory material" by industrial chemists who were introducing new products such as petrochemicals and petroleum distillates "about whose effect on human beings we know very little." This rush to introduce new industrial products, such as solvents, she argued, represented new hazards in the workplace and the general environment. "The quicker the solvent evaporates the greater the contamination of the air," Hamilton said of these new products, "which means that a coating or a degreaser which is advertised as a powerful, quick-drying fluid is one that must be regarded by a physician with suspicion."[8]

Hamilton was also convinced that control techniques, such as respirators or other protective devices, were far from adequate, anticipating similar debates within OSHA (the Occupational Safety and Health Administration) during the 1970s and 1980s. She focused on the impacts from even low exposures or emissions of substances such as lead, anticipating the recognition that for certain toxic substances there is no acceptable threshold. During debates over the decision by the automotive industry to introduce tetraethyl lead in gasoline during the 1920s, Hamilton became a key critic of the claim that the small amounts of lead involved were not significant. In a 1925 article, Hamilton wrote, "I am not one of those who believe that the use of this leaded gasoline can ever be made safe. No lead industry has ever, under the strictest control, lost all its dangers. Where there is lead, some case of lead poisoning sooner or later develops. . . ." The question of when environmental or public health factors needed to be considered was critical for Hamilton. "It makes me hope," Hamilton said of the tetraethyl lead controversy, "that the day is not far off when we shall take the next step and investigate a new danger in industry before it is put into use, before any fatal harm has been done to workmen . . . and the question will be treated as one belonging to the public health from the very outset, not after its importance has been demonstrated on the bodies of workmen."[9]

As her research began to receive attention, Hamilton's standing grew in an area that had largely failed to elicit interest in academic, industry, or government circles. In 1919, she was appointed assistant professor of industrial medicine at Harvard University following Harvard's decision to initiate a degree program in industrial hygiene. The appointment attracted attention, since she was the first woman professor in any field at Harvard and the university did not admit women to its medical school. But Hamilton was chosen partly because there weren't any men interested in the position and the medical field and academic world in general still viewed occupational and environmental issues with little interest.[10]

By the 1920s, with the publication of her classic text *Industrial Poisons in the United States*, her increasing prominence in issues of occupational and environmental health, and her participation in organizations such as the Workers' Health Bureau, Alice Hamilton had become the country's most powerful and effective voice for exploring the environmental consequences of industrial activity. Her interest touched on issues of class, race, and gender in the workplace and the long-term hazards of the production system. She was concerned not only about the visible, acute problems of occupational hazards but also generational issues associated with "race poisons," reproductive toxins such as lead whose "effects are not confined to the men and women who are exposed to it in the course of their work, but are passed on to their offspring."[11] She was able to communicate effectively with industry and government figures because of her sincerity in the goals and substance of her research, while developing a sympathetic relationship with workers due to her compassion and her commitment to change. A reformer in the mold of the settlement house worker (even while at Harvard, Hamilton maintained a "home" at Hull House), and a powerful environmental advocate in an era when the term had yet to be invented, Alice Hamilton situated the question of the environment directly in its urban and industrial context.

NOTES

1. The "I chose medicine" quote is from *Exploring the Dangerous Trades: The Autobiography of Alice Hamilton, M.D.* (Boston: Little, Brown, 1943), p. 38.

2. The "ideal place from which to observe" quote is from Barbara Sicherman, *Alice Hamilton: A Life in Letters* (Cambridge, Mass.: Harvard University Press, 1984), p. 4. The typhoid epidemic issue is also discussed in Wilma Ruth Slaight, "Alice Hamilton: First Lady of Industrial Medicine" (Ph.D. diss., Case Western University, 1974), pp. 24–27.

3. The "here was a subject" quote is from Alice Hamilton, *Exploring the Dangerous Trades*, p. 115.

4. The phossy jaw episode is discussed in Alice Hamilton, *Exploring the Dangerous Trades*, pp. 116–18. See also R. Alton Lee, "The Eradication of Phossy Jaw: A Unique Development of Federal Police Power," *The Historian*, vol. 29, no. 1, November 1966, pp. 1–21; and Alice Hamilton, "Industrial Diseases: With Special Reference to the Trades in Which Women Are Employed," *Charities and the Commons*, vol. 20, September 5, 1908, pp. 655–59.

5. The "foremen deny" quote is from a letter from Alice Hamilton to Jesse Hamilton dated February 26, 1910, as cited in Barbara Sicherman, *Alice Hamilton: A Life in Letters*, p. 157.

6. The "wash hands or scrub nails" quote is from Alice Hamilton, *Exploring the Dangerous Trades*, p. 122. The concept of industrial lead poisoning being "inevitable" is discussed in Alice Hamilton, *The White Lead Industry in the United States, With an Appendix on the Lead-Oxide Industry. Bulletin of the Bureau of Labor, No. 95* (Washington, D.C.: Government Printing Office, 1912), p. 190.

7. The "It seemed natural and right" quote is from Alice Hamilton, *Exploring the Dangerous Trades,* p. 269. The duty "to the producer" quote is from Alice Hamilton, *Industrial Poisons in the United States* (New York: Macmillan, 1925), p. 541.

8. The "laboratory material" and "the quicker the solvent" quotes are from Alice Hamilton, *Exploring the Dangerous Trades*, p. 294. See also Alice Hamilton and Gertrude Seymour, "The New Public Health," *The Survey*, vol. 38, no. 3, April 21, 1917, pp. 59–62, and Alice Hamilton, "The Scope of the Problem of Industrial Hygiene," *Public Health Reports*, vol. 37, no. 42, October 20, 1922, pp. 2604–08.

9. Alice Hamilton, "What Price Safety? Tetra-ethyl Lead Reveals a Flaw in Our Defenses," *The Survey Midmonthly,* vol. 54, no. 6, June 15, 1925, p. 333.

10. Harvard established three informal conditions for Hamilton's appointment: no use of the Harvard Club, no football tickets, and no participation in the commencement procession. Women were admitted to the medical school only after 1945. See Wilma Ruth Slaight, "Alice Hamilton: First Lady of Industrial Medicine," p. 135, and Barbara Sicherman, *Alice Hamilton: A Life in Letters*, pp. 209–18.

11. The "race poisons" discussion is from Alice Hamilton, *Industrial Poisons in the United States*, p. 110.

DAVID R. BROWER

21 Preserving the Hallowed Ground of Dinosaur National Monument (1954)

Look at the Sierra Club, which wants to persuade you to protect Dinosaur and the parks, just as other Congresses have done for so long. What kind of people are in it? Teenage kids, out to climb, hike, and ski; office workers, teachers, professional men—we even have a mailman who comes on our Sierra outings to walk 90 or 100 miles during two weeks in the wilderness. Strange people, slightly odd? Some, perhaps. But also the past president of the American Society of Civil Engineers, the current president of the American Society of Radio Engineers, the next president of the American Chemical Society, the president of a major pharmaceutical house, of a major railroad, of a major mining firm, an Assistant U.S. Attorney General. We have these, too. All of them, whether kids getting away from too much homework or executives getting away from too many telephones ringing on one desk, all have this in common—a love for the beautiful, unspoiled places—places they work hard (at no pay) to preserve, and long after they themselves can no longer enjoy them.

It is a noble human endeavor that leads them to do this. It is this type of endeavor I am hoping I can communicate to you as something

From David Brower, testimony before U.S. Congress, House Committee on Interior and Insular Affairs, January 26, 1954.

every bit as important as the type of enterprise so earnestly supported here—and entirely laudable in its place—the urge to produce, to grow, to develop, to profit, and to spend. This Sierra Club is a good organization, devoted to idealism, and I am proud of it. It is but one of many, all just as good. I wish you were all members. It would cost you only $3.50 per year.

Here are three questions which we feel have not been answered properly yet.

1. What are the important park values in Dinosaur?
2. Would they be destroyed by the Echo Park and Split Mountain dams?
3. Can Dinosaur's scenery be made accessible without dams?

As you may have guessed, our answer is that this area has superlative park values. They would indeed be destroyed by the proposed dams.

The Park Service has said in writing that the effects of these dams upon irreplaceable values of national significance would be deplorable. Deplorable is a mild word to describe what would happen to the scenery in Dinosaur were we to permit these dams to be built there. The Echo Park project alone calls for a dam 525 feet high, backing up 107 miles of reservoir, inundating the intimate, close-up scenes and living space with nearly 6 1/2 million acre feet of water. There would be construction roads in the canyon and above it, tunnels, the whole power installation and transmission lines, the rapid build-up of silt at the upper end of the reservoirs, and the periodic draw-downs of the reservoir to enable it to fulfill its function—a fluctuation that would play hob with fish and wildlife. The piñon pines, the Douglas firs, the maples and cottonwoods, the grasses and other flora that line the banks, the green living things that shine in the sun against the rich colors of the cliffs—these would all go. The river, its surge and its sound, the living sculptor of this place, would be silent forever, and all the fascination of its movement and the fun of riding it, quietly gliding through these cathedral corridors of stone—all done in for good. The tops of the cliffs you could still see, of course. As reservoirs go, it would be a handsome one—but remember the 251 other reservoir sites in the upper basin and the hundreds of reservoir sites elsewhere in the country. We don't want Dinosaur to be just another reservoir. We want it to remain the *only* Dinosaur, which it is now.

If we should accept the amazing statement that Echo Park dam would not destroy Dinosaur, but would only alter Dinosaur, we should also accept such statements as these:

1. A dam from El Capitan to Bridalveil Fall would not destroy Yosemite, but just alter it.
2. Other dams would only alter Yellowstone, Glacier National Park, Mammoth Caves National Park, Kings Canyon National Park.
3. Removal of the rain forest would only alter Olympic National Park.
4. Cutting the 3,000-year-old Big Trees and making them into grapestakes would only alter Sequoia National Park. After all, the ground would still be there, and the sky, and the distant views. All you would have done is alter it, that is, take away its reason for being.

Maybe "alter" isn't the word. Maybe we should just come out with it and say "cut the heart out."

The axiom for protecting the Park System is to consider that it is dedicated country, hallowed ground to leave as beautiful as we have found it, and not country in which man should be so impressed with himself that he tries to improve God's handiwork.

HARRY M. CAUDILL

22 The Rape of the Appalachians (1962)

The same decade that saw the human resources of
the plateau sapped and vitiated by Welfarism, idleness and defeat on the one hand and by sustained out-migration on
the other, also brought the beginning of a terrible new emasculation of
its physical resources. Strip mining, a branch of the industry which
had previously been practiced in such flat coalfields as western Kentucky and southern Illinois, invaded the Cumberlands on a vast scale.

For nearly sixty years the greater part of the region's mineral wealth
had lain in the iron clutch of absentee corporations. They had prospered and bankrupted and prospered again. But through their triumphs
and tragedies, their successes and failures, the corporations had clung
to all the old rights, privileges, immunities, powers and interests vested
in them by their nineteenth-century land and mineral deeds. These
relics from a laissez-faire century were construed to authorize the physical destruction of the land and the abject impoverishment of its inhabitants. With strip mining and its companion, the auger-mining process,
the shades of darkness moved close indeed to the Cumberlands.

The courts have written strings of decisions which not only up-
hold the covenants and privileges enumerated in the ancient deeds
and contracts but which, in the opinion of many lawyers, greatly
enlarge them as well. We have seen that when the mountaineer's

From Harry M. Caudill, "The Rape of the Appalachians," *Night Comes to the Cumberlands:
A Biography of a Depressed Area* (Boston: Little, Brown and Company, 1962), 305–12,
314–18. © 1962 by Harry M. Caudill; renewed 1990 by Anne F. Caudill. Reprinted by
permission of Little, Brown and Company.

ancestor (for the seller is, in most instances, long since dead) sold his land he lived in an isolated backwater. Coal mining was a primitive industry whose methods had changed little in a hundred years and which still depended entirely on picks and shovels. To the mountaineer "mining" meant tunneling into a hillside and digging the coal for removal through the opening thus made. That the right to mine could authorize shaving off and destroying the surface of the land in order to arrive at the underlying minerals was undreamed of by buyers and sellers alike.

But technology advanced. The steam shovel grew into a mighty mechanism and was replaced by gasoline and diesel-powered successors. "Dozers" and other efficient excavators were perfected. Ever cheaper and safer explosives came from the laboratories. These marvelous new tools enabled men to change the earth, abolishing its natural features and reshaping them as whim or necessity might require. And as these developments made possible the radically new application of the privileges granted in the yellowed mineral deeds, the courts kept pace. Year by year they subjected the mountaineer to each innovation in tools and techniques the technologists were able to dream up. First, it was decided that the purchase of coal automatically granted the "usual and ordinary" mining rights; and then that the usual mining rights included authority to cut down enough of the trees on the surface to supply props for the underground workings. This subjected thousands of acres to cutting for which the owners were uncompensated. It gave the companies an immensely valuable property right for which they had neither bargained nor paid.

Next came rulings which gave the companies the power to "divert and pollute" all water "in or on" the lands. With impunity they could kill the fish in the streams, render the water in the farmer's well unpotable and, by corrupting the stream from which his livestock drank, compel him to get rid of his milk cows and other beasts. They were authorized to pile mining refuse wherever they desired, even if the chosen sites destroyed the homes of farmers and bestowed no substantial advantage on the corporations. The companies which held "long-form" mineral deeds were empowered to withdraw subjacent supports, thereby causing the surface to subside and fracture. They could build roads wherever they desired, even through lawns and fertile vegetable gardens. They could sluice poisonous water from the pits onto the crop lands. With impunity they could hurl out from their washeries clouds of coal grit which settled on fields of corn, alfalfa and clover and rendered them worthless as fodder. Fumes from burning slate dumps peeled paint from houses, but the companies were absolved from damages.

The state's highest court held in substance that a majority of the people had "dedicated" the region to the mining industry, and that the inhabitants were estopped to complain of the depredations of the coal corporations, so long as they were not motivated by malice. Since malice seldom existed and could never be proved, this afforded no safeguard at all. The companies, which had bought their coal rights at prices ranging from fifty cents to a few dollars per acre, were, in effect, left free to do as they saw fit, restrained only by the shallow consciences of their officials. When the bulldozer and power shovel made contour strip-mining feasible and profitable in mountainous terrain, the court promptly enforced the companies' right to remove the coal by this unusual and wholly unforeseen method.

The court spurned as unimportant the fact that competent engineers swore only 20 per cent of the coal in a virgin boundary could be recovered even when both strip and auger mining were employed in unison. It brushed aside proof that strip mining destroys the land and eradicates the economic base on which continued residence within the region is predicated. It substantially adjudicated away the rights of thousands of mountaineers to house and home. It bestowed upon the owner of a seam of coal the right to destroy totally the surface insofar as any known system of reclamation is concerned. It delivered into the hands of the coal corporations the present estate and future heritage in the land—in effect an option to preserve or ruin present and future generations. These fateful decisions of the state's highest court, decisions medieval in outlook and philosophy, are now buttressed by the hoary doctrine of *stare decisis* and can be dislodged only by social and political dynamite. And while there is strong reason to suppose that the court as presently constituted views these decisions with uneasiness and dismay, its relatively enlightened judges feel duty-bound to apply them in new appeals. This long line of judicial opinions opened the way for what may prove to be the final obliteration of the plateau's future as a vital part of the nation and its history.

It is probable that this process of judicially straitjacketing the mountaineers for the benefit of the coal companies reached its apogee in a decision handed down by the Court of Appeals on November 15, 1949. The appeal came up from the Circuit Court of Pike County. It involved one of the earliest stripping operations to be undertaken in eastern Kentucky. The Russell Fork Coal Company had cut the top off a mountain on Weddington Fork of Ferrells Creek, leaving ten acres of loose earth, mixed to a great depth with stones and fragments of trees. This vast mass of unstable rubble lay on the upper reaches of a narrow valley, on the floor of which several families made their homes. It was created in an area which had been battered by flash floods throughout its history, so that even the feeblest of minds could have anticipated their recurrence at almost any time. On the night of August 2, 1945, the calamity came in the form of a cloudburst and, foreseeably, thousands of tons of dirt, rocks and shattered tree trunks from the devastated mountain were flung down the hillside into the raging creek. Like a titanic scythe the rolling rubble swept downstream, working havoc among the houses, stores and farms. When the dazed inhabitants recovered sufficiently they sued the coal company for damages on the reasonable assumption that its digging had triggered a misfortune which nature, left undisturbed, would not have visited upon them. The appellate bench reversed the verdict of the jury and the judgment of the trial court. It ruled, in effect, that the rain was an Act of God which the coal operator could not have foreseen and that, had the rain not fallen, the rubble would have remained safely in place. Besides, the stripping had been done in the "same manner as was customary at all strip mines." Usurping the fact-finding prerogative of the jury, the judges, sitting as a self-appointed superjury, found the stripper innocent of wrongdoing and negligence.

In another case several years later, a mountaineer claimed that a company had plowed up his mountainsides, covered his bottomland with rubble, caused his well to go dry and, in his words, had "plumb broke" him. After he had heard all the evidence and arguments of counsel the trial judge dismissed the case. In doing so he told the mountaineer, "I deeply sympathize with you and sincerely wish I could rule for you. My hands are tied by the rulings of the Court of Appeals and under the law I must follow its decisions. The truth is that about the only rights you have on your land is to breathe on it and pay the taxes. For all practical purposes the company that owns the minerals in your land owns all the other rights pertaining to it." . . .

The recovery of coal by the "open-cut" method had previously never been feasible in the mountains, though it had occasionally been practiced in the low hills on the fringes of the plateau. But by 1950, strip mining was not only feasible but was increasingly profitable.

Typically a strip-mine operator needed only a tiny crew of men. He required two bulldozers, one of which could be substantially smaller than the other. He required an air compressor and drill for the boring of holes into the rock overlying the coal. He also required a power shovel for use in loading the coal from the seam into the trucks. These four machines could be operated by as many men. To their wages were added those of a night watchman and two or three laborers, and the crew was complete. With these men and machines the operator first built a road from the nearest highway up the hillside to the coal seam. The bulldozers pursued the seam around the hillside, uprooting the timber and removing all the soil until the coal was reached. Then the dirt was scraped from the sloping mountainside above to expose the crumbling rock. This cut proceeded along the contours of the ridge for half a mile. Then rows of holes were drilled in the rock strata and were tamped with explosives. When the explosives were set off, most of the dirt and rock was blown violently down the mountainside. The remainder lay, soft and crumbly, on top of the coal. The "dozers" then bestrode the shattered "overburden," and with their steel snouts shoved it down the steep slopes. This process left the outer edge of the out-crop exposed. A sheet of coal eight feet thick, fifty feet wide and half a mile long could thus be bared within a few days.

Next, holes were drilled in the glittering black seam of coal. Small charges of dynamite loosened thousands of tons of the mineral, leaving it easily available to the shovel's big dipper. A number of truckers were hired to haul it away, at a cost of perhaps seventy-five cents a ton. It was carried to the nearest ramp or tipple where it was cleaned, sized and loaded into gondolas.

It is instantly apparent that this method of recovery is vastly cheaper than shaft or drift mining. Six or eight men can thus dig more coal from the outcrop than five or six times their number can mine underground. The bulldozers, shovels and drills are expensive, but not more so than their subterranean counterparts. They can produce a ton of coal for little more than half the cost imposed on a competitor in a deep pit. Where the strip mine lies close to the loading ramp so that the haul bill can be minimized the price differential is even more striking.

In the flat country of western Kentucky, where thousands of acres had already been devastated by strip mining, the coal seams lie only thirty to sixty feet beneath the surface. The overburden is scraped off and the coal is scooped out. Inevitably such topsoil as the land affords is buried under towering heaps of subsoil. When the strippers move on, once-level meadows and cornfields have been converted to jumbled heaps of hardpan, barren clay from deep in the earth. This hellish landscape is slow to support vegetation and years elapse before the yellow waste turns green again. In the meantime immense quantities of dirt have crept into the sluggish streams, have choked them, and brackish ponds have formed to breed millions of mosquitoes.

The evil effects of open-cut mining are fantastically magnified when practiced in the mountains. Masses of shattered stone, shale, slate and dirt are cast pell-mell down the hillside. The first to go are the thin remaining layer of fertile topsoil and such trees as still find sustenance in it. The uprooted trees are flung down the slopes by the first cut. Then follows the sterile subsoil, shattered stone and slate. As the cut extends deeper into the hillside the process is repeated again and again. Sometimes the "highwall," the perpendicular bank resulting from the cut, rises ninety feet; but a height of forty to sixty feet is more often found. In a single mile, hundreds of thousands of tons are displaced. . . .

After the coal has been carried away vast quantities of the shattered mineral are left uncovered. Many seams contain substantial quantities of sulphur, which when wet produces toxic sulphuric acid. This poison bleeds into the creeks, killing minute vegetation and destroying fish, frogs and other stream-dwellers. . . .

Within a few years after the "strip operator" has slashed his way into the hillside the unresting elements have carried away most of his discarded overburden. The dirt has vanished, leaving immense expanses of sere brown sandstone and slabs of sickening gray slate. A few straggly clusters of broom sage and an occasional spindly sycamore take root and struggle to survive. . . .

The coal auger made its appearance as a device for removing that portion of the outcrop which could not be reached by stripping. As a rule of thumb ten feet of overburden can profitably be removed for each foot of coal in the seam. When the highwall rose straight up so far it could not be advantageously increased, much of the outcrop remained. The auger allowed the recovery of a large part of the remaining mineral. It is a gigantic drill which bores straight back into the coal seam, spewing out huge quantities of the mineral with each revolution of the screw. The drills range from seventeen inches to six feet in diameter. . . .

Where augering is done in a previously unmined ridge the crumbly "bloom" and a few yards of weathered roofstone is shoved over the hillside. Then the bore holes follow each other in interminable procession around the meandering ridge. They proceed along the edges of sharp spurs, around the "turn of the point," and back to the main ridge again. When the end of the ridge is passed the cutting and boring continues on its reverse side. Thus the bore holes from one side of the mountain extend toward the ends of those drilled from the other side. Under these circumstances coal production is fantastically cheap. A well-financed operation augering in a four- to six-foot seam can realize a net profit of close to a dollar on the ton even in the depressed coal market prevailing as this is written in 1962. A six-foot auger turning uninterruptedly can load fifteen tons in less than one minute. If the fleet of trucks can keep pace with the bulldozers and augers, the profit can be fabulous, amounting to millions of dollars in a few years. Quite naturally the possibility of such quick and easy enrichment has excited many coal companies and the politicians through whom they dominate the state and county governments. . . .

Open-cut strip mining does not always follow the meandering borders of the ridge. A different procedure is used when the vein lies near the top of the hill. Then the strippers blast and carve away the stone and soil overlying the coal, shoving it over the brink of the mountain until at last the entire seam lies black and glistening in the sunlight. Such an operation can transform a razorback spur into a flat mesa. Sometimes the hill's altitude is decreased by 20 per cent while its thickness is much increased. When the strippers have departed and the rains and freezes have flayed such a decapitated mountain for a season or two, it takes on an appearance not unlike the desolate, shattered tablelands of Colorado. But these man-made mesas lie in a rainy area and the layers of loose soil cloaking the slopes will not stay *in situ*. Wraithlike the rubble melts away, only to reappear at countless places downstream. . . .

Under the law strippers are required to replant their wrecked and ravaged acres. The State Department of Conservation recommends short leaf or loblolly pines for the spoil-banks. Conservationists insist that a full year must pass before the young trees are planted. This delay permits the freshly piled soil to settle enough so the trees can take root. The seedlings are approximately five inches long when planted, supposedly at intervals of six feet. Some ten years must elapse before trees growing in such impoverished earth will reach the height of a man's head. In the meantime the rains have clawed the earth about their roots into deep gullies and there is little left for their foliage to protect. Few operators seriously attempt to comply with the reclamation regulations; most are permitted virtually to ignore them.

The effects of strip mining bring an abrupt subsidence of every phase of community life. The community of Upper Beefhide Creek in Letcher County was stripped between 1950 and 1954. Highwalls ten miles long and averaging forty feet in height were created. Earth and rock were tumbled down the mountainsides and raced through fields of grass and corn and blanketed lawns and vegetable gardens. Stones as big as bushels were blasted high into the air like giant mortar shells, to rain down on residences, roads and cornland. One huge rock crashed through the roof of a house, struck a bed dead center and carried the spring and mattress into the earth under the foundation. Another fell on a cemetery, smashing a tombstone and crushing the coffin six feet underground.

_____

Before the avalanches of stone and dirt the population took wings, and seven years after the stripping ceased three quarters of the population had moved away. Before Upper Beefhide Creek was wrecked it comprised a voting precinct, and several hundred men, women and children lived reasonably well within its confines. Some were farmers who sold eggs, milk, butter and other produce in nearby towns and camps. Others worked as miners. A few distilled enough moonshine whiskey to win a measure of local renown for their product. Farmers, miners and moonshiners alike forsook the valley leaving it to a corporal's guard of Old Age pensioners and a handful of children and their dispirited parents.

The long-range impact of such wrecking on the economy of an already poor and backward state is incalculable. While mountain land is now assessed for tax purposes at very low values, strip mining often eliminates it from taxation entirely. Thenceforward the mountaineers who own the surface regard it as worthless for all purposes and decline to pay taxes levied upon it. If the state goes to the expense and effort required to sell the land at a tax sale there are no buyers. Thus the region's schools and other public facilities are deprived of desperately needed revenues, and the taxpayers of more prosperous areas of the state are compelled to produce new funds for support of the "pauper counties" in the plateau. Simultaneously, mud from the spoil-banks congests creeks and rivers and highway culverts and ditchlines. These flood-causing deposits are dredged out by maintenance crews of the Department of Highways, thus draining dollars away from road construction and repair. In effect, the general population is indirectly subsidizing the strippers by paying the bills for much of the damage they inflict.

Practically every ridge, spur and point in the eastern Kentucky coalfield is a candidate for strip and/or auger mining. Many have already been "worked," and the remainder are likely to become spoilbanks within the next few years.

The cumulative effects of the wrecking of a coal-filled mountain stagger the imagination. Let us suppose the ridge contains three seams of coal, and that the company first strip-mines the bottommost seam. A few years later it returns to a higher seam midway up the mountain and cuts highwalls of fifty or sixty feet in its sides. Then to crown its enterprise its shovels and bulldozers slice off the top of the mountain to recover all of the highest seam. Within a dozen years it has dug millions of tons of coal and made a profit of millions of dollars. But in the process it has totally transformed one of earth's terrain features. A relatively stable mountain, whose soil and water were to a high degree protected by grass and trees, has been reduced to a colossal rubble heap.

A few months before this was written I discussed a huge stripping operation with the engineer who was directing it. He was a veteran of nearly forty-five years' experience, and he summed up his lifetime of work in these words: "When I came to this coalfield most of the hills were covered with fine timber and all were full of topgrade coal. Since then we have gutted these old mountains and shaved 'em off clean. Now we are skinning 'em and cutting their heads off!"

LOIS GIBBS

23 What Happened at Love Canal (1982)

The Problem at Love Canal

Almost everyone has heard above Love Canal, but not many people know what it is all about. The Love Canal story is about a thousand families who lived near the site of an abandoned toxic chemical waste dump. More important, it is a warning of what could happen in any American community. We have very little protection against the toxic chemical wastes that threaten to poison our water, our air, and our food. The federal and state governments have agreed to move away everyone who wants to move; but they didn't at first. We had to work to achieve that goal. Love Canal is the story of how government tends to solve a problem, and of how we, ordinary citizens of the United States, can take control of our own lives by insisting that we be heard.

I want to tell you our story—my story—because I believe that ordinary citizens—using the tools of dignity, self-respect, common sense, and perseverance—can influence solutions to important problems in our society. To a great extent, we won our fight. It wasn't easy, that's for sure. In solving any difficult problem, you have to be prepared to fight long and hard, sometimes at great personal cost; but it can be done. It *must* be done if we are to survive as a democratic society—indeed, if we are to survive at all.

From Lois Gibbs, "The Problem at Love Canal," "The Motel People," and "Still Studying the Problem," *Love Canal: My Story* (Albany: State University of New York Press, 1982), 1–2, 8–9, 125–29, 172. Reprinted by permission of Lois Marie Gibbs and the Center for Health, Environment and Justice.

In order to understand what happened at Love Canal, and to understand my part in it, you need to know more about the canal. The best way to introduce you to the canal and its story is, I think, to let you read the statement we wrote explaining ourselves to the thousands of people from all over the world who wrote expressing interest and offering their support and help. You will see that we financed our fight against the federal government and the state of New York with donations from individuals and with the proceeds from T-shirt and cookie-bake sales. You don't need money, but it helps; what you need most are determination, imagination, the conviction that you're right, and the knowledge that you are fighting not only for your family but also for the good of everyone. . . .

If you drove down my street *before Love Canal* (that's what I call what happened to us), you might have thought it looked like a typical American small town that you would see in a TV movie—neat bungalows, many painted white, with neatly clipped hedges or freshly painted fences. The houses are generally small but comfortable; at that time ("before Love Canal" in 1978) they sold for about $30,000. If you came in the summertime, you would have seen men painting their houses or adding an extra room, women taking care of gardens, and children riding bicycles and tricycles on the sidewalks or playing in the backyards.

You would see something quite different today. Since Love Canal, the houses nearest the canal area have been boarded up and abandoned. Many have homemade signs and graffiti, vividly telling what happened to make this a ghost town. The once-neat gardens are overgrown, the lawns uncut. A high chain-link fence surrounds the houses nearest the canal. The area is deserted. The fence is a reminder of the 22,000 tons of poisons buried there, poisons that can cause cancer, that can cause mothers to miscarry or give birth to deformed children, poisons that can make children and adults sick, many of them in ways doctors only dimly understand.

When we moved into our house on 101st Street in 1972, I didn't even know Love Canal was there. It was a lovely neighborhood in a quiet residential area, with lots of trees and lots of children outside playing. It seemed just the place for our family. We have two children—Michael, who was born just before we moved in, and Melissa (Missy), born June 12, 1975. I was twenty-six. I liked the neighborhood because it was in the city but out of it. It was convenient. There was a school within walking distance. I liked the idea of my children being able to walk to the 99th Street School. The school's playground was part of a big, open field with houses all around. Our new neighbors told us that the developers who sold them their houses said the city was going to put a park on the field.

It is really something, if you stop and think of it, that underneath that field were poisons, and on top of it was a grade school and a playground. We later found out that the Niagara Falls School Board knew the filled-in canal was a toxic dump site. We also know that they knew it was dangerous because, when the Hooker Chemical Corporation sold it to them [in 1953] for one dollar, Hooker put a clause in the deed declaring that the corporation would not be responsible for any harm that came to anyone from *chemicals* buried there. That one-dollar school site turned out to be some bargain! . . .

The Motel People

It was now August 1979. Although it had been more than a year, we hadn't given up. Construction began at the north end of the canal.* It was different than when they worked on the southern section, because of the heat of the summer. All the things we worried about earlier now showed up. Residents were becoming ill. After the heavy construction on the north end began, the air was humid, hot, and stagnant, and it reeked of chemicals. Over 50 percent of the children were absent from the day-care centers and the camps because of illness. One adult who hadn't had an asthma attack since he was a child, all of a sudden had one and was taken to the hospital twice during one week.

We kept a daily log. Ninety-seven families had called their physicians, seeking medical attention. A few went to the emergency room, and two children were hospitalized. I can't tell you what it was like on some days. It was hot, and the air would just hang there. The fumes were thick. They made your eyes water, or you coughed. Someone described it as similar to trying to breathe underwater. In the winter the cold wind would come off the river and blow the fumes away. That was bad enough, but in the summer, you knew you were living on a chemical dump.

*Gibbs is referring here to the plan for partial remedial construction of the canal site, which had been approved by the State of New York—before residents had been evacuated from the area. The plan called for a clay pipe drainage system with wells for containing contaminated water and chemicals. As Gibbs notes, residents strongly believed that the system was grossly inadequate. Further, excavation of the canal brought the increased threat of airborne toxicity from the buried chemicals.—Ed.

I called Axelrod* because I was frightened myself. Both my children were sick, and Missy is usually never sick. Michael had a couple of seizures and was running a temperature. His eyes and ears were irritated. One of our office workers was taken to the hospital because she was having difficulty breathing.

Axelrod told me he would investigate. If I would send him what I had, he would see what he could do.

I went across the street to the state task-force office and telecopied a list of ninety-four families' names, addresses, their physicians' names, whether they saw their physician, or whether they just contacted him by phone, their symptoms, and their diagnoses when they had seen a physician. When I called him the next day, he said he had talked to four physicians. They said that it was something going around and that I shouldn't be concerned. I was really upset with that. The health department had had contact with many of the physicians in Niagara County. They knew which ones would be sympathetic and which ones wouldn't. He may have contacted four physicians, and those four physicians probably said that to him, but he knew the four to contact who would come out and say what he wanted to hear. So, Axelrod said there was no problem, that it was something going around and not to worry about it.

A few residents were temporarily evacuated. When we went to court to try to stop the construction, the judge accepted the state's safety plan. Those who felt ill or who felt discomfort could leave the area for forty-eight hours. A few of the residents decided to go because they were frightened. They didn't want their families to stay in the area during the construction. They were evacuated to Niagara University, a college near Bloody Run. The people didn't know how long they could stay out, but they knew they did not want to come back to Love Canal. They knew that they were sick and blamed it directly on the construction.

The residents were now more anxious than ever—and far more upset. Families were sick, but no one would acknowledge a problem. We decided to do something in the form of protest in order to bring everyone together and get the media back again. That was the only thing that had helped us. We planned a candlelight ceremony to celebrate the first anniversary. We asked the Ecumenical Task Force on

*David Axelrod, a New York State public health official—Ed.

Love Canal to arrange for a minister to conduct the service. They refused. No one wanted to be involved. Debbie Cerrillo called the head of her church, who agreed. We held it in the evening at dusk. Many of the media people covered it. The weather was slightly foggy, with a misty rain. It fit everyone's mood. The service left us with a feeling of closeness. Although I am not very religious, the idea that we were all together, whether praying to God or just knowing someone else cared, set the whole mood.

Unfortunately, the following week we needed more than prayers. The New York State Health Department issued a press release stating that they had found dioxin in the leachate collected in the drainage system.

Once again, there was panic. "What should we do? Where do we go? Who could we talk to?" There was no one. The state did not have any health department personnel, nor anyone from their laboratories. They did what they usually did: released the news on a Friday in hopes that the residents would calm down by Monday.

A state task force meeting was set for August 21. David Axelrod would be there. The task force meeting was to be closed to the residents. Only task force members were supposed to attend. I told the residents they had as much right to be there as anyone else, that I couldn't ask every question they might have. We preferred a public meeting, but the task force refused. I explained why the meeting should be open. I told the residents to go to the task force meeting, stand outside, bang on the door, force their way in. I told them not to be put off because they weren't wanted there. If they made enough noise, they would be let in. The meeting was held in a big gymnasium in the housing project just west of the Canal. The room was so large that every time anyone talked, it echoed. The residents banged on the doors and eventually were allowed in. They sat in front of the U-shaped table but they just couldn't hear anything that was going on. They were too far away; when somebody spoke up, it echoed. [William] Hennessy [commissioner of the New York Department of Transportation] told the residents to move closer to the table. The residents were inches away from the commissioners, which made them nervous and made me happy. I took a dead branch from across the street. Vegetation was dying in the neighborhood, but no one seemed to care; no one seemed to want to check it. I was going to make sure he saw it, and that he touched it. I put the stick in a plastic bag and I set it underneath my seat, waiting for the right time.

The meeting began and Commissioner Hennessy opened the meeting. He said a few things about nothing in particular. Then I began to go down my list of questions. I had a long discussion with Axelrod about the health studies and their inadequacies. I kept badgering him about the miscarriages and the women who were contemplating pregnancy. I told him about my neighbor's miscarriage. I believed that if she had been out of the area prior to conceiving, her baby might have survived. Axelrod answered with the stupid statement that she had weighed the risks, that she was an intelligent young lady. She knew the risk. I got angry and said: "We *don't know* what the risk is. *You* tell *me* what the risk is. If I were to get pregnant, what would be my chance of having a miscarriage?" He said I knew there had been miscarriages. Finally, he gave in and said the miscarriage rate in Love Canal—my chance of a miscarriage—was thirty-five to forty-five percent. When the residents who were sitting there heard this, they began yelling. If the percentage was that high, then why the hell were they still here? Patti Grenzy was crying but determined. She said she was out temporarily, and had no intention of moving back. Someone had mentioned the dioxin findings, and people shouted: "What does that mean? Are we going to be exposed? What are you doing to us? Don't you care? We are people. We didn't ask for this. We are victims. And you're minimizing it! You're playing everything down!"

Marie Pozniak got very upset. She has a severely asthmatic daughter, and other medical problems in her family. She was sitting inches from Axelrod. She stood up and said, "In view of the new dioxin findings, Commissioner Axelrod, does that mean that you are going to relocate my family?" Axelrod just put his head down and held it in his hands. She kept after him, "Answer me! Does that mean that you are going to relocate me?" He just hung his head, until she finally told him to pick up his head and answer her, that she wouldn't stop until he answered. He said, "No, we are not going to relocate you, Mrs. Pozniak, in view of the dioxin findings." At that, she picked up Dr. Axelrod's cardboard name tag, ripped the "doctor" part off, and threw it at him. She said he didn't deserve a title like "Doctor" or "Commissioner." She ran to the door, where her husband met her, and they left.

I pulled out the twig I had brought and laid it on the table. I asked him what killed this vegetation around Love Canal. He said he didn't know, but according to the reports he had gotten from the DEC [Department of Environmental Conservation], it was winterkill. I explained to him that this particular branch had died that *spring*. It had grown leaves and the leaves turned brown, curled up, and died. It hadn't been below forty degrees. I asked him to explain that. He said he couldn't explain it, that he didn't know; but he would be willing to investigate, if I wanted him to.

The residents, once again, became excited. Everything was chaotic. It was like an opera or a musical, with those up front questioning the commissioners like lead singers, and every once in awhile the audience would cry out just as if they were the chorus. At this time, Commissioner Hennessy said: "I am closing the meeting. We are leaving." I looked at him and said, "No. I still have fourteen points to bring up, questions that have not been answered." Commissioner Hennessy said: "I'm sorry, but the meeting is closed. We have a plane to catch." (They had their own plane. They don't use a regular commercial flight.) It was just an excuse; Commissioner Axelrod was telling us too much. They didn't want us to have the information. They all stood up and started to walk away. I just sat there looking at them. I couldn't believe they were leaving. I threw my papers on the desk and said: "Where the hell do you think you're going?" They said that I was welcome to come to Albany and bring up anything I wanted. I could spend as much time as necessary; but they had a plane to catch, and were sorry. I went over to Axelrod. I was tempted to hit one of them. I'm not a violent person, but I could have hit them with no problem. I paced back and forth, I was so angry. Then I walked away. . . .

Still Studying the Problem

. . . The small children suffered the most. They did not understand *chemicals*, *dioxin*, or exactly how they might be harmed. Even though parents explained many times, the children couldn't understand what they couldn't see or touch but could sometimes smell. The odor around the canal was normal to the children. They could not comprehend exactly what their mothers were telling them. Many had nightmares imagining what "chemicals" looked like and then having an imaginary "thing" attack them. Many children lost their sense of security. Mom was not home as she used to be. Either Dad or a baby-sitter was caring for them. Some of the children went to three different schools and had to keep adjusting and making new friends. Children who attended high school since ninth grade and wanted to graduate with their classes were pulled out of school in their junior or senior year because the family moved to a new home in a different district or a different state.

Families moved in and out of hotels several times. Small children had problems adjusting. Mom told them they couldn't bring their toys, that she would get new ones because the toys might be contaminated, or there were too many toys for the small hotel rooms. Children wanted to go home to their own rooms where things were familiar and have Mom greet them at the door after school, back to their friends, their bikes, and their own small worlds.

From the beginning, signs of insecurity surfaced in many children. Some had behavioral problems in school. Some sucked their thumbs, wet their beds, had nightmares, or cried at every little thing. The total psychological damage to our children has not been measured, but it will stay with them for a long time. Many may need help in the future to cope with their problems.

EILEEN MAURA McGURTY

24 The Origins of the Environmental Justice Movement (1997)

In the summer of 1978, Robert Burns and his two sons drove liquid tanker trucks along the rural roads in thirteen North Carolina counties and through remote sections of the Fort Bragg Military Reservation. Driving at night to avoid detection, they opened the bottom valve of the tanker and discharged liquid contaminated with polychlorinated biphenyls (PCBs) removed from the Ward Transformer Company in Raleigh onto the soil along the road shoulders. This violation of the Toxic Substance Control Act (TSCA) continued for nearly two weeks until 240 miles of road shoulders were contaminated. Robert Ward had hired the Burnses to illegally dispose of the contaminated liquid in an attempt to avoid the escalating cost of disposal that was due, in part, to increasing regulation of hazardous waste.[1] Since the contamination occurred on state-owned property, North Carolina was responsible for remediation. Within a few months after detecting the contamination, the state devised a plan calling for the construction of a landfill in Warren County, a rural area in northeastern North Carolina with a majority of poor, African-American residents. Warren County also suffered the most contamination of any of the thirteen counties affected by the illegal disposal. A farmer in the

From Eileen Maura McGurty, "From NIMBY to Civil Rights: The Origins of the Environmental Justice Movement," *Environmental History* 2, no. 3 (July 1997): 301–3, 305–23. Reprinted by permission of the Forest History Society and the American Society for Environmental History.

small community of Afton, facing a foreclosure and bankruptcy, sold his property to the state for use as a final resting place for the contaminated soil.[2]

The announcement of this disposal site sparked intense resistance from county residents concerned with the possible contamination of their groundwater and the potential threat to local economic development from the stigma of a hazardous waste facility. After three years of legal battles unsuccessfully waged by Warren County against North Carolina and the U.S. Environmental Protection Agency (EPA), the state was permitted to begin construction of the landfill in the summer of 1982. When it became apparent that the standard processes of recourse would not stop the forty thousand cubic yards of soil from being buried at the site, citizens of Warren County changed their oppositional strategy to disruptive collective action. In the process of planning for the protest events, they also shifted their primary rationale for opposing the site. While threats to groundwater and the local economy were still worries for the citizens, the disruptive action focused on environmental racism. Protesters argued that Warren County was chosen, in part, because the residents were primarily poor and African-American. As one activist put it, "The community was politically and economically unempowered; that was the reason for the siting. They took advantage of poor people and people of color."[3] The citizens garnered support from regional and national civil rights leaders and organized protest events daily during the six-week period while soil was delivered to the landfill. The unrelenting protests resulted in a delay and disruption of the landfilling project, with nearly five hundred arrests and significant state and national media coverage, but they failed to stop the landfill.

Despite the failure of the protests to reach the immediate objective, the controversy over the Warren County landfill had a major impact on contemporary environmental activism and the environmental policy agenda. The events in Warren County are proclaimed by activists and policymakers alike as the birth of the environmental justice movement.[4] Environmental justice activists argue that the inequitable distribution of environmental degradation and systematic exclusion of the poor and people of color from environmental decision making is perpetuated by traditional environmental organizations, also known as mainstream environmentalism, and by environmental regulatory agencies.[5] The topic seemed to explode overnight, creating the perception that environmental justice has shaped an original challenge to the contemporary environmental discussion. In reality, potential negative social impacts of both environmental degradation and regulatory policies have been at the core of environmental discussions since the onset of the modern environmental era. Charges of racism, exclusion, elitism, and regressive policies had been leveled against mainstream environmentalists and regulatory agencies prior to the emergence of the activism identified as "environmental justice."

These conflicts first emerged between 1968 and 1975, a period of heightened environmental and social activism. Within this context, the conflict in Warren County transformed the relationship between mainstream environmentalists and the civil rights movement. Civil rights leaders incorporated an environmental aspect into the civil rights agenda, motivated by the nature of the toxic contamination, the national and local political landscape, and the direct conflict with government agencies responsible for environmentally related decisions. As civil rights leaders with influence among African-Americans and within the established political system integrated the new notion of environmental racism into their program, the cause gained legitimacy and strength. In addition to the transformation of the African-American agenda, the local, primarily white residents working against the landfill incorporated civil rights claims as part of their environmental cause in order to keep their opposition alive with the help of experienced civil rights activists. Although the bulwark between civil rights and environmentalism began to weaken, the conflicts of the period from 1968 to 1975 did not completely disappear with the emergence of the contemporary environmental justice movement. The well-established, mainstream environmental organizations did not have any part in either the embrace of environmentalism by civil rights activists or the embrace of a civil rights agenda by local environmentalists. As a result, the "marriage of social justice with environmentalism" remains a rocky union between ambivalent partners. . . .

During the six weeks of protests in Warren County, North Carolina, in the autumn of 1982, white land owners joined together with black residents and civil rights activists to produce a significant disruptive collective action. The process of coming together transformed the two parties in the coalition and loosened the strict boundaries between environmental and civil rights causes. Civil rights activists embraced an environmental perspective as a result of a toxic threat to the daily lives of African-Americans and through their direct conflict with government agencies responsible for environmental decisions. Local whites, who began their opposition with the narrow focus of keeping hazardous waste out of their community, expanded their resistance to include a concern for inadvertent racist ramifications of some environmental policies. The political landscape for African-Americans at the local and national level, the emerging toxic construct, and the economic instability of the county all contributed to the transformative moment. This new movement for environmental justice emerged from the lived experience of the residents of this rural, poor county in North Carolina and their connections to powerful African-Americans, not from mainstream environmental groups. This union of two causes which emerged from the Warren County events was partly in conflict with the traditional environmental organizations involved in the case. The conflict is still reflected in the ongoing tension between the two causes as they seek common ground.

The Remediation Process: Expediency and Uncertainty

The Toxic Substance Control Act of 1976 banned the manufacture of PCBs and regulated the disposal of PCB-contaminated soil in landfills. Within these federal constraints, there were still several options available to North Carolina in its effort to clean up the 240 miles of contaminated soil. The soil could be moved to an approved hazardous waste landfill. With the nearest site located in Emelle, Alabama, this option was assumed to be too expensive. Since the contamination was spread throughout thirteen counties, the state could have constructed multiple landfills. The logistic complications and probable expense deemed this option unfeasible as well, forcing the state to find one site. Government officials examined state-owned property within the central counties and issued a plea to citizens and local governments to volunteer tracts of land. Over ninety sites were examined as potential locations.[6]

Within a few months, the choices were limited to two sites. One of these was the Afton site in Warren County owned by Carter and Linda Pope. As early as October 1978, the Division of State Property began negotiations with the Popes and signed an option to buy on December 1, 1978.[7] The second site was a six-acre section of the Chatham County sanitary landfill. Since the Chatham County site was publicly owned, final approval to sell the property was subject to input by county residents. At a public hearing on December 11, 1978, they voiced strong opposition to the plan to sell part of the landfill to the state. The following day, the county commissioners withdrew their offer, and the state submitted its request to the EPA for a permit to construct the landfill on the Popes' farm.[8]

The choice of the Warren County site was shaped by the state's need to immediately deal with the contamination and uncertainty over how to pay for this remediation. The drive for expediency emerged in part from concerns about a potential public health crisis and the possibility of a significant loss to the agriculturally dependent communities adjacent to the contaminated roads. These two issues, coupled with a desire to avoid a public relations debacle, motivated the state to move as quickly as possible.[9] The Comprehensive Emergency Response, Compensation and Liability Act of 1980, popularly known as Superfund, had not yet been conceived, although the North Carolina contamination catastrophe added to the impetus for its eventual passage in 1980. In 1978, there was no federal assistance available, but by the time the landfill was actually constructed in 1982, the North Carolina roadways had been placed on the "National Priority List" of contaminated sites in need of remediation, making their cleanup eligible for 90 percent funding through Superfund. Four years earlier, when the state was searching for answers, no one could have foreseen this complete transformation in environmental policy.

The Popes' land was available, relatively inexpensive, and the sale was not subject to public review. Purchase of the property also helped the state avoid the sticky problem of using eminent domain. While it was important to state officials that the landfill be located in a sparsely populated area, finding a location with little potential for resistance was not a major concern. Expediency was vital, but in 1978 there was not much reason to expect that public outcry would significantly delay the project. Based on the experience of hazardous waste management in the 1970s, waste facility siting faced only limited obstacles from local residents and had not encountered a major difficulty.[10] While Warren County was one of five counties in North Carolina with a majority of African-American residents, it was also among the poorest and agriculturally least productive. Given the agricultural downturn and economic recession of the 1970s and the already problematic economic situation in the county, it was not surprising that a farmer in Warren County was willing to sell his property to the state in an effort to regain financial security. . . .

The Initial Opposition: "Not in My Backyard!"

The initial protest in Warren County began typically, as a narrowly defined, self-interested response to a local threat: "We don't want that facility in our backyards." Residents were primarily concerned with public health repercussions from potential groundwater contamination and negative economic impacts of a waste facility near their homes. The fear of contamination was fueled by the timing of the North Carolina incident: the dumping of the PCB-contaminated liquid occurred exactly at the same time when hazardous waste became a household word as a result of the Love Canal catastrophe in August 1978. . . .

The infusion of the hazardous waste issue into public discourse through the Love Canal news coverage had two impacts. First, the toxic threat itself was always lurking in the background; no one had immunity from the silent killer, not whites, not blacks, not the wealthy, not the poor. Second, the government was implicated in the victimization of citizens by toxic materials. Distrust of the agency with the official environmental label became the rallying cry for the new activists. The direct connection of the North Carolina contamination with the Love Canal catastrophe reinforced both of these notions. The already strong connection between the two cases of contamination increased when PCBs were identified as part of the toxins at Love Canal. In December 1978, when county residents read in the newspaper that the state had submitted a permit application for a landfill site in Warren County, they responded based on these newly formed constructs and vehemently resisted the plan.

Warren County Citizens Concerned about PCBs (Concerned Citizens) became one of many local groups opposed to the hazardous waste facility, countering "facts" from the state and the EPA with their own data showing the flaws in the state's plan. In this way, they were like numerous other opponents of locally unwanted land uses, worried that a hazardous waste facility would ruin the natural resources upon which they depended and destroy their already shaky economy. The post-Love Canal activism also created an aggregate of resistance groups that developed a new synergy. On regional and national levels, networks sprang up quickly to put local activists in touch with each other and to disseminate the most up-to-date information about the emerging field of hazardous waste management and remediation. These groups had access to information and also had experience in organizing against toxic contamination. Concerned Citizens were in need of both, and the emerging activist networks provided the necessary information for them to organize significant resistance.[11]

The "not in my back yard" (NIMBY) response diagnosed the problem as a technical issue: where best to put the soil? Citizens pressed for alternative solutions based on technical information they could trust from experts who were not affiliated with state or federal agencies. The technical arguments against the Warren County site presumed that a suitable site did exist someplace else; the unacceptable properties of the Afton site were often compared to the properties of other locations, both real and hypothetical:

> We think that the site chosen for the PCBs should be safe beyond any reasonable doubt whatsoever. In as much as there appear to be sites elsewhere in the state of North Carolina that can handle PCBs, we feel that it is only reasonable that the state would look at those sites and reject the Pope site.[12]

Better yet, according to citizens, why not truck the contaminated soil to the chemical waste landfill in Emelle, Alabama? The site had been approved by the EPA, had already been built, and had been operating successfully. In January 1979, Chemical Waste Management (CWM), owners of the Emelle landfill, estimated that shipment and disposal of the contaminated soil would cost $8.8 million.[13] It seemed to citizens that the only reason for not using the Alabama site was the high cost involved. Citizens were outraged that the state would jeopardize their health, the health of future generations, and the shaky economy in order to save money. How could the state put a price tag on the value of lives in Warren County? In 1979, shipment to Alabama, no matter what the cost, became the official position of Concerned Citizens. Ken Ferrucio, the leader of the group, made this clear at an EPA-sponsored public hearing: "PCB on the shoulders and PCB in temporary storage [should] be sent to Alabama, one of the three legal national dumping sites where I understand every precaution has been taken, unlike the situation here in Warren County."[14]

Residents of Warren County traveled to the landfill in Alabama to see if it was an acceptable place for the contaminated soil and found it suitable: "They buried this stuff 70 feet deep with 630 feet of clay under that."[15] The technical arguments were clearly an "anywhere but here" discussion. Once the county entered the judiciary system with its civil suit against the state and the EPA, it was forced to continue in this vein, arguing over technical problems with the site and flaws in the design of the landfill. If the county did not agree that a safe disposal method was possible, as was presumed under the federal regulations, then what would the state do to remediate the problem? There had to be a solution; it was unthinkable that this situation could not be fixed with the application of sound science. As a result, once the court ruled that the design improvements transformed the Warren County property into an acceptable site, the county was forced to accept the landfill. In the spring of 1982, the county withdrew its suit after securing the design changes and gaining the deed to the 120 acres of the Pope farm which was not to be used for the landfill. The court lifted the injunction, and the state began construction of the landfill in June, with the contaminated soil scheduled to begin arriving at the site in September.[16]

The Coalition Is Formed

Late in the summer of 1982, with the soil delivery looming, the citizens made a drastic shift in their strategy by moving toward disruptive collective action. Protests were not generally a part of the cultural experience of the white members of the group, and when faced with the reality of organizing a direct action, Concerned Citizens realized that it lacked expertise. In fact, demonstrations in the South were typically associated with black civil rights activism often leveled against local whites. During the tumultuous 1960s in Warren County, many confrontations between black and white residents occurred in the middle of Warrenton on Main Street. Prior to its association with black civil rights groups, Concerned Citizens reached out to both Ronald Reagan and Jesse Helms. . . .

Given the long history of racial discrimination and tension, it was most astonishing that a largely white opposition group in a rural southern county would reach out to black protest leaders for help and advice to revive their movement. It was even more astonishing that many whites, although not all, stayed and participated in the meetings, marches, and acts of civil disobedience. The nature of toxic contamination, the political climate in the county, and the tenacity and coalition-building skills of opposition leaders made these unlikely partners collaborate.

The white land owners involved in Concerned Citizens were distressed over the potential contamination of groundwater and the destruction of economic development plans. More importantly, Warren County residents were angry that a decision about the use of county land had been made without their input. Anger about the loss of local control over land use decisions was a powerful mobilizing factor.[17] This central issue in hazardous waste policy became the key to transforming the Warren County case from just another NIMBY resistance to a defining moment for the environmental justice movement. Fear of losing control over a local decision motivated Concerned Citizens to change their strategy to direct action and to build a coalition with civil rights activists. . . .

In addition to anger over losing control of a local land use decision, the long-standing animosity between black residents and the white county board also played a significant role in building the coalition. When the county board settled the case with the state, the 1982 elections were only a few months away. The court settlement gave blacks in the county another reason to vote against the largely white political establishment. Black residents had struggled to gain equal representation in county decision making since the passage of the Voting Rights Act of 1965, which removed prerequisites for registering and voting.[18] After 1965, there was a significant increase in the number of blacks registered to vote in the county, and by 1976 an equal number of blacks and whites were registered. . . . The same African-Americans who led the voter registration campaign in the county played key roles in the direct action protests at the landfill during the autumn of 1982, and the two issues of black political power and landfill opposition were inextricably linked.[19] In the time between the county's withdrawal of the suit and the general election of 1982, the overall number of voters registered in Warren County increased by 30 percent; 65 percent of the overall increase came from nonwhite registrants.[20] Since race still determined the outcome of elections, the huge increase of black registered voters changed the political landscape. In November 1982, African-Americans won a majority of offices in the county, including a majority of seats on the county board, the sheriff, the registrar of deeds, and the state assembly representative. After the election results, the *Durham Herald* proclaimed the county "Free at Last!"[21]

In the summer of 1982, while Concerned Citizens were building a coalition with local civil rights activists familiar with direct action campaigns, the local chapter of the NAACP [National Association for the Advancement of Colored People] brought another suit against the state, arguing that the high percentage of minority residents was one factor influencing the decision to site the landfill in Warren County. Given that there were nearly eight hundred thousand acres of land with clay soils less permeable than those in Warren County and that the state had to request three waivers to qualify for a permit for the Warren County site, the NAACP argued that there must have been other than technical reasons for choosing the site in Afton. The plaintiffs argued that the large black population in Warren County was the other reason for the state's decision, but the court did not agree:

> There is not one shred of evidence that race has at any time been a motivating factor for any decision taken by any official—State, federal or local—in this long saga. . . . . Although population *density* was understandably a criteria in the selection process, absolutely nothing indicates that the racial makeup of the population influenced the decision. Failure of the plaintiffs to raise any question of race throughout the laborious process of public hearings and earlier lawsuits leads to the conclusion that its injection at this late hour is a last-ditch effort to forestall or prevent the project from being completed.[22]

In fact, the issue had been raised by Warren County residents at the 1979 EPA hearing and in public statements by the local NAACP chapter, but no one on either side of the controversy was ready to delve into its implications. The state did not take these sentiments seriously enough to even dispute them, nor did Warren County attempt to marshal evidence in support of the claims. Instead, black and white citizens supported the official stance of the county board who were pursuing the case in court. As the county became more immersed in the court cases and the environmental impact statement, the discussion became more centered on the technical merits of the site and the quality of the landfill design. Out of necessity, landfill opponents engaged more fully in the language of environmental law. There was no room in that language for the larger social issue of environmental racism. In July 1982, when they attempted to raise the issue of discrimination, the court easily dismissed it for lack of any earlier serious discussion on the topic. . . .

Leon White, who had orchestrated much of the voter registration drive in Warren County, had many years of experience in organizing civil rights demonstrations and had the institutional support of the UCC [United Church of Christ] behind him. One of the most significant impacts from the involvement of White was his connection with the Reverend Benjamin Chavis, the renowned leader of the "Wilmington Ten."[23] As a member of White's UCC congregation located in Warren County, Chavis became an important symbolic leader for local blacks involved in the protests. He delivered a motivational speech to the group, and on the third day of the protests he was arrested while leading a group of activists in blocking Department of Transportation trucks.[24]

Chavis evoked respect from African-Americans, caution from law enforcement, and intense interest from the media. Locals felt that participation from Chavis meant he was still connected to his roots in northeastern North Carolina. Because he had a national reputation, it also meant that their local struggle was meaningful in a larger arena. Although law enforcement officials were not surprised by his participation nor taken off guard by it, Chavis gave the action a serious connotation, with a potential for extreme disruption, and perhaps even violence. His position also gave the newly embraced environmental issue legitimacy among African-Americans. After his brief experience with the Warren County residents, Chavis became the chief crusader among civil rights leaders combating what he called "environmental racism." Several years later, he convinced the UCC to fund an extensive study of the relationship between the location of toxic waste and the racial composition of the surrounding community. The result, *Toxic Waste and Race*, became a cornerstone of the environmental justice movement. The participation of Chavis, his influential position with African-Americans, his influence in national policy arenas, and his dynamic personality catapulted the new linkage between environmentalism and civil rights into the minds and hearts of a multitude of Americans—blacks, whites, civil rights activists, and environmentalists.[25]

In addition to expertise from the UCC, local opponents received support from the Southern Christian Leadership Conference (SCLC), the organization associated with Martin Luther King and the nonviolent civil rights actions of the 1950s and 1960s. The initial involvement of the SCLC led to the arrest of Walter E. Fauntroy, a nonvoting member of Congress from the District of Columbia, and increased media attention associated with this unusual occurrence.[26] When Fauntroy returned to Washington, he initiated the first government-sponsored inquiry into the correlation of race and income with landfill sites. The subsequent General Accounting Office (GAO) study influenced Chavis to support the more extensive *Toxic Waste and Race* and started the drive toward documenting discrimination in siting and in environmental hazards. Although questions remain about the validity of the results and the use of the conclusions for forming public policy, the GAO study has had a large impact on the development of the environmental justice movement and on the resulting changes in policy.[27] Because an influential black political leader like Fauntroy was in a position to marshal government resources on behalf of Warren County activists, the environmental justice movement took its first step toward documenting its central claim.

With the assistance of experienced civil rights organizers, a direct action campaign against the landfill was waged from September 15 through October 12, 1982. The number of participants ranged from a handful to several hundred, and the protest successfully disrupted the orderly and efficient completion of the landfill. . . .

The power of the protests came from the repertoire of actions honed by civil rights activists two decades earlier.[28] Observers saw the similarities immediately:

> The whole thing was a revival of the whole civil rights stuff—the tone, the look, the cants, the point. It was more like a civil rights protest than any NIMBY opposition. I had been to other NIMBY type meetings in wealthy communities with all kinds of technical stuff about why not near them. There was some of that [in Warren County] but the tone of the marches was more "you are doing this to us because we're poor and black."[29]

Participants were familiar with the pattern for activism and could easily fall into its rhythm. Although not all whites in the county were willing to join, the actions of the civil rights movement were familiar to both blacks and whites. Meetings at the local black Baptist church (located less than two miles from the landfill site), the high visibility of well-known African-American activists, the incorporation of prayer into all the protests, and the long-distance march—from Warrenton to Raleigh—were all part of an established program of civil rights activism familiar to both county residents and activists from other places who joined the locals.

The landfill situation also presented an opportunity for dramatic action. When the Department of Transportation trucks brought the contaminated soil from the road shoulders to the landfill, the protesters lay down on the road in front of the oncoming vehicles. None of the Warren County residents participating in the protests had ever "put their bodies on the line" in such a literal sense. This tactic of symbolically blocking the source of the contamination delayed the project and raised the visibility of the events, inviting more extensive media coverage and encouraging others to join the protests.[30]

Environmental Racism: Not in African-American Backyards!

African-Americans saw the hazardous waste landfill as an environmental problem for their county, but they did not align this environmentalism with their perception of traditional, mainstream environmentalism. As one participant explained, trying to distance herself from mainstream environmentalism, "African-Americans are not concerned with endangered species because we are an endangered species." The concern of the local activists seemed more closely aligned with public health, with threats to the places where people live, work, and play. The concept of contamination by synthetic chemicals enabled the addition of an environmental aspect to the civil rights framework, especially fears of both groundwater contamination and potential economic devastation from the stigma of the landfill. These two issues resonated with past experiences of African-Americans in the county: blacks had been victims of past transgressions at the hands of whites in power, resulting in excessive poverty, physical suffering, and even death. The landfill was the latest manifestation of their experience for the past several centuries. One participant, a local civil rights activist since the early 1960s, stated the case bluntly: "They use black people as guinea pigs. Anytime there is something that is going to kill, we'll put it in the black area to find out if it kills and how many. They don't care. They don't value a black person's life."[31]

Changing discriminatory land use decisions had been part of an earlier civil rights agenda, but the civil rights framing of the Warren County case added environmental, social, economic, and political dimensions to the problem. The contamination was thrust upon the community by the state and federal governments. Since government had failed many times in the recent past to protect blacks, it was not difficult to believe that another failure was imminent. Civil rights activists adopted an environmental perspective to protect African-Americans, their health, and the resources upon which they depended. This environmental viewpoint was in opposition to the government agencies that were charged with taking protective action, but did not protect all citizens equally.[32] . . .

Although not central to the landfill opposition, two mainstream environmental organizations did play a very small role in the landfill siting controversy: the state chapter of the Sierra Club and the Conservation Council of North Carolina, an influential organization started in 1969 by scientists, lawyers, and academics. While both groups offered suggestions to state officials about how to handle the cleanup and how to design the landfill, neither organization participated extensively, and both distanced themselves from the Warren County citizens once the protests began.

If an environmental perspective meant being against the environmental agencies and having a focus on hazards that threaten public health, then alliances with the mainstream environmental organizations were not necessary for the joining of civil rights with environmentalism. In fact, the tactics advocated by landfill opponents did not sit well with the traditional environmentalists in the state. They were uncomfortable with emphasizing the social dimensions of environmental issues over the technical and legal dimensions, and they were unwilling to engage in direct action.[33] The Sierra Club and the Conservation Council stayed on the sidelines, trying to work with the state and the EPA to find a resolution to this very difficult problem. While mainstream environmentalists focused on technical problems and eschewed direct action, environmentalism was transformed by the collective actions in Warren County. As a result, mainstreamers emerged as "outsiders" to the environmental justice movement, not setting the agenda, but responding to the agenda established by civil rights activists who embraced an environmental perspective through the actions in Warren County.

As the diagnosis of the problem began to include discriminatory siting based on race, the problem grew into something larger than Warren County's landfill. There were many Warren Counties out there, and perhaps many of these poor, predominately black communities were host to hazardous waste facilities. As Golden Frinks, an experienced organizer, explained:

> I did not know anything about it, so I did a little research. I called Atlanta and told Albert [Love] what I was involved in and wanted him to put it in the ear of Lowery. That I thought it was a good movement and thought he should become involved. I also wanted him to find out if there were other toxic waste dumps in black communities. They found it in South Carolina.[34]

This new definition of the problem had an important implication for Warren County: the shipment of the contaminated soil to Emelle, Alabama, was no longer a viable option. As it turned out, the largest hazardous waste facility in the nation had major compliance and regulatory problems and was also located in a poor town with a predominately African-American population.[35] Environmental racism cemented the problem within a victimization framework, where the injustices done impacted a class of victims beyond the local residents, enabling these residents to downplay the NIMBY aspect of their resistance. For white activists, poverty and ruralism marked residents as among the politically powerless. Environmental racism was the catalyst to a more comprehensive framework, but it was also the cause of a major chasm in the environmental justice movement, which became entrenched in trying to determine which factor, race or class, was a better indicator of the location of environmental hazards. This ongoing conflict within environmental justice began in Warren County.[36] . . .

The heritage of civil rights activism in the county impacted the organizing of the landfill opposition. Warren County activists were able to link with powerful African-American elites by renewing associations with earlier civil rights activism. Through reforms resulting from this activism, these individuals had gained access to official political institutions. These positions of power enabled the fledgling movement to raise a new issue—distributive justice of environmental hazards—in public policy debates. As these African-American elites rallied behind a cause that linked environmental integrity and economic justice, they embraced the notion that Tom Bradley had articulated a decade earlier: "The problems of poverty and environmental quality are inextricably intertwined."

Actions on behalf of environmental quality were not necessarily "distractions from the problems of black and brown Americans," but were instead an integral part of making daily life healthy, safe, and economically secure. Such a notion helped to blur the distinction between environmentalism and social justice causes. While this transformation did not eliminate elitism in the mainstream organizations or the potential regressive impacts from several environmental reforms advocated by these groups, challenges are now made by activists who have incorporated an environmental awareness into their cause and who can envision alternatives. Warren County and the unlikely coalition that formed there began the process of overcoming these limitations of the environmental movement.

NOTES

1. Robert Burns and his two sons were found guilty of violating TSCA. The elder Burns spent five years in prison, while his two sons received a probation term of five years. Robert Ward was found not guilty; however, he was found liable under CERCLA [Comprehensive Emergency Response, Compensation, and Liability Act] and ordered to pay damages to the Environmental Protection Agency and the state of North Carolina. As of 1995, the damages remain unpaid. Al Hanke, telephone interview by author, 15 March 1995; William Meyer, interview by author, tape recording, Raleigh, N.C., 25 May 1994.

2. PCBs are a group of over two hundred chlorinated hydrocarbons that had been used primarily in electrical transformers and capacitors since Monsanto began manufacturing them in 1929. They had a unique set of chemical properties (low flammability, low electrical conductivity, and high degree of chemical stability) that made them commercially attractive for the electrical industry, but that also led to many of the problems associated with their environmental and health hazards. Since PCBs are among the most stable chemicals, they remain for decades once released into the environment. They are not water soluble and easily accumulate in sediments, especially the fatty tissues of organisms. As a result, their concentration magnifies upward through the food chain. Thus, PCBs were ubiquitous in the environment and in human tissue by 1975. The Toxic Substances Control Act of 1976 banned the manufacture of PCBs and regulated their disposal. The intent was to eventually halt all use of PCBs. Marshall Lee Miller, "Toxic Substances," *Environmental Law Handbook*, 7th ed., ed. J. Gordon Arbuckle (Rockville, Md.: Government Institute, Inc., 1983).

3. Dollie Burwell, interview by author, Warren County, N.C., 22 May 1994.

4. "The protests marked the first time African Americans had mobilized a national, broad-based group to oppose what they defined as environmental racism." Robert D. Bullard, "Environmental Justice for All," in *Unequal Protection: Environmental Justice and Communities of Color,* ed. R. D. Bullard (San Francisco: Sierra Club Books, 1994), 5–6. "Warren County is important because activities there set off the national environmental justice movement." Benjamin Chavis, foreword to *Confronting Environmental Racism: Voices from the Grassroots*, ed. Robert D. Bullard (Boston: South End Press, 1993), 3. "The 1982 demonstration against the siting of polychlorinated biphenyl (PCB) landfill in Warren County, North Carolina, was a watershed event in the environmental equity movement." U.S. Environmental Protection Agency, *Environmental Equity: Reducing Risks for All Communities*, vol. 1, EPA 230-R-92-008 (Washington, D.C.: GPO, 1992), 6.

5. Commonly referred to as the "Group of Ten," the ten largest environmental organizations are the Wilderness Society, Sierra Club, National Audubon Society, National Wildlife Federation, Natural Resources Defense Council, Environmental Defense Fund, Defenders of Wildlife, National Parks and Conservation Association, Izaak Walton League, and Environmental Policy Institute. See Robert Gottlieb, *Forcing the Spring: The Transformation of the American Environmental Movement* (Washington, D.C.: Island Press, 1993) for a full explanation of the

collaborative efforts of the Group of Ten and their power in setting the national environmental policy agenda.

6. Department of Crime Control and Public Safety, "Final Environmental Impact Statement," 13 November 1982, RC-CCPS, File 236, Division of Records, State of North Carolina Archives, Raleigh, N.C.

7. J. K. Sherron, Negotiating Diary for PCB Storage Site, 1978, and J. K. Sherron to Carl Pope, 28 November 1978, RC-AG, File 2363, Division of Records, State of North Carolina Archives, Raleigh, N.C.

8. County of Chatham, Public Hearing Before County Commissioners, 11 December 1978, tape recording, RC-CCPS, File 236, Division of Records, State of North Carolina Archives, Raleigh, N.C.; Department of Crime Control and Public Safety, "Final Environmental Impact Statement."

9. Department of Crime Control and Public Safety, "Application for Cooperative Agreement between the U.S. Environmental Protection Agency and the State of North Carolina for the Construction of PCB Landfill and the Clean-up of PCB Contaminated Soil Along N.C. Roadways Using CERCLA or Superfunds," April 1982, RC-CCPS, File 697, Division of Records, State of North Carolina Archives, Raleigh, N.C.; David Levy, interview by author, tape recording, Washington, D.C., 16 December 1994; Meyer, interview; C. Gregory Smith, interview by author, Raleigh, N.C., 24 May 1994; John Moore to Dr. Martin Hines, 15 August 1978, RC-CCPS, File 697, Division of Records, State of North Carolina Archives, Raleigh, N.C.

10. Despite the long history of NIMBY resistance to locally unwanted land uses, hazardous waste facilities had not created a public outcry which hindered the implementation of policy until after Love Canal. See Andrew Szasz, *Ecopopulism: Toxic Waste and the Movement for Environmental Justice* (Minneapolis: University of Minnesota Press, 1994). For a historical perspective on NIMBY, see William B. Meyer, "NIMBY" Then and Now: Land-Use Conflict in Worcester, Massachusetts, 1876–1900," *Professional Geographer* 47 (1995): 298–308.

11. Ken Ferruccio, interview by author, tape recording, Warrenton, N.C., 24 May 1994; *Warren (N.C.) Record*, "Mass Arrests Made by Patrol," 22 September 1982, 1.

12. U.S. Environmental Protection Agency, "Public Hearing before the Environmental Protection Agency on the Matter of the Application to Dispose of Soil Contaminated with PCBs at a Selected Site in Warren County, North Carolina," January 1979, RG-CCPS, File 697, Division of Records, State of North Carolina Archives, Raleigh, N.C., 154.

13. Herbert L. Hyde to Governor James B. Hunt, memorandum, 23 January 1979, RG-CCPS, File 697, Division of Records, State of North Carolina Archives, Raleigh, N.C.

14. U.S. Environmental Protection Agency, "Public Hearing," 100.

15. Ibid., 149.

16. *Warren County v. State of North Carolina*, Civil Action No. 79-560-CIV-5, U.S. District Court, Eastern District of North Carolina, Raleigh Division, RC-AG, File 2363, Division of Records, State of North Carolina Archives, Raleigh, N.C.

17. N. Freudenberg, *Not in Our Backyards! Community Action for Health and the Environment* (New York: Monthly Review Press, 1984); Michael R. Greenberg and Richard F. Anderson, *Hazardous Waste Sites: The Cred-*

ibility Gap (New Brunswick, N.J.: Center for Urban Policy Research, 1984); Kent Portney, *Siting Hazardous Waste Treatment Facilities: The NIMBY Syndrome* (New York: Auburn House, 1991); Frank J. Popper, "The Environmentalists and the LULUS," in *Resolving Locational Conflict*, ed. Robert Lake (New Brunswick, N.J.: Center for Urban Policy Research, 1987).

18. For background on the Voting Rights Act, see U.S. Commission on Civil Rights, *The Voting Rights Act: Unfulfilled Goals* (Washington, D.C.: U.S. Commission on Civil Rights, 1981).

19. Burwell, interview; Charles Lee, interview by author, tape recording, New York, 8 February 1995; Mary Guy Harris, interview by author, tape recording, Red Hill, N.C., 2 September 1994; Florence and Edward Somerville, interview by author, tape recording, Afton, N.C., 30 August 1994; Leon White, interview by author, Warren County, N.C., 22 May 1994.

20. Voter Registration Records file, Board of Election Office, County of Warren, Warrenton, N.C.

21. "Free at Last," *Durham Herald*, 8 December 1982, 1.

22. *National Association for the Advancement of Colored People of Warren County, et al. v. Anne Gorsuch, et al.*, Civil Action No. 82-768-CIV-5, U.S. District Court, Eastern District of North Carolina, Raleigh Division, RC-AG, File 2363, Division of Records, State of North Carolina Archives, Raleigh, N.C., 9–10.

23. For details on Chavis, his struggles against wrongful imprisonment, the Wilmington Ten, and his political battles, see Lennox S. Hinds, *Illusions of Justice: Human Rights Violations in the United States* (Iowa City: School of Social Work, University of Iowa, 1978), and "Chavis Battling Reagan Policies," *Raleigh News and Observer*, 4 April 1982, 3:D.

24. His home was in Oxford, North Carolina, in a county adjacent to Warren and about twenty miles from the proposed landfill. By February 1997, Chavis had left the UCC and become a member of the Nation of Islam.

25. Chavis is often credited with coining the term *environmental racism*. For examples of his statements about environmental justice, see forewords in Bullard, *Confronting Environmental Racism*, and United Church of Christ, Commission for Racial Justice, *Toxic Waste and Race in the United States: A National Report on the Racial and Socioeconomic Characteristics of Communities Surrounding Hazardous Waste Sites* (New York: United Church of Christ, 1987); Charles Lee, ed., *Proceedings: The First People of Color Environmental Leadership Summit* (New York: United Church of Christ, 1992); House Committee on the Judiciary, Subcommittee on Civil and Constitutional Rights, *Environmental Justice: Hearings*, 103d Cong., 1st Sess., 1993, 11–14.

26. Marguerite Ross Barnett, "The Congressional Black Caucus: Illusions and Realities of Power," in *The New Black Politics: The Search for Political Power*, ed. Michael B. Preston, L. J. Henderson Jr., and Paul Puryear (New York: Longman, 1982), 28–54; Walter E. Fauntroy, interview by author, tape recording, Washington, D.C., 14 December 1994.

27. Sylvia N. Tesh and Bruce A. Williams summarized the five potential problems with the GAO report and the follow-up study completed by the UCC: (1) no examination of racial composition of the communities at the time of the dumping; (2) use of Zip codes to define a community leads to various sized communities exposed to hazards; (3) neither

report distinguished among new, state-of-the-art sites and aging, poorly run sites; (4) use of crude measures for both race and class; and (5) no demonstration made that living near hazardous wastes has an effect on one's health, by assuming that location leads to exposure, which leads to health effects. "Science, Identity Politics and Environmental Racism," unpublished manuscript, n.d., Department of Urban and Regional Planning, University of Illinois at Urbana-Champaign, 10–13 (author's personal file). The GAO attempted to overcome some of these shortfalls with an updated study, *Hazardous and Nonhazardous Waste: Demographics of People Living Near Waste Facilities,* GAO/RCED-95-84, June 1995. For a complete discussion of design and methodology for studies of the correlation between race and location, see Rae Zimmerman, "Issues of Classification in Environmental Equity: How We Manage is How We Measure," *Fordham Urban Law Journal* 21 (1994): 633–69.

28. Don Griffin, interview by author, tape recording, Charlotte, N.C., 19 January 1995; Jack Harris, interview by author, tape recording, Warrenton, N.C., 29 August 1994; Jane Sharpe, interview by author, tape recording, Chapel Hill, N.C., 20 January 1995.

29. Richard Hart, interview by author, tape recording, Chapel Hill, N.C., 18 January 1995.

30. Ferruccio, interview; Burwell, interview; Mary Guy Harris, interview.

31. Mary Guy Harris, interview.

32. Ballance, interview; Luther Brown, interview by author, tape recording, Soul City, N.C., 8 June 1994; Burwell, interview; Somerville, interview; White, interview.

33. Levy, interview; Sharpe, interview.

34. Golden Frinks, interview by author, tape recording, Edenton, N.C., 19 January 1995.

35. Connor Baily, Charles E. Faupel, and James H. Gundlach, "Environmental Politics in Alabama's Blackbelt," in *Confronting Environmental Racism: Voices from the Grassroots*, ed. Robert D. Bullard (Boston: South End Press, 1993), 107–22.

36. The most recent GAO report summarizes the ten most significant studies, showing varied and conflicting results. The new data from the GAO report itself indicate that "minorities and low-income people were not over represented near the majority of nonhazardous municipal landfills." *Hazardous and Nonhazardous Waste*, 4. For a strong argument against the evidence of environmental racism, see Vicki Been, "Locally Unwanted Land Uses in Minority Neighborhoods: Disproportionate Siting or Market Dynamics?" *Yale Law Journal* 103 (1994): 1383–1422.

V The Environ- mental Era

Responses to Nature in Distress

Mourning the broken balance,
the hopeless prostration of the earth
Under men's hands and their minds,
The beautiful places killed like rabbits
to make a city . . .
—Robinson Jeffers, "The Broken Balance"[1]

In the summer of 1999, Disney's Animal Kingdom sprouted up on a patch of soggy ground outside of Orlando, Florida. Behold the Disney imagination: just one 500-acre section of the park "brings to life" Kenya's 700,000-acre Masai Mara. Animal Kingdom offers first-rate "edutainment"—a hybrid of merrily satisfying fun and edifying enrichment for the whole family. Rooted in the World's Fair tradition, edutaining attractions now abound in America, but nobody does it better than Disney: "On safaris, riverboat rides and jungle trails, visitors can observe animals in natural settings, participate in exciting adventures and learn about the dangers facing wildlife worldwide."[2] The star attractions of Animal Kingdom are exotic, endangered species who have been saved from dwindling habitat, exposure to global climate change, and various other more insidious threats. Here in this artificially natural environment, they thrive.

It is a perfect fit, really; animals animated. Disney has been doing nature ever since Bambi, so this new park represents a culmination of sorts. And a second chance: Animal Kingdom came in the wake of Disney's failed attempt in the early 1990s to build a theme park near Manassas around the bright and bloody motif of the American Civil War. Obstructing the growth of Disney's World is akin to interfering with evolution. Having lost the third Battle of Bull Run, Disney determined to do its eco-project "with sensitivity," according to CEO Michael Eisner.[3] So the entire Kingdom is environmentally correct, featuring, for example, "recycled water" in the lagoons and exhibits telling visitors of the contributions that Disney makes to environmental conservation and encouraging them to follow the corporate example.

Long before Animal Kingdom, there were the garbarge-feeding bears of Yellowstone, who entertained visitors for decades. Frank Jay Haynes postcard image, author's collection.

Animal Kingdom represents the ultimate expression of nature romanticism, which has always preferred "natural settings" and well-planned "adventure" to unruly swamps and serendipity. Should we be distressed that in the postmodern age, a megabyte-driven, concrete-and-plaster nature facsimile is becoming as close as we believe we want or need to get to nature? It seems the perfect nature for a culture more removed from it than ever. As we have already seen, whatever the natural universe is—all of its biological, chemical, geophysical, mystical glory—stands apart from our own conceptions. Now, nature is what we say it is. And Animal Kingdom may be a metaphor for what American culture has made of it: the properly landscaped mall, the nature store within it, petting zoos, a rainforest CD-Rom, an SUV cruising into a Serengeti sunset. In its shimmering, feigning postmodern glory, nature is an emotional refuge, beautifully packaged. Nature in general, as D. W. Meinig has said of landscape in particular, is "an attractive, important, and *ambiguous* term."[4]

Artificial constructions of nature have become ubiquitous while the real thing has shriveled. In the second half of the twentieth century, Americans witnessed a seemingly endless stream of grim environmental news: acidified lakes, diminishing biodiversity caused by habitat loss, oil spills, toxic waste dumps, global warming, the ozone hole. But as it always has, the romantic image of nature reassures us. As the scope and nature of environmental problems have worsened, that inspiration has become more desperately needed than ever. Hence, Animal Kingdom. As Jennifer Price has argued, our nature constructions say much more about us—our fears and anxieties of degraded nature, our good taste in consuming nature—than they do about nature itself.[5] Take, as an added example, any manufactured, manicured subdivision in America. Please. Here, corporate landscapers replace 150-year-old oak and hemlock trees with perfectly vertical factory seedlings.[6] The builders of these bucolic communities insist on planting the trees precisely perpendicular to the horizon, not a degree off.

Beyond Animal Kingdom and suburban cul-de-sacs, Americans in the second half of the twentieth century responded in a multitude of ways to worsening environmental degradation. Part V offers a wide-ranging sampling of expressions from that age of mounting concern, when the more holistic and disquieting terms of "environment" and ecology supplanted "nature." Lyrical and literary reflections, bureaucratic, antibureaucratic, and professional responses, and philosophical redefinitions together provide a window on a time when Americans struggled to come to terms with a shrinking, besieged natural world. Robinson Jeffers offers a poetic elegy to the sudden loss of the passenger pigeon that symbolized how dramatic ecological change had become in the modern era; Lynn White probes the religious dimensions of environmental degradation; freethinker Edward Abbey challenges the more-tourists-is better paradigm of national park management and signals the emergence of a more militant environmental defense; an excerpt from Leslie Marmon Silko's classic Native American novel,

Ceremony, indicts modern civilization for its apparent contempt of indigenous people and the land itself; and Andree Collard's ecofeminism critiques patriarchy's exploitation of women and Earth.

Also included are more official, technocratic responses: the National Environmental Policy Act (1969), a landmark piece of legislation designed to help remedy the problem of severe human impact on the environment; and an excerpt from an American Forestry Association compendium, which holds fast to the axiom that science, technology, and better management can solve any environmental challenge. There is, too, a passage from Ron Arnold, an advocate of the "wise use" movement that emerged in the 1980s and 1990s as a virulent reaction to the rising tide of environmentalism and increased governmental regulation of the nation's public lands. Like the family visit to Animal Kingdom, these writings reveal as much about our civilization as they do a natural world in distress.

————

Robinson Jeffers belongs to the "Lost Generation" of writers who grew so deeply disenchanted with the increasingly banal culture and repressive forces of 1920s America that they literally withdrew from it—in Jeffers's case, to the remote isolation of the northern California coast.[7] As with many of this generation of American literati, Jeffers's "awakening" to a sharper consciousness came through the convulsive horror of World War I. Not subscribing to the antiwar sentiments of some of his contemporaries, Jeffers initially volunteered for service. But by 1916 the horrifically modern nature of the war had become clear; the aspiring poet had a family, and he wavered. Jeffers was seeking reclassification with Selective Service when the Armistice was declared. The first modern global conflict had forced in upon his mind deep questions about the nature of humanity. Jeffers came to the sobering conclusion that war was a natural condition of men. His ambivalence and torment over the Great War, Jeffers later wrote, "made the world and [my] own mind much more real and intense." It "brought a kind of awakening" to the hypocrisy of humanity in the modern age.[8] How could men such as President Woodrow Wilson proclaim international progress in the face of such slaughter? Forget other men; man's inhumanity to the universe was unforgivable. Jeffers saw the modern condition, epitomized by the war, as an affront to life itself.[9]

Although he never saw battle, Jeffers's personal anguish over the World War thus became for him an intellectual and emotional watershed. He resigned himself to the extreme fallibility of the human species and focused his mind's eye upon the place where he and his wife, Una Jeffers, had arrived in December 1914, "just after the world began its violent change." As he later recalled, on the still romantically isolated coast of northern California,

> for the first time in my life, I could see people living—amid magnificent unspoiled scenery—essentially as they did in the Idyls or the sagas, or in Homer's Ithaca. Here was life purged of the ephemeral accretions. . . . Here was contemporary life that was also permanent life, and not shut from the modern world but conscious of it and related to it, capable of expressing its spirit but unencumbered by the mass of poetically irrelevant details and complexities that make a civilization.[10]

Recalling Thoreau at Walden, this passage goes to the heart of what Jeffers saw at Big Sur, while suggesting also the hope that he had for his work. The poem that was Big Sur caught the essence of the beauty, integrity, and perpetuity that life should hold but which men had placed at risk. Standing on the rocky coast, Jeffers felt that essential tension of modern life at a stage far more advanced than Thoreau had seen on the surface of Walden Pond. Jeffers may have separated himself from society, but, like Thoreau and Annie Dillard, he could not cease to ponder it. Here, for the next several decades, Jeffers would mimic the seascape's capacity to "express the spirit" of that place "between permanent and contemporary life." Here he lived his work in the emotional space between nature and the world. Jeffers would distill awesome literary reflections of natural wonder, permeated increasingly with his inescapable awareness of a menacing civilization.

It was one thing to urge romantically, as Jeffers did in his poems of the 1920s and 1930s, the "beauty of things go on, go on," to celebrate the "roots of millennial trees [that] fold me in the darkness." But by the end of World War II, Jeffers was musing less upon craggy coastlines and was turning a sharp pen upon the human world. In doing so the poet lost favor with much of his audience and his publishers. He stubbornly refused "to tell lies in verse" or to "feign any emotion [he] did not feel."[11] Rather, "How shall one dare to live?" was the Thoreauvian question he posed in "Gale in April."

From his post-Great War beginnings, Jeffers's style had always been bold and primal. The "horrible beauty and stark elemental power" of his work, as one anthology described it, seem to have been inspired by both the rugged Big Sur seascape and a deeply religious background.[12] His father was a Presbyterian minister in Pittsburgh and came from a long line of fiercely dogmatic Calvinists who preached the fiery, righteous damnation of sinners. Although he ultimately abandoned Christianity, an apocalyptic cast colored much of Jeffers's work, particularly after about 1940.[13] That religious impulse also helped lead Jeffers to judge the human race guilty of unspeakable iniquities. From Manifest Destiny to the Nazi death camps, modern men had demonstrated an arrogant lust for power time and again. It became clear to Jeffers that Nature had served as both weapon and victim in that gruesome epic. Prefiguring the hard political edge of the Beat poets to come, Jeffers named names. That particularity demonstrated the historical continuum of the human condition and the futility of hoping for anything more noble.[14]

To fill the spiritual and intellectual void of Calvinist Christianity, to answer the grim destructiveness of humanity, Jeffers embraced a philosophy of inhumanism. His world view recognized the "splendor of inhuman things" and declared that humanity is but "a moving lichen/on the cheek of the round stone."[15] Conceit—that was the essential character flaw in Homo sapiens. "A day will come," Jeffers wrote in the highly controversial *The Double Axe*, "when the earth/will scratch herself and rub off humanity." Fear not death, urged Jeffers, for that day would bring redemption. The earthly end of our individual human lives was more significant than the death of, say, a snail, only in that our demise would return us to our "better nature, the nobler/elements, earth, air and water."[16] The snail needs no such deliverance.

In the meantime, it is oneness—with rocks and trees, reptiles and amphibians, insects and stars—this divine sense of *connectedness with all*, Jeffers believed, that was the highest state of mind and soul to which men could aspire. Indeed, "seeing beyond and around the human race" was for Jeffers the key to maintaining "emotional sanity" in the face of human history.[17] One might think of inhumanism as Aldo Leopold writ large—on the tablet of the galaxy.

"Passenger Pigeons" (Selection 25) is framed by these large themes: life and death, the magnificence of the universe, and the self-inflated significance of humanity. In this poem, Jeffers offers a sardonic, feigned supplication to Death to spare the human species. It is a sort of history of human-induced death, through eons of time: from the passenger pigeon to its ultimate expression in the splitting and exploding of the atom. Invoking the late-nineteenth-century white prairies of rotting bison bones, he darkly suggests that the same fate may well await humanity. A litany of modern human achievements that have made us go farther and faster with more deadly force than ever before only intensifies the distressing rhetorical question to which he has been leading: Human extermination? It was possible, even likely. But what of it? The Earth and the universe of which it is only one part will barely notice and may not mind our passing.

Rachel Carson's *Silent Spring* and the growing environmental consciousness of the 1960s prompted a broad search among historians, ecologists, and other critics for, as Lynn White, Jr., put it, "the historical roots of our ecologic crisis." In his influential 1967 article written for the journal *Science* (Selection 26), White laid blame squarely at the door of Judeo-Christian teleology. Christianity, White theorizes, suppressed or destroyed outright pagan animistic religions the world over that held all things in nature to be sacred and alive, supplanting them with the belief that men stood above and apart from the rest of a mechanistic universe. He argues that humanity has lived the past 1,700 years largely under the Judeo-Christian paradigm that has both advanced the exploitation of lands and people and justified ideologically the commandeering, destructive impulse. More than any other single force, White charges, Christianity, with its anthropocentrism and religiously charged, scientifically sanctioned exploitative conquest of various parts of the globe, is at the center of the current dismal state of environmental affairs. In White's view, the installation of Adam as the crowning act of Creation was Christianity's original ecological sin.

Not so fast. In his final paragraphs, White recounts that nearly a millennium ago a much different set of ideas about humans and nature emerged in Christian thought but, because of the strength of the forces they opposed, failed to reverse the course of events. The ecological teachings of Saint Francis of Assisi were repressed and romanticized by the dominant Christian ideology that assumed that endless scientific, technological, and industrial growth is a game plan phoned in by God. Francis put forth the principles of Creation's divinity and the imperative of ecological humility. He could see it coming in the thirteenth century: the brutal estrangement of men from God's holy work and, not inconsequently, from one another.

The great realization in Lynn White's article, however, is that the crisis of the planet is rooted not in the inadequacy of laws, nor in science and technology and capitalism, but rather in a failure of the human soul—a potentially transformative idea, but slow to take root among American environmentalists, comfortably situated in the realm of secular humanism. Nearly thirty years after White's article, a broadly multidenominational movement to reconnect religion and ecology finally took hold.[18] Recognizing that virtually every religious sect—Judaism and Christianity included—has from the beginning deemed Creation to be sacred, religious leaders began to come together in the 1990s to confront what they saw at bottom as a crisis of the spirit. For their part, environmentalists increasingly acknowledged what so much of twentieth-century environmental history has painfully illustrated: laws are never enough.

As a native of the place, I have come to wonder something about the warm and lovely but wholly prosaic landscape of southwestern Pennsylvania. What is it about this region of mined-out hillsides and industrialized river valleys that has generated in the twentieth century some of the most eloquent and powerful writing about both nature and the troubled relationship between modern Americans and the natural world? The place that Hamlin Garland once called "hell with the lid off" seems to inspire critical thinking about the sublime technological power, environmental cost, and human sacrifice of the modern industrial age. No surprise, perhaps, since this is a place where as late as 1942 people drove with their headlights on at noon because of the thickness of the smoke, and where women used to sweep daily from their houses and sidewalks the soot that fell like dew, three shifts and twenty-four hours per day. Then again, it may be geographical coincidence that links the work of Robinson Jeffers, Rachel Carson, Annie Dillard, and Edward Abbey; indeed, all moved away, finding the spiritual epicenters of their nature writing in places far from Pittsburgh. Moreover, their environmental literature has less to do with a sense of that place than with more universal concerns. From what Carson called a "sense of wonder" has come the sharply critical view of the chasm that has opened up between civilization and the nonhuman world.

In the case of Ed Abbey, call it a sense of outrage. How, and from whence, comes a socially challenged, malcontent lover of the wild such as Abbey? As his brother Howard recalled, the temperament of the father, Paul Revere Abbey, forecast that of the son: "anti-capitalist, anti-religion, anti-prevailing opinion, anti-booze, anti-war, and anti-anyone who didn't agree with him."[19] Paul Abbey was a fiercely independent soul who would take any job to sustain his family without government help, who found religion in the movement of a rabbit through the woods, who would quote Walt Whitman to anyone who would listen. From this coarse and craggy man Edward Abbey received his great skill as a social critic. An artistic sensibility derived from Abbey's mother, Mildred, who raised a family, gathered and sowed wildflower seeds, taught school, and played the organ for the local choir.[20] From the woods came everything else. The Big Woods, actually, for that was the moniker the Abbey children hung on the thicket of Appalachian wilderness that bordered the nearby tiny mountain town of Home, Pennsylvania, where they grew up. "Dark glens of mystery and shamanism," as Abbey later described the area.[21]

The industrial landscape of the Pittsburgh region, ca. 1930, from whence numerous "nature writers" have come. Author's collection.

Although one could still get lost in the Big Woods, the Abbeys and their neighbors knew their way: where and how to trap raccoons and cultivate wildflowers, when to tap the maple trees. Born and raised in a place as close to frontier living as one could get in the twentieth century, Edward Abbey is a purely unvarnished American figure. His rugged background had given life not only to an unyielding love of wild nature but also to an antiestablishment individualism, a Jeffersonian belief that a little mischievous anarchy in a higher cause was noble and righteous and good for the country. By the time he was twenty, Abbey had begun a life in opposition to the state and all of its works. The FBI started its Abbey File after seeing a notice he posted on a bulletin board at Indiana State Teachers College calling for civil disobedience against what President Dwight Eisenhower would soon refer to as the "military industrial complex."[22] Clearly he was a man not only defiant but a beat ahead of his time.

Although he carried the earthy spirit of Appalachia for the rest of his life and returned to the mountains often in his final years,[23] Abbey found home away from Home in the lonely and forbidding desert of the Southwest. It was the West—especially its southwest corner—that gave life to his twenty-one books of fiction and essays that collectively represent a mix of natural history and principled, occasionally caustic social commentary. Abbey began his life in the West in 1947 as a student at the University of New Mexico. Like much of America, Albuquerque in the postwar era was a place of heady growth and blinding optimism. A sprawling complex of military bases and nuclear weapons sites from Roswell to Los Alamos fueled the region's rapid development. In the early years of the Cold War, the city exemplified everything that was right with America.

Abbey, however, did not see the region or his country in the same blithely optimistic light. He was more philosophically attuned to Beatnik poets such as Allen Ginsberg than the corporate manager-in-training young men of the late 1940s were supposed to be. Like the Beats who rejected the middle-class conformity of gray flannel suits, suburban ranch homes, and fallout shelters, Abbey resisted America's intoxicating, insatiable consumerism and oozing growth across the countryside. He saw what *Life* magazine called "the flowering of American capitalism" as "the ideology of a cancer cell" that was eating away at the traditional goodness of his country, at its very soul.[24] For Abbey, the soul was the land, and the land was the West. As one biographer recounted, Abbey did not see the mythical, heroic West of popular fiction writers Zane Grey and Louis L'Amour.[25] Instead, he saw a region that, while still representing the ideals of freedom, personal liberty, and renewed democracy that historian Frederick Jackson Turner celebrated a half-century earlier, was rapidly becoming something else. This "slickrock desert" that lay "beyond the end of the roads,"[26] this last best hope for American freedom, was being turned over to Pentagon overlords and the agribusiness, cattle, energy, timber, and tourism industries. The American West was being incorporated. He could not bear to look—without, that is, taking up his pen against these changes.

Beginning with his Master's thesis and continuing for the next forty years, Abbey's fiction and essays promulgated the notion of political anarchy targeted at these perceived enemies of the land. In *Jonathan Troy*, his first (and admittedly bad) novel, the author revealed his love of the natural world (in this case, his mountain home) and his penchant for anarchistic characters who would fight to save, as he later said, all of "the most beautiful [places] on Earth."[27] Troy mourns the kind of environmental damage being documented in those years by Harry Caudill, speaking of the "slow sulfurous creek . . . boney piles of waste from the mines, of yellow rock and red ash, with flames creeping like blue spirits from pits and craters in the smoldering mass."[28]

In his books about the West, Abbey challenged the moral authority and very legitimacy of those making the same kind of mess of things there. East or West, the root of all evils, Abbey asserted, was the "excesses of the nation-state" that served neither the environment nor the common people of the West. He declared that to save the region from ruin would require complete "decentralization of the State's political, economic and military power."[29] Abbey had no illusions that the state would relinquish power willingly; its hand would need to be forced, subversively. So in love with the West was Abbey, so passionate in carrying the torch of American individualism that he saw in that landscape, he could advocate—most famously in an incendiary work of fiction called *The Monkey Wrench Gang*—acts of "Eco-Defense" such as the relatively modest gesture of removing survey stakes that ends our selection from *Desert Solitaire*. Although Abbey had not intended it, the former book helped to give life to the militant environmental group Earth First!, which advocated "eco-tage" (for example, forest occupation and tree-spiking to prevent clear-cutting).

His position was not an ill-considered reactionary one. As James Bishop has chronicled, Abbey read and thought long and hard about the "morality of violence," pondering the question of whether violence against the property of the state or corporation was justified when those institutions had wrought injury upon treasured environments that people had called home. Abbey argued that Americans had "the right to resist and . . . the obligation . . . to defend that which we love." A serious student of history, he determined that to defend against voracious development the land—the primal font of democracy, as Frederick Jackson Turner most famously argued—was utterly American. For the purpose of such resistance was not only to save the land, but also to regenerate populist democracy.[30]

Arches National Monument (later National Park) in Utah, where Edward Abbey spent several seasons trying to subvert "industrial tourism." Photographs by Mary Ellen Magoc.

Abbey the radical, then, might also be viewed as the truest conservative, dedicated to the restoration of Jeffersonian Old America: small-town rural living, deep affection for and rootedness in the land, and independence for a responsible citizenry. He remained stubbornly committed to those ideals in the face of the sweeping inexorability of the industrial corporate technocracy and welfare state that came to define America in the second half of the twentieth century. Selective, creative acts of violence, or the threat thereof, would serve as the most effective means of shaking the institutions of power so as to constrain or even reduce their totalitarian tendencies.[31]

Sprawling subdivisions, one form of the kind of progress deplored by Edward Abbey, have reached their way into such remote corners of the nation as the perimeter of Yellowstone National Park. Photo by Tim Crawford. *Courtesy Tim Crawford and Greater Yellowstone Coalition, Bozeman, Montana*

Abbey's social criticism sharpened with his two seasons in 1956–57 as a park ranger in Utah's Arches National Park, resulting in *Desert Solitaire* (Selection 27). His ruminations on his happiness with his job in the "most beautiful place on earth" are rudely interrupted by the "madman" road surveyor who has come to fulfill the Master Plan. Exemplifying the larger American myth of Progress in the postwar era, the Master Plan calls for roads to bring more millions of tourists to Arches. To transform America's national parks into cash cows—that, in Abbey's view, seems to be the mission of the politicians and bureaucratic stewards of the system in the postwar era. In confronting the dilemma of democratic access versus preservation—a debate as old as the parks themselves[32]—Abbey typically pulls no punches. He casts his net of culpability far and wide: automobiles, park rangers, and lazy, overpopulating Americans are together leading the parks headlong into a nightmarish world of asphalt, concrete, and steel.

His plan to forestall that nightmare had about as much chance of being enacted as the Black Panther Party's platform did in 1968.

Nevertheless, to stem the onslaught, Abbey argues, Americans had to be challenged. A patriot and visionary, Abbey was also a realist who bore no illusions about the momentum of Progress. He would doubtless have been amazed to see that by the late 1990s some of his ideas appeared prophetic: the Park Service began to curtail the numbers of automobiles, roads, jet skis, and snowmobiles allowed in the most congested parks; and further, the government was actively considering the destruction of several hydroelectric dams in the West.

It is strange what images some books conjure up. In message and tone, *Desert Solitaire* has always recalled for me Dr. Seuss's classic children's book of the same era, *The Lorax* (1971).[33] This is the story of the grumpy, curmudgeonly creature who berates "the Old Oncler" for having cut down all the truffula trees and destroyed the land where the "grickle grass used to grow"—all in the name of "biggering and biggering" because "money, money is what everyone needs." Like Abbey, the Lorax makes a nuisance of himself, pleading and nagging for an end to what he sees as a continual, mindless path of progress-for-progress's sake, a course that breeds a mountain of stuff for human consumption but in the end a diminished quality of life. Finally, the Old Oncler comes to his senses. He wants the Lorax and the truffula trees to return. They won't, he concludes, unless you, dear reader, do something.

_____

The environmental crisis of the 1960s coincided with one of the periodic infatuations of Americans with Native American culture. From John G. Neihardt's *Black Elk Speaks* to T. C. McLuhan's *Touch the Earth* to Paula Gunn Allen's *The Sacred Hoop*, Native American works drew sharp contrasts between indigenous and Euro-American perceptions of the natural world.[34] Leslie Marmon Silko's *Ceremony* (Selection 28) is one of those books of extraordinarily rare power that can provoke emotionally painful reflection and personal transformation. I am not alone in this assessment. In the first of a long series of letters he and Silko wrote to each other, Pulitzer Prize-winning poet James Wright called it "one of the four or five best books I have ever read about America." His "very life [meant] more to [him]" because of Silko's first novel.[35]

Ceremony is a fictional exploration of a Laguna Pueblo Indian man's struggle to regain wholeness of mind, body, and spirit in the aftermath of World War II. On one level, this book can be read as an Indian analog of MacKinlay Kantor's novel, *Glory and Me*, which became the basis for the classic 1946 film, *The Best Years of Our Lives*. Kantor's story probes the severe emotional, physical, and economic challenges faced by many returning servicemen.[36] Likewise, *Ceremony* is centered on the story of Tayo, who returns from combat experience psychologically tortured and physically traumatized. Wracked by horrible memories of the war and by the "vague feeling that he knew something which he could not remember," Tayo is further devastated by what he sees upon his return home: drought in the land and degradation of his fellow veterans. He becomes mysteriously ill. Neither modern medicine, nor alcohol, nor sexual gratification can heal him, for it is Tayo's soul that is deeply wounded.

Only the wisdom of Laguna culture can restore him to wholeness. Tayo seeks the counsel of the elder, Ku'oosh, who suggests that the people themselves by their behavior had brought about the sickness in the land, that somehow the evil was linked with his own malaise, and that there lay in the earth the key to a healing redemption:

> This is where we come from, see. This sand, this stone, these trees, the vines, all the wildflowers. This earth keeps us going. . . . These dry years you hear some people complaining, you know, about the dust and the wind, and how dry it is. But the wind and the dust, they are part of life too, like the sun and the sky. You don't swear at them. It's people, see. They're the ones. The old people used to say that droughts happen when people forget, when people misbehave.[37]

Tayo finds comfort in basic sensory impressions of the pueblo: an adobe wall against his back, white gypsum dust between his fingers, "the world of crickets and wind and cottonwood trees." He begins to feel "almost alive again."[38] Ku'oosh then leads him to the mountains to medicine man Betonie, who takes Tayo on a journey of stories and ancient ceremonial healing rituals that begin to restore his health.

We find Tayo lying alone on a mountain, waking up from a rude encounter with a pair of Texas cattlemen. Although the Texans decide to pass on the fun of torturing an Indian in favor of poaching a mountain lion, their voices acutely open the gates of consciousness for Tayo. Instantly, he comes to understand what has befallen himself, his people, and the homeland. These near-final pages of *Ceremony* assail the spiritual impoverishment, technocratic reason, and numbing materialism that are hallmarks of the Nuclear Age. That is where, in the end, Silko leads Tayo to find peace: in the painfully astonishing revelation of what had become of the beautiful, "bright and alive" yellow uranium rock. He recalls Old Grandma telling him of having seen the brilliant flash of the Trinity Test on the early morning of July 16, 1945, as the world was propelled into the Nuclear Age. Because of a rock mined from his people's own homeland, humans could now instantaneously annihilate life on the planet.

In Tayo's epiphany on the mountain, he realizes the source of his haunting sense that somehow his fate was linked to that of the Japanese whom he had been asked to kill, but with whom he now felt he shared some ancient affinity. The global universality of the atomic bomb's destructive power, and the yellow uranium ore from which it is made, force the light of day. Now he can clearly see the connectedness of all life—an old truth from which he and his people had been blinded by the idolatrous ways of "the destroyers" who had long ago ensnared the whites. The malady was all of one piece: the degradation of his culture, his own illness, the faces of dying Japanese, and the sickness in his land. And only a return to the ancient ways could restore the full Laguna awareness that, as Silko has stated elsewhere, the fate of "the people and the land are inseparable."[39]

Central to the myths, stories, and traditions of Silko's culture, the notion of indivisibility has been largely foreign to the rest of us in the western world. Silko herself did not wholly appreciate the layered dimensions of oneness, nor the degree of its rupture, until after she wrote *Ceremony*. It was the desire to understand the ancient linkage of her Laguna country and its people that incited and informed the writing of the book. As she later wrote, in the Laguna world view:

> Rocks and clay are part of the Mother. They emerge in various forms, but at some time before, they were smaller particles or great boulders. At a later time they may again become what they once were. Dust.
>
> A rock shares this fate with us and with animals and with plants as well. A rock has being or spirit, although we may not understand it. The spirit may differ from the spirit we know in animals or plants or in ourselves. In the end we all originate from the depths of the earth. Perhaps this is how all beings share in the spirit of the Creator. We do not know.[40]

Coinciding with, and indirectly prompting, the popular revitalization of Native American consciousness in the late 1960s was a steady accumulation of environmental maladies. This grim litany of disasters was punctuated by smog in Los Angeles, the setting afire of a layer of oil and chemicals on the surface of the Cuyahoga River in Cleveland, and the largest oil spill in American history off the coast of Santa Barbara, California. Scientific studies and organized movements throughout the country brought to light numerous other crises of varying severity and scope. The term "nature" had denoted the preservation of national parks and wild lands: Nature Out There. The more expansive "environment" now suggested the protection of public health and the restoration of a deteriorating quality of life. These issues increasingly pushed their way into the headlines in the late 1960s and 1970s. The accumulation of ecological distress in the human environment resulted in the passage of an unprecedented wave of legislation. Hundreds of local, state, and federal laws were passed from the mid-1960s through the 1970s on issues from clean air and water to endangered species and toxic chemicals. This flurry of environmental legislation delivered the problems over to a wide range of experts to manage and regulate—epidemiologists, toxicologists, risk-assessment managers, cost-benefit analysts. Bureaucrats were to enforce the laws and gavel-wielding judges would interpret them.

The years 1969 and 1970 proved critical in the development of the envronmental policy structure. In 1969, Congress passed the National Environmental Policy Act (NEPA) (Selection 29), which officially recognized the significant impact that government had on the environment. The law created the Council on Environmental Quality in the Office of the President and more important, required every federal agency to prepare and circulate for public comment Environmental Impact Statements (EIS) on any proposed legislative or agency action affecting the quality of the environment. The passage of NEPA symbolized the apogee of a process begun during the Progressive Era of turning environmental problems over to scientific and technical experts. As public interest and environmental organizations were soon to discover, the EIS process, while significant, was vulnerable to manipulation by public agencies and private interests intent on pursuing a project. Its highly technical and complex nature proved enormously challenging to both participating citizens and interpreting judges.

Passage of NEPA set the stage for executive creation the following year of the Environmental Protection Agency (EPA). Establishment of the EPA consolidated and reorganized the federal government's mounting responsibilities to regulate air and water quality as well as nuclear, toxic chemical, and solid waste disposal. By the end of the 1970s the

EPA constituted the largest regulatory apparatus in the federal government. EPA scientists and public officials carefully studied and confidently pronounced the acceptable levels of mercury, dioxin, benzene, trichlorethynol, and other carcinogenic substances that the public should accept as safe and as part of the cost of a modern industrialized society. "Risk assessment," it came to be called. Such scientifically sound but numbingly technocratic approaches designed to reassure the public mind became the watchwords at the EPA and other environmental agencies. Complex and expensive though the scientific approach was, to prevent pollution at its source would have been infinitely more problematic.

As we saw in Part III, ecology was born in response to the scientific atomization of the natural world. That did not end with the creation of the environmental regulatory structure; indeed, the technical specialization of environmental problems emerged from nature's fragmentation. In an excerpt from *Natural Resources for the 21st Century* (Selection 30), published by the American Forestry Association (AFA), one can sense how strongly held the managerial view of nature remains in the minds of the professionals who are accountable for its stewardship. For natural resource specialists who composed this collection—hydrologists, wildlife managers, foresters, and the like—"nature" elicits discussions of baseline populations, natural capital, anticipated reproduction rates, habitat requirements, wolf supply, and so on. Nature is measurable and manageable. We know by now from whence such calculating precision comes. The AFA's compartmentalized and calculated view of the natural world stands on the firm shoulders of Descartes, Newton, and Bacon, who combined science, religion, and capitalism to separate heaven and earth.[41] During the Progressive Era, that paradigm separated good animals from bad, crops from weeds, sublime scenery from extractable resources. To make the most of nature and to do its work more efficiently, scientific managers separated nature into parts and calculated its loss by the numbers.

And they always did it objectively, ostensibly removing nature from the passions of politics and special interests. Editors of the AFA book argue that their work is largely free of "value judgments."[42] What happens to science once it leaves the laboratory, they suggest, is the work of others—politicians, economists, and corporate managers. Moreover, throughout this collection, recognition of ethical questions or serious distress to a particular resource is met with the reassurance that "better information" and technology, properly applied, "performs like a capital investment" to solve the problem.[43] The goal of nature managers is to "make natural resources more productive and plentiful."[44] Gifford Pinchot redux. It is a reassuring view, especially for those who say it. Who wants to believe that their job is to reduce the supply of ducks and trees? There is in the AFA's collection an intrepid, unflinching, and now almost anachronistic confidence in technology to solve virtually any environmental problem. Too much carbon dioxide in the atmosphere? We can design whole forests and new species to absorb excess carbon.[45] Native Americans "overfishing their quota" in the Great Lakes? They lack the complement of scientists and technicians to "manage the resource."[46] The scientific-technocratic panacea lives.

———

Although ecologists abound in these agencies and organizations, there is an enormous gap between the EPA-AFA style of commanding stewardship of nature and the more spiritual vein of ecological thought. Those differences center fundamentally on the matter-versus-spirit of nature. Head or heart, Western reason versus Eastern mysticism—the question runs deep into human history and throughout our culture. On the ground, in the real world, the mechanistic still largely rules, but it is being chased. In the early 1970s "deep ecology" emerged as a challenge to the notion that professionalized modern environmentalism—legal, scientific, and technocratic action—could remedy the ecological crisis. Deep ecologists argued that "shallow ecology," signified by well-meaning environmental laws and reasonably effective mainstream environmental groups, was woefully inadequate.

The new school called for relearning the old language of biocentrism. "Shallow ecologists," in the view of deep ecologists, "encourage the destructiveness and wastefulness of industrial society even as they seek to reform it . . . [They] argue that environmental regulations based on emission standards and tolerances represent licenses to pollute," as Peter Borelli has summarized.[47] Echoing Jeffers, taking Leopold's land ethic further, deep ecologists argue that the culture and language and importance of humanity are no greater or lesser than those of birds and wolves and fungi.[48] As Michael Tobias has said, "From the biosphere's perspective, the whole point of Homo sapiens is their armpits, aswarm with 24.1 billion bacteria."[49] Deep ecology, then, demands a complete reassessment of the human relationship with nature.

Many deep ecologists suggest misplaced fear as the ultimate source for much of the violence we do to ourselves and the earth. If one accepts that Earth is us, we may conclude that our treatment of the planet is a form of collective self-loathing. As long as we speak of life-giving, life-destroying natural events in militaristic terms—the battle against garden pests, the assault by El Niño-triggered bad weather—we know that fear is having its way with us. Like William Bartram, deep ecologists seek revelation in the slithering creatures of the planet and suggest that humans can truly learn from the natural world only when they accept an egalitarian universe. Our "profound unnaturalness," as Alice Walker has called it, has led us to assume that making the world over in polyethylene fiber optics is a good thing.[50] Deep ecologists bore into the American assumption that Earth is here for the taking. They propose that we limit our take from the natural world to that which allows for "abundant subsistence" and to those things we can re-create ourselves. But how to delimit the former? Middle-class Americans shrink from the suggestion that they now live in decadent abundance. We struggle "to make ends meet," that is, to pay for five hundred satellite television stations. As David Potter has written, the right of plenty is at the core of what we call the American character.[51]

The presumption of endless material bounty rests on the related assumed birthright of Americans to extract, cultivate, and develop natural resources to the fullest extent possible for the benefit of civilization. To be sure, that ideology, despite the growing consensus of Americans that there is an ecological crisis, has not dissolved. On the contrary, beginning in the late 1970s ardent advocates of unfettered free-market capitalism reacted assiduously to the blossoming of the environmental movement, the growing acceptance of ecological ideas in America, and especially the enlarged environmental regulatory structure of government at all levels. The strength of the reaction was evidenced in the late 1970s phenomenon known as the Sagebrush Rebellion, in which mostly large private interests (the cattle and mining industries, most notably) attempted to derail the increasingly environmentally sensitive federal management of public lands in the West. Their antigovernment message and deep financial coffers helped in 1980 to elect Ronald Reagan, who brought a deregulatory emphasis to Washington.

The ideals and fervency of free marketers evolved by the mid-1980s into a movement known as "wise use." Its leaders emphatically disavow any philosophical connection to Gifford Pinchot, the coiner of that phrase. Pinchot, in the eyes of wise users, was "just another bureaucrat who believed 'conservation' had to come by 'government control of resources.' "[52] The force of the wise-use movement emerged not only from well-funded large corporate interests but also from the legitimate fears and anxieties of small farmers and ranchers throughout the country whose economic livelihoods became increasingly precarious in the New Global Economy. Many became convinced that environmental regulations were at the root of their troubles. By the turn of the twenty-first century, the wise-use movement had focused much of the angst and bitterness of rural America on the central idea that environmentalism was undermining the American way of life. We hear a distillation of wise-use ideas from Ron Arnold, author of the 1996 polemic, *A Wolf in the Garden: The Land Rights Movement and the New Environmental Debate* (Selection 31). Wise-use thinkers and activists promised a vehement challenge to any notion of an environmental paradigm shift in the new century. (And increasingly succeeding: as I write, a wise-use attorney is poised to assume the role of U.S. Secretary of the Interior.) In its most extreme manifestation, fringe elements of the wise-use movement took to the old frontier impulse to violently resist a perceived overextension of federal authority. In the mid-1990s officials throughout the country, especially in the West, were reporting death threats and sporadic incidents of violent attacks against public employees charged with managing public lands.[53]

Finally, at the opposite end of the environmental philosophical continuum, there is ecofeminism. After a generation of exploratory literature and scholarship, a definitive ecofeminism remains elusive. Wide and deep, this school of thought grew out of both the movement for women's liberation from a patriarchal society in the 1960s and 1970s, and the perception by many women that the same male-dominated civilization that oppressed them also lay at the root of a threatening environmental crisis. Ecofeminism's central theme is that domination of, and violence toward, women and the earth are inextricably linked. In a brief excerpt from *Rape of the Wild: Man's Violence against Animals and the Earth* (Selection 32), Andrée Collard delivers a blistering indictment of that patriarchal paradigm.

The literary roots of what Collard calls "patriarchal ecocide" were unearthed by scholars such as Annette Kolodny. In her landmark study, *The Lay of the Land: Metaphor as Experience and History in American Life and Letters* (1984), Kolodny surveyed the literary terrain of male adventurers, explorers, and developers of this continent, finding that the language of conquest helped to establish the metaphor of "land-as-woman, both mother and mistress, [which lies] at the root of our aggressive and exploitative [environmental] practices."[54] She explains that male violence toward the earth in America is linked to that of woman because men long ago made a habit of seeing the continent as feminine and therefore ripe for subjugation. Kolodny argues that the "psychological patterns of regression and violation" associated with the four-hundred-year-old Virgin Myth figured forcefully in the course of environmental change in America.[55] Whatever role the psychosexual aggressions of men have played in the capitalizing of the continent one cannot quantify. Plainly, however, as feminist scholars such as Collard, Susan Griffin, and Mary Daly have argued, the alluring language of a virginal yet fruitful feminine continent is now dangerously anachronistic.

_____

Historians may chronicle, writers may brood, scientists may manage, and bureaucrats may regulate, but what do the rest of us have to do with nature? In their study of American environmental attitudes in

Artificial constructions of nature in American culture include the delineation of what is sacred and what is exploitable. This aerial view vividly illustrates that division, showing the border between Yellowstone National Park (left) and the clear-cut areas of the Targhee National Forest (right). Photograph by Tim Crawford. *Courtesy Tim Crawford and Greater Yellowstone Coalition, Bozeman, Montana*

the early 1990s, Edward O. Wilson and Stephen R. Kellert argued that the genetic human trait to have contact "with the rest of the living world" may be diminishing as nature has become simply unnecessary and irrelevant in the postmodern age. The *natural* impulse is atrophying, leading to "indifference or even hostility" toward the environment.[56] Thus, our redefinitions of nature reflect not only what is happening to it but also to us. The more our civilization covers over nature, the more removed from it we become, and, consequently, the more inclined we are to reinvent and reproduce facsimiles of it. Although nature writers and literary scholars may argue for a biocentric reenvisioning of nature and culture and suggest, as SueEllen Campbell has, that "all desire is not human,"[57] here in the land of too much milk and honey, every desire is human and *natural*. The fusion of nature and culture is so strong that we cannot distinguish the nature that is of our own making: the indoor rock climb, the wide-mouth bass over the mantel. Consider the "American Wilderness Experience," the first attempt to simulate wilderness in, of all places, a suburban shopping mega-mall, in California. Located forty miles east of Hollywood in the Ontario Mills mall, the American Wilderness Experience—or AWE, as its promoters prefer—guarantees an edutaining, "totally immersive wilderness experience . . . a unique blend of technology, ecology, and wildlife discovery."[58]

Nature is indeed what we say it is. In a provocative article ostensibly about sport fishing, Dana Phillips ponders the question to which this chapter has been sadly leading all along: "Is nature necessary?"

> Can an expression like "the natural world" have any meaning, if we have solved the puzzle of our estrangement from nature by making strange nature itself? In one New England state, biologists stock some streams with hatchery-bred albino trout ("mutants"): albino trout are popular with anglers, who find them easier to catch because they're so much easier to see . . . albino trout are stocked in streams just as hamburger is stocked in grocery stores, except that the hamburger probably has a longer shelf-life. . . . Such encounters with artifice, where one expects to see the real thing, suggest that we have found a substitute for "the natural world": in the postmodern world, nature no longer seems to be necessary.[59]

With albino trout, Animal Kingdom, and the American Wilderness Experience, who needs nature? Have we reached, in the words of Bill McKibben, "the end of nature"?[60]

Cynicism creeps in. Polls tell us that Americans overwhelmingly describe themselves as "environmentalists." We want to do the right thing. Yet, what is that? One person's natural refuge is a wise user's frontier. Moreover, most of us are connected to nature most of the time only by the artifice of mass culture. The exponential growth of nature catalogs, nature stores, and nature Web sites selling an amazing array of nature products testifies to that.[61] The escalating volume and deepening meaning of nature in television programming and Hollywood films parallel the rising popular concern over environmental issues.[62] Television programming, particularly, provides a reliable barometer of this popular concern for nature. Programs such as *Lassie* and *Green Acres* of the 1950s and 1960s gave us warm and zany takes on pastoral and outdoor themes. By the 1990s the environmental apocalypse had seeped into a wide range of dramas from *Northern Exposure* to *Dr. Quinn, Medicine Woman*, and nature documentaries and cable channels proliferated.[63] If, as critics such as McKibben and Campbell are correct, we have reached a point where nature is simply beside the point, the solace and affirmation of concern we get through the nineteen-inch screen of our culture is merely a palliative for our suppressed anxiety. We cling to an idyllic image of nature only to be rudely confronted by daily reports of icebergs falling off the edge of the Antarctic and two-headed frogs found in Minnesota lakes. In such a world, how long will our well-worn constructions of nature suffice?

In the end one must hope for more—that the combination of laws and regulations, scientists and regulators, righteous judges, conscientious corporations, and engaged citizens will overcome the ecological crisis. In an age of divided highways and split atoms, former farmlands and virtual communities, there is no going back to nature. We are in it. As Ted Kaczinski (the "Unabomber") proved rather hopelessly, this civilization is going nowhere. And as we have seen in Part V, some of the most brilliant and disturbing American nature writing is about that human world. The most profound of these writings challenge us to confront the hallmarks of modern America: the frenetic pace of humans, endless material accumulation, technological prowess, and scientific confidence. Across the dominant paradigm nature writers have sliced. They remind us that while we have intoxicated ourselves with the delusion of human mastery and the pursuit of happiness, in the geologic blink of an eye Americans have come precariously close to fracturing the bonds of heaven and earth that prevailed for countless preceding millennia. They urge us to search beyond the scientific and legalistic realms of parts per billion and liability mitigation for the ultimate spiritual and cultural roots of the dilemma. They suggest, finally, that the stories of humans and the places we inhabit bear the power to heal the breach and deliver us from the edge of apocalypse.

NOTES

1. Robinson Jeffers, "The Broken Balance," excerpted from *Not Man Apart, Lines from Robinson Jeffers: Photographs of the Big Sur Coast*, edited by David R. Brower (San Francisco: Sierra Club Books, 1965), 87.
2. Jane Ciabattari, "Step into the African Wild," *Parade* (February 22, 1998): 4–5.
3. Ibid., 5.
4. D. W. Meinig, "The Beholding Eye: Ten Versions of the Same Scene," in D. W. Meinig and John Brinckerhoff Jackson, eds., *In the Interpretation of Ordinary Landscapes* (New York: Oxford University Press, 1979), 1 (emphasis mine). On the broad notion of the vernacular landscape in America, see also the classic works by J. B. Jackson, *Discovering the Vernacular Landscape* (New Haven: Yale University Press, 1984); John F. Stilgoe, *Common Landscapes of America, 1580–1845* (New Haven: Yale University Press, 1984); and George F. Thompson, ed., *Landscape in America* (Austin: University of Texas Press, 1995).
5. Jennifer Price, *Flight Maps: Adventures with Nature in Modern America* (New York: Basic Books, 1999), see especially chapters 1–3.
6. The author speaks from personal experience (North Hills of Pittsburgh, April–May 1997). The names of these places all run together: Laurel Ridge, Pine Meadows, Laurel Meadows . . . I continue to look for one called Disappearing Woodlands.
7. Among the good accounts of the Lost Generation are Loren Baritz, ed., *The Culture of the Twenties* (1970); Roderick Nash, *The Nervous Generation: American Thought, 1917–1930* (1969); and Houston Baker, Jr., *Modernism and the Harlem Renaissance* (1987).
8. Robinson Jeffers, autobiographical "holograph" in Jeffers Collection, Humanities Research Center, University of Texas, Austin, 1918, in James Shebl, *In This Wild Water: The Suppressed Poems of Robinson Jeffers* (Pasadena, CA: Ward Ritchie Press, 1976), 9. Shebl also cites Melba Berry Bennett, *The Stone Mason of Tor House* (Menlo Park, CA: Ward Ritchie Press, 1966), 86.
9. Shebl, *In This Wild Water*, 10.
10. Jeffers, *Not Man Apart*, 30. The short quotation is excerpted from, as Brower notes, "a preface to a proposed book of poems and photographs"; the longer quotation is from the introduction that Jeffers wrote to *The Selected Poetry of Robinson Jeffers* (New York: Random House, 1938).
11. Jeffers, quoted by Shebl, *In This Wild Water*, 11.
12. Norman Foerster, ed., *American Poetry and Prose* (New York: Houghton Mifflin, 1934), 1444.
13. Frederic I. Carpenter, *Robinson Jeffers* (New York: Twayne Publishers, 1962), 22.
14. Shebl, *In This Wild Water*, see especially the first chapter.

15. Robinson Jeffers, *Themes in My Poems* (San Francisco: Book Club of California, 1956), viii, quoted by Shebl, *In This Wild Water*, 11.

16. Robinson Jeffers, *The Double Axe and Other Poems* (New York: Random House, 1948).

17. Quoted by Shebl, *In This Wild Water*, 31.

18. Trebbe Johnson, "The Second Creation Story: Redefining the Bond between Religion and Ecology," *Sierra* 83 (November/December 1998): 50–57. Most of this issue is devoted to the subject.

19. Quoted by James Bishop, Jr., *Epitaph for a Desert Anarchist: The Life and Legacy of Edward Abbey* (New York: Atheneum Press, 1994), 56.

20. Bishop, *Epitaph*, 54–56.

21. Ibid., 56, 58.

22. C. Wright Mills, *The Power Elite* (1956). See also President Eisenhower's farewell address of 1961 in which he warned the nation of the "military industrial complex."

23. Bishop, *Epitaph*, 76–78.

24. Ibid., Abbey quote on p. 20. The quintessential example of the Beatnik spirit is Ginsberg's "Howl," *Howl and Other Poems* (San Francisco: City Lights Pocket Bookshop, 1956). Gray flannel suits refers to Sloan Wilson's *The Man in the Gray Flannel Suit* (1955), a novel about a New York middle-class businessman.

25. Bishop, *Epitaph*, 86.

26. Edward Abbey, *Desert Solitaire: A Season in the Wilderness* (New York: Ballantine, 1968), 2.

27. Ibid., 1.

28. Edward Abbey, quoted from *Jonathan Troy* by Bishop, *Epitaph*, 96.

29. Abbey, quoted by Bishop, *Epitaph*, 90.

30. Bishop, *Epitaph*, 106–9.

31. Edward Abbey, *One Life at a Time, Please* (New York: Henry Holt, 1978), 179–80.

32. See Elizabeth McKinsey, *Niagara Falls: Icon of the American Sublime* (New York: Cambridge University Press, 1985); and Alfred Runte, *National Parks: The American Experience* (Lincoln: University of Nebraska Press, 1987, 2d rev. ed.).

33. Theodore Geisel (Dr. Seuss), *The Lorax* (New York: Random House, 1971). Although hundreds of elaborately illustrated, stridently well-meaning ecological picture books for children have been published since *The Lorax*, none has exceeded the simple brilliance of this classic.

34. In *Touch the Earth: A Portrait of Indian Self-Existence*, compiled by T. C. McLuhan (New York: Simon and Schuster, 1971), 15.

35. James Wright to Leslie Silko, August 28, 1978, *The Delicacy and Strength of Lace: Letters between Leslie Marmon Silko and James Wright*, edited and with Introduction by Anne Wright (St. Paul: Graywolf Press, 1986), 3.

36. Martin A. Jackson, "The Uncertain Peace: *The Best Years of Our Lives* (1946)," in John E. O'Connor and Martin A. Jackson, eds., *American History/American Film: Interpreting the Hollywood Image* (New York: Ungar, 1979); David A. Gerber, "Heroes and Misfits: The Troubled Social Reintegration of Disabled Veterans in *The Best Years of Our Lives*," *American Quarterly* 46, no. 4 (December 1994): 545–74.

37. Leslie Marmon Silko, *Ceremony* (New York: Viking Penguin, 1977), 47.

38. Ibid., 109.

39. Leslie Marmon Silko, *Yellow Woman and Beauty of the Spirit: Essays on Native American Life Today* (New York: Simon and Schuster, 1996), 85.

40. Leslie Marmon Silko, "Landscape, History, and the Pueblo Imagination," in Cheryll Glotfelty and Harold Fromm, eds., *The Ecocriticism Reader: Landmarks in Literary Ecology* (Athens: University of Georgia Press, 1996), 265.

41. Carolyn Merchant, *The Death of Nature: Women, Ecology, and the Scientific Revolution* (San Francisco: Harper and Row, 1980).

42. R. Neil Sampson and Fred Deneke, Introduction to *Natural Resources for the 21st Century* (Covelo, CA: Island Press, 1990), 5.

43. Peter C. Myers, Foreword to *Natural Resources*, xiii–xiv; and Sampson and Deneke, *Natural Resources*, 1, 3.

44. Sampson and Deneke, *Natural Resources*, 5.

45. Perry Gagenstein, "Forests," chapter 4, in Sampson and Deneke, *Natural Resources*, 97–98.

46. William G. Gordon, "Fisheries," chapter 9, in Sampson and Deneke, *Natural Resources*, 231.

47. Peter Borelli, originally in Borelli's "The Ecophilosophers," *The Amicus Journal* 10, no. 2 (Spring 1988): 30–39; reprinted as "Environmental Philosophy," in Carolyn Merchant, ed., *Major Problems in American Environmental History* (Lexington, MA: D. C. Heath and Company, 1993), 560.

48. Michael Foucault, *Politics, Philosophy, Culture: Interviews and Other Writings, 1977–1984*, trans. Alan Sheridan (New York: Routledge, 1988), 59; Bill Devall, personal correspondence, October 17, 1988; Bill Devall and George Sessions, *Deep Ecology: Living as if Nature Mattered* (Salt Lake City: Gibbs M. Smith, 1985).

49. Michael Tobias, ed., *Deep Ecology* (San Diego, CA: Avant Books, 1984), 23, quoted by SueEllen Campbell, "The Land and Language of Desire," in *The Ecocriticism Reader*, 132–33. Campbell (p. 132) and Tobias (p. 39). Arne Naess is the Norwegian philosopher who coined the phrase "deep ecology."

50. Alice Walker, from "Everything Is a Human Being," in *Living by the Word: Selected Writings by Alice Walker, 1973–1987* (New York: Harcourt Brace Jovanovich, 1988), 148.

51. David M. Potter, *People of Plenty: Economic Abundance and the American Character* (Chicago: University of Chicago Press, 1954).

52. "Wise Use: What do we believe?" (www.eskimo.com/~rarnold/wiseuse.html, November 2, 1999).

53. See David Helvarg, *The War against the Greens: The Wise-Use Movement, the New Right, and Anti-Environmental Violence* (San Francisco: Sierra Club Books, 1997); and the Web site for Public Employees for Environmental Responsibility, http://www.peer.org/wise_use/violence.html.

54. Cheryll Glotfelty, "Literary Studies in an Age of Environmental Crisis," Introduction to Glotfelty and Fromm, eds., *The Ecocriticism Reader*, xxix.

55. Annette Kolodny, "Unearthing Herstory," in Glotfelty and Fromm, eds., *The Ecocriticism Reader*, 177. This article reprints excerpts of *The Lay of the Land: Metaphor as Experience and History in American Life and Letters* (Chapel Hill: University of North Carolina Press, 1984).

56. Quote belongs to William K. Stevens, "Are Birds and Trees Our Best Friends?" *Pittsburgh Post-Gazette*, December 9, 1993, special from the *New York Times*. Stevens reviews Edward O. Wilson and Stephen R. Kellert, *The Biophilia Hypothesis* (New Haven: Yale University Press, 1993).

57. Campbell, "The Land and Language of Desire," in Glotfelty and Fromm, eds., *The Ecocriticism Reader*, 136.

58. B. J. Bergman, "The Great Indoors," *Sierra* (March/April 1998): 82.

59. Dana Phillips, "Is Nature Necessary?" in Glotfelty and Fromm, eds., *The Ecocriticism Reader*, 214–15.

60. Bill McKibben, *The End of Nature* (New York: Random House, 1989).

61. Price, *Flight Maps*, 167–206.

62. See for example, Chris J. Magoc, "The Machine in the Wasteland: Progress, Pollution, and the Pastoral in Rural Based Television, 1954–1971," *Journal of Popular Film and Television* 19, no. 1 (Spring 1991): 25–34. In the late 1980s the Environmental Media Association organized for the specific purpose of encouraging the infusion of environmental themes in all media (Culver City, CA: Tides Foundation, 1989).

63. Among the many "environmental" storylines on *Northern Exposure* (CBS, 1990–1995), I recall these: Ed's nuclear nightmare; the human body as a microcosm of a healthy environment, where millions of insects naturally make themselves at home; and the continuing story of "the Bubble Man," whose reaction to environmental toxicity forced him to live in a hermetically sealed home. Among her many crises, in one episode the star of *Dr. Quinn* (CBS, 1993–1998) discovered the source of community sickness to be mercury poisoning by an evil mine owner. She solves the problem by having the sinister capitalist agree to a holding pond for the waste.

25 Passenger Pigeons (1949)

Slowly the passenger pigeons increased, then suddenly
    their numbers
Became enormous, they would flatten ten miles of forest
When they flew down to roost, and the cloud of their rising
Eclipsed the dawns. They became too many, they are all dead,
Not one remains.
                And the American bison: their hordes
Would hide a prairie from horizon to horizon,
    great heads and storm-cloud shoulders, a torrent of life—
How many are left? For a time, for a few years, their bones
Turned the dark prairies white.
                      You, Death, you watch
    for these things,
These explosions of life: they are your food,
They make your feasts.
                But turn your great rolling eyes
    away from humanity,
Those grossly craving black eyes. It is true we increase.
A man from Britain landing in Gaul when Rome
    had fallen,
He journeyed fourteen days inland through that beautiful
Rich land, the orchards and rivers and the looted villas:
    he reports that he saw

No living man. But now we fill up the gaps,
In spite of wars, famines and pestilences we are quite
suddenly
Three billion people: our bones, ours too, would make
Wide prairies white, a beautiful snow of unburied bones:
Bones that have twitched and quivered in the nights of love,
Bones that have been shaken with laughter and hung slack
in sorrow, coward bones
Worn out with trembling, strong bones broken on the rack,
bones broken in battle,
Broad bones gnarled with hard labor, and the little bones
of sweet young children, and the white empty skulls,
Little carved ivory wine-jugs that used to contain
Passion and thought and love and insane delirium, where now
Not even worms live.
Respect humanity, Death, these
shameless black eyes of yours,
It is not necessary to take all at once—besides that,
you cannot do it, we are too powerful,
We are men, not pigeons; you may take the old, the useless
and helpless, the cancer-bitten and the tender young,
But the human race has still history to make. For look—
look now
At our achievements: we have bridled the cloud-leaper lightning,
a lion whipped by a man, to carry our messages
And work our will, we have snatched the live thunderbolt
Out of God's hands. Ha? That was little and last year—
for now we have taken
The primal powers, creation and annihilation; we make
new elements, such as God never saw,
We can explode atoms and annul the fragments, nothing left
but pure energy, we shall use it
In peace and war—"Very clever," he answered,
in his thin piping voice,
Cruel and a eunuch.
Roll those idiot black eyes of yours
On the field-beasts, not on intelligent man,
We are not in your order. You watched the dinosaurs
Grow into horror: they had been little efts in the ditches

and presently became enormous, with leaping flanks
And tearing teeth, plated with armor, nothing could
           stand against them, nothing but you,
Death, and they died. You watched the sabre-tooth tigers
Develop those huge fangs, unnecessary as our sciences,
           and presently they died. You have their bones
In the oil-pits and layer-rock, you will not have ours.
           With pain and wonder and labor we have bought intelligence
We have minds like the tusks of those forgotten tigers,
           hypertrophied and terrible,
We have counted the stars and half understood them,
           we have watched the farther galaxies fleeing away
           from us, wild herds
Of panic horses—or a trick of distance deceived the prism—
           we outfly falcons and eagles and meteors,
Faster than sound, higher than the nourishing air;
           we have enormous privilege, we do not fear you,
We have invented the jet-plane and the death-bomb
           and the cross of Christ—"Oh," he said, "surely
You'll live forever"—grinning like a skull, covering his mouth
           with his hand—"What could exterminate you?"

LYNN WHITE, JR.

26 The Historic Roots of Our Ecologic Crisis (1967)

Medieval View of Man and Nature

Until recently, agriculture has been the chief occupation even in "advanced" societies; hence, any change in methods of tillage has much importance. Early plows, drawn by two oxen, did not normally turn the sod but merely scratched it. Thus, cross-plowing was needed and fields tended to be squarish. In the fairly light soils and semiarid climates of the Near East and Mediterranean, this worked well. But such a plow was inappropriate to the wet climate and often sticky soils of northern Europe. By the latter part of the seventh century after Christ, however, following obscure beginnings, certain northern peasants were using an entirely new kind of plow, equipped with a vertical knife to cut the line of the furrow, a horizontal share to slice under the sod, and a moldboard to turn it over. The friction of this plow with the soil was so great that it normally required not two but eight oxen. It attacked the land with such violence that cross-plowing was not needed, and fields tended to be shaped in long strips.

In the days of the scratch-plow, fields were distributed generally in units capable of supporting a single family. Subsistence farming was the presupposition. But no peasant owned eight oxen: to use the

From Lynn White, Jr., "The Historic Roots of our Ecologic Crisis," *Science* (March 10, 1967): 8–14. © 1967. Reprinted by permission of the American Association for the Advancement of Science.

new and more efficient plow, peasants pooled their oxen to form large plow-teams, originally receiving (it would appear) plowed strips in proportion to their contribution. Thus, distribution of land was based no longer on the needs of a family but, rather, on the capacity of a power machine to till the earth. Man's relation to the soil was profoundly changed. Formerly man had been part of nature; now he was the exploiter of nature. Nowhere else in the world did farmers develop any analogous agricultural implement. Is it coincidence that modern technology, with its ruthlessness toward nature, has so largely been produced by descendants of these peasants of northern Europe?

This same exploitive attitude appears slightly before A.D. 830 in Western illustrated calendars. In older calendars the months were shown as passive personifications. The new Frankish calendars, which set the style for the Middle Ages, are very different: they show men coercing the world around them—plowing, harvesting, chopping trees, butchering pigs. Man and nature are two things, and man is master.

These novelties seem to be in harmony with larger intellectual patterns. What people do about their ecology depends on what they think about themselves in relation to things around them. Human ecology is deeply conditioned by beliefs about our nature and destiny —that is, by religion. To Western eyes this is very evident in, say, India or Ceylon. It is equally true of ourselves and of our medieval ancestors.

The victory of Christianity over paganism was the greatest psychic revolution in the history of our culture. It has become fashionable today to say that, for better or worse, we live in "the post-Christian age." Certainly the forms of our thinking and language have largely ceased to be Christian, but to my eye the substance often remains amazingly akin to that of the past. Our daily habits of action, for example, are dominated by an implicit faith in perpetual progress which was unknown either to Greco-Roman antiquity or to the Orient. It is rooted in, and is indefensible apart from, Judeo-Christian teleology. The fact that Communists share it merely helps to show what can be demonstrated on many other grounds: that Marxism, like Islam, is a Judeo-Christian heresy. We continue today to live, as we have lived for about 1,700 years, very largely in a context of Christian axioms.

What did Christianity tell people about their relations with the environment?

While many of the world's mythologies provide stories of creation, Greco-Roman mythology was singularly incoherent in this respect. Like

Aristotle, the intellectuals of the ancient West denied that the visible world had had a beginning. Indeed, the idea of a beginning was impossible in the framework of their cyclical notion of time. In sharp contrast, Christianity inherited from Judaism not only a concept of time as nonrepetitive and linear but also a striking story of creation. By gradual stages a loving and all-powerful God had created light and darkness, the heavenly bodies, the earth and all its plants, animals, birds, and fishes. Finally, God had created Adam and, as an afterthought, Eve to keep man from being lonely. Man named all the animals, thus establishing his dominance over them. God planned all of this explicitly for man's benefit and rule: no item in the physical creation had any purpose save to serve man's purposes. And, although man's body is made of clay, he is not simply part of nature: he is made in God's image.

Especially in its Western form, Christianity is the most anthropocentric religion the world has seen. As early as the second century both Tertulian and Saint Irenaeus of Lyons were insisting that when God shaped Adam he was foreshadowing the image of the incarnate Christ, the Second Adam. Man shares, in great measure, God's transcendence of nature. Christianity, in absolute contrast to ancient paganism and Asia's religions (except, perhaps Zoroastrianism), not only established a dualism of man and nature but also insisted that it is God's will that man exploit nature for his proper ends.

At the level of the common people this worked out in an interesting way. In Antiquity every tree, every spring, every stream, every hill had its own *genius loci*, its guardian spirit. These spirits were accessible to men, but were very unlike men; centaurs, fauns, and mermaids show their ambivalence. Before one cut a tree, mined a mountain, or dammed a brook, it was important to placate the spirit in charge of that particular situation, and to keep it placated. By destroying pagan animism, Christianity made it possible to exploit nature in a mood of indifference to the feelings of natural objects.

It is often said that for animism the Church substituted the cult of saints. True; but the cult of saints is functionally quite different from animism. The saint is not *in* natural objects; he may have special shrines, but his citizenship is in heaven. Moreover, a saint is entirely a man; he can be approached in human terms. In addition to saints, Christianity of course also had angels and demons inherited from Judaism and perhaps, at one remove, from Zoroastrianism. But these were all as mobile as the saints themselves. The spirits *in* natural objects, which formerly had protected nature from man, evaporated. Man's effective monopoly on spirit in this world was confirmed, and the old inhibitions to the exploitation of nature crumbled.

When one speaks in such sweeping terms, a note of caution is in order. Christianity is a complex faith, and its consequences differ in differing contexts. What I have said may well apply to the medieval West, where in fact technology made spectacular advances. But the Greek East, a highly civilized realm of equal Christian devotion, seems to have produced no marked technological innovation after the late seventh century, when Greek fire was invented.* The key to the contrast may perhaps be found in a difference in the tonality of piety and thought which students of comparative theology find between the Greek and the Latin Churches. The Greeks believed that sin was intellectual blindness, and that salvation was found in illumination, orthodoxy— that is, clear thinking. The Latins, on the other hand, felt that sin was moral evil, and that salvation was to be found in right conduct. Eastern theology has been intellectualist, Western theology has been voluntarist. The Greek saint contemplates; the Western saint acts. The implications of Christianity for the conquest of nature would emerge more easily in the Western atmosphere.

The Christian dogma of creation, which is found in the first clause of all the Creeds, has another meaning for our comprehension of today's ecologic crisis. By revelation, God had given man the Bible, the Book of Scripture. But since God had made nature, nature also must reveal the divine mentality. The religious study of nature for the better understanding of God was known as natural theology. In the early Church, and always in the Greek East, nature was conceived primarily as a symbolic system through which God speaks to men: the ant is a sermon to sluggards; rising flames are the symbol of the soul's aspiration. This view of nature was essentially artistic rather than scientific. While Byzantium preserved and copied great numbers of ancient Greek scientific texts, science as we conceive it could scarcely flourish in such an ambience.

However, in the Latin West by the early thirteenth century natural theology was following a very different bent. It was ceasing to be the decoding of the physical symbols of God's communication with man and was becoming the effort to understand God's mind by discovering

---

*An inflammable mixture used by the Byzantine Greeks in warfare. It burned fiercely even under water.—Ed.

how his creation operates. The rainbow was no longer simply a symbol of hope first sent to Noah after the Deluge: Robert Grosseteste, Friar Roger Bacon, and Theodoric of Freiberg produced startlingly sophisticated work on the optics of the rainbow, but they did it as a venture in religious understanding. From the thirteenth century onward, up to and including Leibnitz and Newton, every major scientist, in effect, explained his motivations in religious terms. Indeed, if Galileo had not been so expert an amateur theologian he would have got into far less trouble: the professionals resented his intrusion. And Newton seems to have regarded himself more as a theologian than as a scientist. It was not until the late eighteenth century that the hypothesis of God became unnecessary to many scientists.

It is often hard for the historian to judge, when men explain why they are doing what they want to do, whether they are offering real reasons or merely culturally acceptable reasons. The consistency with which scientists during the long formative centuries of Western science said that the task and the reward of the scientist was "to think God's thoughts after him" leads one to believe that this was their real motivation. If so, then modern Western science was cast in a matrix of Christian theology. The dynamism of religious devotion, shaped by the Judeo-Christian dogma of creation, gave it impetus.

An Alternative Christian View

We would seem to be headed toward conclusions unpalatable to many Christians. Since both *science* and *technology* are blessed words in our contemporary vocabulary, some may be happy at the notions, first, that, viewed historically, modern science is an extrapolation of natural theology; and, second, that modern technology is at least partly to be explained as an Occidental, voluntarist realization of the Christian dogma of man's transcendence of, and rightful mastery over, nature. But, as we now recognize, somewhat over a century ago science and technology—hitherto quite separate activities—joined to give mankind powers which, to judge by many of the ecologic effects, are out of control. If so, Christianity bears a huge burden of guilt.

I personally doubt that disastrous ecologic backlash can be avoided simply by applying to our problems more science and more technology. Our science and technology have grown out of Christian attitudes toward man's relation to nature which are almost universally held not only by Christians and neo-Christians but also by those who fondly regard themselves as post-Christians. Despite Copernicus, all the cosmos rotates around our little globe. Despite Darwin, we are *not*, in our hearts, part of the natural process. We are superior to nature, contemptuous of it, willing to use it for our slightest whim. The newly elected Governor of California, like myself a churchman but less troubled than I, spoke for the Christian tradition when he said (as is alleged), "when you've seen one redwood tree, you've seen them all." To a Christian a tree can be no more than a physical fact. The whole concept of the sacred grove is alien to Christianity and to the ethos of the West. For nearly two millennia Christian missionaries have been chopping down sacred groves, which are idolatrous because they assume spirit in nature.

What we do about ecology depends on our ideas of the man-nature relationship. More science and more technology are not going to get us out of the present ecologic crisis until we find a new religion, or rethink our old one. The beatniks, who are the basic revolutionaries of our time, show a sound instinct in their affinity for Zen Buddhism, which conceives of the man-nature relationship as very nearly the mirror image of the Christian view. Zen, however, is as deeply conditioned by Asian history as Christianity is by the experience of the West, and I am dubious of its viability among us.

Possibly we should ponder the greatest radical in Christian history since Christ: Saint Francis of Assisi. The prime miracle of Saint Francis is the fact that he did not end at the stake, as many of his left-wing followers did. He was so clearly heretical that a General of the Franciscan Order, Saint Bonaventura, a great and perceptive Christian, tried to suppress the early accounts of Franciscanism. The key to an understanding of Francis is his belief in the virtue of humility—not merely for the individual but for man as a species. Francis tried to depose man from his monarchy over creation and set up a democracy of all God's creatures. With him the ant is no longer simply a homily for the lazy, flames a sign of the thrust of the soul toward union with God; now they are Brother Ant and Sister Fire, praising the Creator in their own ways as Brother Man does in his.

Later commentators have said that Francis preached to the birds as a rebuke to men who would not listen. The records do not read so: he urged the little birds to praise God, and in spiritual ecstasy they flapped their wings and chirped rejoicing. Legends of saints, especially the Irish saints, had long told of their dealings with animals but always, I believe, to show their human dominance over creatures. With

Francis it is different. The land around Gubbio in the Apennines was being ravaged by a fierce wolf. Saint Francis, says the legend, talked to the wolf and persuaded him of the error of his ways. The wolf repented, died in the odor of sanctity, and was buried in consecrated ground.

What Sir Steven Ruciman calls "the Franciscan doctrine of the animal soul" was quickly stamped out. Quite possibly it was in part inspired, consciously or unconsciously, by the belief in reincarnation held by the Cathar heretics who at that time teemed in Italy and southern France, and who presumably had got it originally from India. It is significant that at just the same moment, about 1200, traces of metempsychosis are found also in western Judaism, in the Provençal *Cabbala*. But Francis held neither to transmigration of souls nor to pantheism. His view of nature and of man rested on a unique sort of pan-psychism of all things animate and inanimate, designed for the glorification of their transcendent Creator, who, in the ultimate gesture of cosmic humility, assumed flesh, lay helpless in a manger, and hung dying on a scaffold.

I am not suggesting that many contemporary Americans who are concerned about our ecologic crisis will be either able or willing to counsel with wolves or exhort birds. However, the present increasing disruption of the global environment is the product of a dynamic technology and science which were originating in the Western medieval world against which Saint Francis was rebelling in so original a way. Their growth cannot be understood historically apart from distinctive attitudes toward nature which are deeply grounded in Christian dogma. The fact that most people do not think of these attitudes as Christian is irrelevant. No new set of basic values has been accepted in our society to displace those of Christianity. Hence we shall continue to have a worsening ecologic crisis until we reject the Christian axiom that nature has no reason for existence save to serve man.

The greatest spiritual revolutionary in Western history, Saint Francis, proposed what he thought was an alternative Christian view of nature and man's relation to it: he tried to substitute the idea of the equality of all creatures, including man, for the idea of man's limitless rule of creation. He failed. Both our present science and our present technology are so tinctured with orthodox Christian arrogance toward nature that no solution for our ecologic crisis can be expected from them alone. Since the roots of our trouble are so largely religious, the remedy must also be essentially religious, whether we call it that or not. We must rethink and refeel our nature and destiny. The profoundly religious, but heretical, sense of the primitive Franciscans for the spiritual autonomy of all parts of nature may point a direction. I propose Francis as a patron saint for ecologists.

EDWARD ABBEY

27 Polemic: Industrial Tourism and the National Parks (1968)

I like my job. The pay is generous; I might even say munificent: $1.95 per hour, earned or not, backed solidly by the world's most powerful Air Force, biggest national debt, and grossest national product. The fringe benefits are priceless: clean air to breathe (after the spring sandstorms); stillness, solitude and space; an unobstructed view every day and every night of sun, sky, stars, clouds, mountains, moon, cliffrock and canyons; a sense of time enough to let thought and feeling range from here to the end of the world and back; the discovery of something intimate—though impossible to name—in the remote. . . .

The ease and relative freedom of this lovely job at Arches follow from the comparative absence of the motorized tourists, who stay away by the millions. And they stay away because of the unpaved entrance road, the unflushable toilets in the campgrounds, and the fact that most of them have never even heard of Arches National Monument. (Could there be a more genuine testimonial to its beauty and integrity?) All this must change.

From Edward Abbey, "Polemic: Industrial Tourism and the National Parks," *Desert Solitaire: A Season in the Wilderness* (New York: Ballantine Books, 1968), 45, 48–52, 54–60, 62–63, 65–67. © 1968 by Edward Abbey, renewed 1996 by Clarke Abbey. Reprinted by permission of Don Congdon Associates.

I'd been warned. On the very first day Merle and Floyd had mentioned something about developments, improvements, a sinister Master Plan. Thinking that *they* were the dreamers, I paid little heed and had soon forgotten the whole ridiculous business. But only a few days ago something happened which shook me out of my pleasant apathy.

I was sitting out back on my 33,000-acre terrace, shoeless and shirtless, scratching my toes in the sand and sipping on a tall iced drink, watching the flow of evening over the desert. Prime time: the sun very low in the west, the birds coming back to life, the shadows rolling for miles over rock and sand to the very base of the brilliant mountains. I had a small fire going near the table—not for heat or light but for the fragrance of the juniper and the ritual appeal of the clear flames. For symbolic reasons. For ceremony. When I heard a faint sound over my shoulder I looked and saw a file of deer watching from fifty yards away, three does and a velvet-horned buck, all dark against the sundown sky. They began to move. I whistled and they stopped again, staring at me. "Come on over," I said, "have a drink." They declined, moving off with casual, unhurried grace, quiet as phantoms, and disappeared beyond the rise. Smiling, thoroughly at peace, I turned back to my drink, the little fire, the subtle transformations of the immense landscape before me. On the program: rise of the full moon.

It was then I heard the discordant note, the snarling whine of a jeep in low range and four-wheel-drive, coming from an unexpected direction, from the vicinity of the old foot and horse trail that leads from Balanced Rock down toward Courthouse Wash and on to park headquarters near Moab. The jeep came in sight from beyond some bluffs, turned onto the dirt road, and came up the hill toward the entrance station. Now operating a motor vehicle of any kind on the trails of a national park is strictly forbidden, a nasty bureaucratic regulation which I heartily support. My bosom swelled with the righteous indignation of a cop: by God, I thought, I'm going to write these sons of bitches a ticket. I put down the drink and strode to the housetrailer to get my badge.

Long before I could find the shirt with the badge on it, however, or the ticket book, or my shoes or my park ranger hat, the jeep turned in at my driveway and came right up to the door of the trailer. It was a gray jeep with a U.S. Government decal on the side—Bureau of Public Roads—and covered with dust. Two empty water bags flapped at the bumper. Inside were three sunburned men in twill britches and engineering boots, and a pile of equipment: transit case, tripod, survey rod, bundles of wooden stakes. (*Oh no!*) The men got out, dripping with dust, and the driver grinned at me, pointing to his parched open mouth and making horrible gasping noises deep in his throat.

"Okay," I said, "come on in."

It was even hotter inside the trailer than outside but I opened the refrigerator and left it open and took out a pitcher filled with ice cubes and water. As they passed the pitcher back and forth I got the full and terrible story, confirming the worst of my fears. They were a survey crew, laying out a new road into the Arches.

And when would the road be built? Nobody knew for sure; perhaps in a couple of years, depending on when the Park Service would be able to get the money. The new road—to be paved, of course—would cost somewhere between half a million and one million dollars, depending on the bids, or more than fifty thousand dollars per linear mile. At least enough to pay the salaries of ten park rangers for ten years. Too much money, I suggested—they'll never go for it back in Washington.

The three men thought that was pretty funny. Don't worry, they said, this road will be built. I'm worried, I said. Look, the party chief explained, you *need* this road. He was a pleasant-mannered, soft-spoken civil engineer with an unquestioning dedication to his work. A very dangerous man. Who *needs* it? I said; we get very few tourists in this park. That's why you need it, the engineer explained patiently; look, he said, when this road is built you'll get ten, twenty, thirty times as many tourists in here as you get now. His men nodded in solemn agreement, and he stared at me intently, waiting to see what possible answer I could have to that.

"Have some more water," I said. I had an answer all right but I was saving it for later. I knew that I was dealing with a madman.

———

As I type these words, several years after the little episode of the gray jeep and the thirsty engineers, all that was foretold has come to pass. Arches National Monument has been developed. The Master Plan has been fulfilled. Where once a few adventurous people came on weekends to camp for a night or two and enjoy a taste of the primitive and remote, you will now find serpentine streams of baroque automobiles pouring in and out, all through the spring and summer, in numbers that would have seemed fantastic when I worked there: from 3,000 to 30,000 to 300,000 per year, the "visitation," as they call it, mounts ever upward. The little campgrounds where I used to putter around reading three-day-old newspapers full of lies and watermelon seeds have now been consolidated into one master campground that looks, during the busy season, like a suburban village: elaborate housetrailers of quilted aluminum crowd upon gigantic camper-trucks of Fiberglas and molded plastic; through their windows you will see the blue glow of television and hear the studio laughter of Los Angeles; knobby-kneed oldsters in plaid Bermudas buzz up and down the quaintly curving asphalt road on motorbikes; quarrels break out between campsite neighbors while others gather around their burning charcoal briquettes (ground campfires no longer permitted—not enough wood) to compare electric toothbrushes. . . .

Progress had come at last to the Arches, after a million years of neglect. Industrial Tourism has arrived.

What happened to Arches Natural Money-mint is, of course, an old story in the Park Service. All the famous national parks have the same problems on a far grander scale, as everyone knows, and many other problems as yet unknown to a little subordinate unit of the system in a backward part of southeastern Utah. And the same kind of development that has so transformed Arches is under way, planned or completed in many more national parks and national monuments. . . .

———

There may be some among the readers of this book, like the earnest engineer, who believe without question that any and all forms of construction and development arc intrinsic goods, in the national parks as well as anywhere else, who virtually identify quantity with quality and therefore assume that the greater the quantity of traffic, the higher the value received. There are some who frankly and boldly advocate the eradication of the last remnants of wilderness and the complete subjugation of nature to the requirements of—not man—but industry. This is a courageous view, admirable in its simplicity and power, and with the weight of all modern history behind it. It is also quite insane. I cannot attempt to deal with it here.

There will be other readers, I hope, who share my basic assumption that wilderness is a necessary part of civilization and that it is the primary responsibility of the national park system to preserve *intact and undiminished* what little still remains.

Most readers, while generally sympathetic to this latter point of view, will feel, as do the administrators of the National Park Service, that although wilderness is a fine thing, certain compromises and adjustments are necessary in order to meet the ever-expanding demand for outdoor recreation. It is precisely this question which I would like to examine now.

The Park Service, established by Congress in 1916, was directed not only to administer the parks but also to "provide for the enjoyment of same in such manner and by such means as will leave them unimpaired for the enjoyment of future generations." This appropriately ambiguous language, employed long before the onslaught of the automobile, has been understood in various and often opposing ways ever since. The Park Service, like any other big organization, includes factions and factions. The Developers, the dominant faction, place their emphasis on the words "*provide for the enjoyment.*" The Preservers, a minority but also strong, emphasize the words "*leave them unimpaired.*" It is apparent, then, that we cannot decide the question of development versus preservation by a simple referral to holy writ or an attempt to guess the intention of the founding fathers; we must make up our own minds and decide for ourselves what the national parks should be and what purpose they should serve.

The first issue that appears when we get into this matter, the most important issue and perhaps the only issue, is the one called *accessibility*. The Developers insist that the parks must be made fully accessible not only to people but also to their machines, that is, to automobiles, motorboats, etc. . . .

What does accessibility mean? Is there any spot on earth that men have not proved accessible by the simplest means—feet and legs and heart? Even Mt. McKinley, even Everest, have been surmounted by men on foot. (Some of them, incidentally, rank amateurs, to the horror and indignation of the professional mountaineers.) The interior of the Grand Canyon, a fiercely hot and hostile abyss, is visited each summer by thousands and thousands of tourists of the most banal and unadventurous type, many of them on foot—self-propelled, so to speak—and the others on the backs of mules. Thousands climb each summer to the summit of Mt. Whitney, highest point in the forty-eight United States, while multitudes of others wander on foot or on horseback through the ranges of the Sierras, the Rockies, the Big Smokies, the Cascades and the mountains of New England. Still more hundreds and thousands float or paddle each year down the currents of the Salmon, the Snake, the Allagash, the Yampa, the Green, the Rio Grande, the Ozark, the St. Croix and those portions of the Colorado which have not yet been destroyed by the dam builders. And most significant, these hordes of nonmotorized tourists, hungry for a taste of the difficult, the original, the real, do not consist solely of people young and athletic but also of old folks, fat folks, pale-faced office clerks who don't know a rucksack from a haversack, and even children. The one thing they all have in common is the refusal to live always like sardines in a can—they are determined to get outside of their motorcars for at least a few weeks each year.

This being the case, why is the Park Service generally so anxious to accommodate that other crowd, the indolent millions born on wheels and suckled on gasoline, who expect and demand paved highways to lead them in comfort, ease and safety into every nook and corner of the national parks? For the answer to that we must consider the character of what I call Industrial Tourism and the quality of the mechanized tourists—the Wheelchair Explorers—who are at once the consumers, the raw material and the victims of Industrial Tourism.

Industrial Tourism is a big business It means money. It includes the motel and restaurant owners, the gasoline retailers, the oil corporations, the road-building contractors, the heavy equipment manufacturers, the state and federal engineering agencies and the sovereign, all-powerful automotive industry. These various interests are well organized, command more wealth than most modern nations, and are represented in Congress with a strength far greater than is justified in any constitutional or democratic sense. (Modern politics is expensive—power follows money.) Through Congress the tourism industry can bring enormous pressure to bear upon such a slender reed in the executive branch as the poor old Park Service, a pressure which is also exerted on every other possible level—local, state, regional—and through advertising and the well-established habits of a wasteful nation.

When a new national park, national monument, national seashore, or whatever it may be called is set up, the various forces of Industrial Tourism, on all levels, immediately expect action—meaning specifically a road-building program. Where trails or primitive dirt roads already exist, the Industry expects—it hardly needs to ask—that these be developed into modern paved highways. . . .

Great though it is, however, the power of the tourist business would not in itself be sufficient to shape Park Service policy. To all accusations of excessive development the administrators can reply, as they will if pressed hard enough, that they are giving the public what it wants, that their primary duty is to serve the public, not preserve the wilds. "Parks are for people" is the public-relations slogan, which decoded means that the parks are for people-in-automobiles. Behind the slogan is the assumption that the majority of Americans, exactly like the managers of the tourist industry, expect and demand to see their national parks from the comfort, security, and convenience of their automobiles.

Is this assumption correct? Perhaps. Does that justify the continued and increasing erosion of the parks? It does not. Which brings me to the final aspect of the problem of Industrial Tourism: the Industrial Tourists themselves.

They work hard, these people. They roll up incredible mileages on their odometers, rack up state after state in two-week transcontinental motor marathons, knock off one national park after another, take millions of square yards of photographs, and endure patiently the most prolonged discomforts: the tedious traffic jams, the awful food of park cafeterias and roadside eateries, the nocturnal search for a place to sleep or camp, the dreary routine of One-Stop Service, the endless lines of creeping traffic, the smell of exhaust fumes, the ever-proliferating Rules & Regulations . . .

Hard work. And risky. Too much for some, who have given up the struggle on the highways in exchange for an entirely different kind of vacation—out in the open, on their own feet, following the quiet trail through forest and mountains, bedding down at evening under the stars, when and where they feel like it, at a time when the Industrial Tourists are still hunting for a place to park their automobiles.

Industrial Tourism is a threat to the national parks. But the chief victims of the system are the motorized tourists. They are being robbed and robbing themselves. So long as they are unwilling to crawl out of their cars they will not discover the treasures of the national parks and will never escape the stress and turmoil of the urban-suburban complexes which they had hoped, presumably, to leave behind for a while.

How to pry the tourists out of their automobiles, out of their back-breaking upholstered mechanized wheelchairs and onto their feet, onto the strange warmth and solidity of Mother Earth again? This is the problem which the Park Service should confront directly, not evasively, and which it cannot resolve by simply submitting and conforming to the automobile habit. The automobile, which began as a transportation convenience, has become a bloody tyrant (50,000 lives a year), and it is the responsibility of the Park Service, as well as that of everyone else concerned with preserving both wilderness and civilization, to begin a campaign of resistance. The automotive combine has almost succeeded in strangling our cities; we need not let it also destroy our national parks.

It will be objected that a constantly increasing population makes resistance and conservation a hopeless battle. This is true. Unless a way is found to stabilize the nation's population, the parks cannot be saved. Or anything else worth a damn. Wilderness preservation, like a hundred other good causes, will be forgotten under the overwhelming pressure of a struggle for mere survival and sanity in a completely urbanized, completely industrialized, ever more crowded environment. For my own part I would rather take my chances in a thermonuclear war than live in such a world.

Assuming, however, that population growth will be halted at a tolerable level before catastrophe does it for us, it remains permissible to talk about such things as the national parks. Having indulged myself in a number of harsh judgments upon the Park Service, the tourist industry, and the motoring public, I now feel entitled to make some constructive, practical, sensible proposals for the salvation of both parks and people.

(1) No more cars in national parks. Let the people walk. Or ride horses, bicycles, mules, wild pigs—anything—but keep the automobiles and the motorcycles and all their motorized relatives out. We have agreed not to drive our automobiles into cathedrals, concert halls, art museums, legislative assemblies, private bedrooms and the other sanctums of our culture; we should treat our national parks with the same deference, for they, too, are holy places. . . .

I can foresee complaints. The motorized tourists, reluctant to give up the old ways, will complain that they can't see enough without their automobiles to bear them swiftly (traffic permitting) through the parks. But this is nonsense. A man on foot, on horseback or on a bicycle will see more, feel more, enjoy more in one mile than the motorized tourists can in a hundred miles. . . .

(2) No more new roads in national parks. After banning private automobiles the second step should be easy. Where paved roads are already in existence they will be reserved for the bicycles and essential in-park services, such as shuttle buses, the trucking of camping gear and concessioners' supplies. Where dirt roads already exist they too will be reserved for nonmotorized traffic. Plans for new roads can be discarded and in their place a program of trail-building begun, badly needed in some of the parks and in many of the national monuments. . . .

Once people are liberated from the confines of automobiles there will be a greatly increased interest in hiking, exploring, and back-country packtrips. Fortunately the parks, by the mere elimination of motor traffic, will come to seem far bigger than they are now—there will be more room for more persons, an astonishing expansion of space. This follows from the interesting fact that a motorized vehicle, when not at rest, requires a volume of space far out of proportion to its size. To illustrate: imagine a lake approximately ten miles long and on the average one mile wide. A single motorboat could easily circumnavigate the lake in an hour; ten motorboats would begin to crowd it; twenty or thirty, all in operation, would dominate the lake to the exclusion of any other form of activity; and fifty would create the hazards, confusion, and turmoil that makes pleasure impossible. Suppose we banned motorboats and allowed only canoes and rowboats; we would see at once that the lake seemed ten or perhaps a hundred times bigger. The same thing holds true, to an even greater degree, for the automobile. Distance and space are functions of speed and time. . . .

(3) Put the park rangers to work. Lazy scheming loafers, they've wasted too many years selling tickets at toll booths and sitting behind desks filling out charts and tables in the vain effort to appease the mania for statistics which torments the Washington office. Put them to work. They're supposed to be rangers—make the bums range; kick them out of those overheated air-conditioned offices, yank them out of those overstuffed patrol cars, and drive them out on the trails where they should be, leading the dudes over hill and dale, safely into and back out of the wilderness. It won't hurt them to work off a little office fat; it'll do them good, help take their minds off each other's wives, and give them a chance to get out of reach of the boss—a blessing for all concerned.

They will be needed on the trail. Once we outlaw the motors and stop the road-building and force the multitudes back on their feet, the people will need leaders. . . .

Excluding the automobile from the heart of the great cities has been seriously advocated by thoughtful observers of our urban problems. It seems to me an equally proper solution to the problems besetting our national parks. Of course it would be a serious blow to Industrial Tourism and would be bitterly resisted by those who profit from that industry. Exclusion of automobiles would also require a revolution in the thinking of Park Service officialdom and in the assumptions of most American tourists. But such a revolution, like it or not, is precisely what is needed. The only foreseeable alternative, given the current trend of things, is the gradual destruction of our national park system.

Let us therefore steal a slogan from the Development Fever Faction in the Park Service. The parks, they say, are for people. Very well. At the main entrance to each national park and national monument we shall erect a billboard one hundred feet high, two hundred feet wide, gorgeously filigreed in brilliant neon and outlined with blinker lights, exploding stars, flashing prayer wheels and great Byzantine phallic symbols that gush like geysers every thirty seconds. (You could set your watch by them.) Behind the fireworks will loom the figure of Smokey the Bear, taller than a pine tree, with eyes in his head that swivel back and forth, watching You, and ears that actually twitch. Push a button and Smokey will recite, for the benefit of children and government officials who might otherwise have trouble with some of the big words, in a voice ursine, loud and clear, the message spelled out on the face of the billboard. To wit:

HOWDY, FOLKS. WELCOME. THIS IS YOUR NATIONAL PARK, ESTABLISHED FOR THE PLEASURE OF YOU AND ALL PEOPLE EVERYWHERE. PARK YOUR CAR, JEEP, TRUCK, TANK, MOTORBIKE, SNOWMOBILE, MOTORBOAT, JETBOAT, AIRBOAT, SUBMARINE, AIRPLANE, JETPLANE, HELICOPTER, HOVERCRAFT, WINGED MOTORCYCLE, ROCKETSHIP, OR ANY OTHER CONCEIVABLE TYPE OF MOTORIZED VEHICLE IN THE WORLD'S BIGGEST PARKING LOT BEHIND THE COMFORT STATION IMMEDIATELY TO YOUR REAR. GET OUT OF YOUR MOTORIZED VEHICLE, GET ON YOUR HORSE, MULE, BICYCLE OR FEET, AND COME ON IN.

ENJOY YOURSELVES. THIS HERE PARK IS FOR PEOPLE.

The survey chief and his two assistants did not stay very long. Letting them go in peace, without debate, I fixed myself another drink, returned to the table in the backyard and sat down to await the rising of the moon.

My thoughts were on the road and the crowds that would pour upon it as inevitably as water under pressure follows every channel which is opened to it. Man is a gregarious creature, we are told, a social being. Does that mean he is also a herd animal? I don't believe it, despite the character of modern life. The herd is for ungulates, not for men and women and their children. Are men no better than sheep or cattle, that they must live always in view of one another in order to feel a sense of safety? I can't believe it.

We are preoccupied with time. If we could learn to love space as deeply as we are now obsessed with time, we might discover a new meaning in the phrase *to live like men*.

At what distance should good neighbors build their houses? Let it be determined by the community's mode of travel: if by foot, four miles; if by horseback, eight miles; if by motorcar, twenty-four miles; if by airplane, ninety-six miles.

Recall the Proverb: "Set not thy foot too often in thy neighbor's house, lest he grow weary of thee and hate thee."

The sun went down and the light mellowed over the sand and distance and hoodoo rocks "pinnacled dim in the intense inane." A few stars appeared, scattered liberally through space. The solitary owl called.

Finally the moon came up, a golden globe behind the rocky fretwork of the horizon, a full and delicate moon that floated lightly as a leaf upon the dark slow current of the night. A face that watched me from the other side.

The air grew cool. I put on boots and shirt, stuffed some cheese and raisins in my pocket, and went for a walk. The moon was high enough to cast a good light when I reached the place where the gray jeep had first come into view. I could see the tracks of its wheels quite plainly in the sand and the route was well marked, not only by the tracks but by the survey stakes planted in the ground at regular fifty-foot intervals and by streamers of plastic ribbon tied to the brush and trees.

Teamwork, that's what made America what it is today. Teamwork and initiative. The survey crew had done their job; I would do mine. For about five miles I followed the course of their survey back toward headquarters, and as I went I pulled up each little wooden stake and threw it away, and cut all the bright ribbons from the bushes and hid them under a rock. A futile effort, in the long run, but it made me feel good. Then I went home to the trailer, taking a shortcut over the bluffs.

28 | The Fate of All Living Things (1977)

He lay there and hated them. Not for what they wanted to do with him, but for what they did to the earth with their machines, and to the animals with their packs of dogs and their guns. It happened again and again, and the people had to watch, unable to save or to protect any of the things that were so important to them. He ground his teeth together; there must be something he could do to still the vague, constant fear unraveling inside him: the earth and the animals might not know; they might not understand that he was not one of them; he was not one of the destroyers. He wanted to kick the soft white bodies into the Atlantic Ocean; he wanted to scream to all of them that they were trespassers and thieves. He wanted to follow them as they hunted the mountain lion, to shoot them and their howling dogs with their own guns. The destroyers had sent them to ruin this world, and day by day they were doing it. He wanted to scream at Indians like Harley and Helen Jean and Emo that the white things they admired and desired so much—the bright city lights and loud music, the soft sweet food and the cars—all these things had been stolen, torn out of Indian land: raw living materials for their ck'o'yo manipulation. The people had been taught to despise themselves because they were left with barren land and dry rivers. But they were wrong. It was the white people who had nothing; it was the white people who were suffering as thieves do, never able to forget that their

From Leslie Marmon Silko, *Ceremony* (New York: Signet, 1977), 212–14, 256–58. © 1977 by Leslie Silko. Reprinted by permission of Viking Penguin, a division of Penguin Putnam.

pride was wrapped in something stolen, something that had never been, and could never be, theirs. The destroyers had tricked the white people as completely as they had fooled the Indians, and now only a few people understood how the filthy deception worked; only a few people knew that the lie was destroying the white people faster than it was destroying Indian people. But the effects were hidden, evident only in the sterility of their art, which continued to feed off the vitality of other cultures, and in the dissolution of their consciousness into dead objects: the plastic and neon, the concrete and steel. Hollow and lifeless as a witchery clay figure. And what little still remained to white people was shriveled like a seed hoarded too long, shrunken past its time, and split open now, to expose a fragile, pale leaf stem, perfectly formed and dead. . . .

———————

Waves of heat caught him, and his legs and lungs were vapor without sensation; only his memory of running and breathing kept him moving and alive. He stumbled and ran behind the sun, not following but dragged with it across arroyos, over mesas and hills. At sundown he was lying on the sand at the bottom of the long mesa, feeling the heat recede from the air and from his body into the earth. The wind came up and he shivered.

He crawled through the strands of barbed wire. Twilight was giving way to darkness. He scooped water off the top of thick green moss that clogged the steel water trough under the windmill. The water was still warm from the sun and it tasted bitter. He sat on the edge of the trough and looked across the wide canyon at the dark mine shaft. Maybe the uranium made the water taste that way. The sandstone and dirt they had taken from inside the mesa was piled in mounds, in long rows, like fresh graves.

Old Grandma told him while he was still sick and weak, lying in the darkened room. She shuffled in and sat down on the edge of his bed. "I have been thinking of something," she said. "It happened while you were gone. I had to get up, the way I do, to use the chamber pot. It was still dark; everyone else was still sleeping. But as I walked back from the kitchen to my bed there was a flash of light through the window. So big, so bright even my old clouded-up eyes could see it. It must have filled the whole southeast sky. I thought I was seeing the sun rise again, but it faded away, and by that time all the dogs around here were barking, like the time that bear was prowling around the trash pile. You remember that, sonny, how they barked. 'My, my,' I said to myself, 'I never thought I would see anything so bright again.' " She was patting his arm as she talked, tapping out the story with her hand. "Your auntie laughed at me when I told her what I saw. But later on that day, Romero came around. He said he saw it too. So bright that it blinded him for a moment; then later on he could still see it flashing when he closed his eyes." She paused, as if she were trying to think of the right words. "You know, I have never understood that thing I saw. Later on there was something about it in the newspaper. Strongest thing on this earth. Biggest explosion that ever happened—that's what the newspaper said." She was shaking her head slowly from side to side. "Now I only wonder why, grandson. Why did they make a thing like that?"

"I don't know, Grandma," he had answered then. But now he knew.

He had been so close to it, caught up in it for so long that its simplicity struck him deep inside his chest: Trinity Site, where they exploded the first atomic bomb, was only three hundred miles to the southeast, at White Sands. And the top-secret laboratories where the bomb had been created were deep in the Jemez Mountains, on land the Government took from Cochiti Pueblo Los Alamos, only a hundred miles northeast of him now, still surrounded by high electric fences and the ponderosa pine and tawny sandrock of the Jemez mountain canyon where the shrine of the twin mountain lions had always been. There was no end to it; it knew no boundaries; and he had arrived at the point of convergence where the fate of all living things, and even the earth, had been laid. From the jungles of his dreaming he recognized why the Japanese voices had merged with Laguna voices, with Josiah's voice and Rocky's voice; the lines of cultures and worlds were drawn in flat dark lines on fine light sand, converging in the middle of witchery's final ceremonial sand painting. From that time on, human beings were one clan again, united by the fate the destroyers planned for all of them, for all living things; united by a circle of death that devoured people in cities twelve thousand miles away, victims who had never known these mesas, who had never seen the delicate colors of the rocks which boiled up their slaughter.

He walked to the mine shaft slowly, and the feeling became overwhelming: the pattern of the ceremony was completed there. He knelt and found an ore rock. The gray stone was streaked with powdery yellow uranium, bright and alive as pollen; veins of sooty black formed lines with the yellow, making mountain ranges and rivers across the stone. But they had taken these beautiful rocks from deep within the earth and they had laid them in a monstrous design, realizing destruction on a scale only *they* could have dreamed.

He cried the relief he felt at finally seeing the pattern, the way all the stories fit together—the old stories, the war stories, their stories— to become the story that was still being told. He was not crazy; he had never been crazy. He had only seen and heard the world as it always was: no boundaries, only transitions through all distances and time.

29 | The National Environmental Policy Act

The National Environmental Policy Act, 1969
*Pub. Law No. 91–190, 83 Stat. 852 (1970) codified at 42
U.S.C. §4331 (1982). Selected provisions.*

§4331. Congressional declaration of national environmental policy

(a) The Congress, recognizing the profound impact of man's activity on the interrelations of all components of the natural environment, particularly the profound influences of population growth, high-density urbanization, industrial expansion, resource exploitation, and new and expanding technological advances and recognizing further the critical importance of restoring and maintaining environmental quality to the overall welfare and development of man, declares that it is the continuing policy of the Federal Government, in cooperation with State and local governments, and other concerned public and private organizations, to use all practicable means and measures, including financial and technical assistance, in a manner calculated to foster and promote the general welfare, to create and maintain conditions under which man and nature can exist in productive harmony, and fulfill the social, economic, and other requirements of present and future generations of Americans.

(b) In order to carry out the policy set forth in this chapter, it is the continuing responsibility of the Federal Government to use all practicable means, consistent with other essential considerations of national

From the National Environmental Policy Act, *Pub. Law No. 91-190, 83 Stat. 852 (1970)
codified at 42 U.S.C. §4331 (1982).*

policy, to improve and coordinate Federal plans, functions, programs, and resources to the end that the Nation may—

(1) fulfill the responsibilities of each generation as trustee of the environment for succeeding generations;

(2) assure for all Americans safe, healthful, productive, and esthetically and culturally pleasing surroundings;

(3) attain the widest range of beneficial uses of the environment without degradation, risk to health or safety, or other undesirable and unintended consequences;

(4) preserve important historic, cultural, and natural aspects of our national heritage, and maintain, wherever possible, an environment which supports diversity and variety of individual choice;

(5) achieve a balance between population and resource use which will permit high standards of living and a wide sharing of life's amenities; and

(6) enhance the quality of renewable resources and approach the maximum attainable recycling of depletable resources.

(c) The Congress recognizes that each person should enjoy a healthful environment and that each person has a responsibility to contribute to the preservation and enhancement of the environment.

§4332. Cooperation of agencies; reports; availability of information; recommendations; international and national coordination of efforts

The Congress authorizes and directs that, to the fullest extent possible: (1) the policies, regulations, and public laws of the United States shall be interpreted and administered in accordance with the policies set forth in this chapter, and (2) all agencies of the Federal Government shall—

(A) utilize a systematic, interdisciplinary approach which will insure the integrated use of the natural and social sciences and the environmental design arts in planning and in decisionmaking which may have an impact on man's environment;

(B) identify and develop methods and procedures, in consultation with the Council on Environmental Quality . . . , which will insure that presently unquantified environmental amenities and values may be given appropriate consideration in decisionmaking along with economic and technical considerations;

(C) include in every recommendation or report on proposals for legislation and other major Federal actions significantly affecting the quality of the human environment, a detailed statement by the responsible official on—

    (i) the environmental impact of the proposed action,

    (ii) any adverse environmental effects which cannot be avoided should the proposal be implemented,

    (iii) alternatives to the proposed action,

    (iv) the relationship between local short-term uses of man's environment and the maintenance and enhancement of long-term productivity, and

    (v) any irreversible and irretrievable commitments of resources which would be involved in the proposed action should it be implemented.

Prior to making any detailed statement, the responsible Federal official shall consult with and obtain the comments of any Federal agency which has jurisdiction by law or special expertise with respect to any environmental impact involved. Copies of such statement and the comments and views of the appropriate Federal, State, and local agencies, which are authorized to develop and enforce environmental standards, shall be made available to the President, the Council on Environmental Quality and to the public as provided by section 552 of title 5, and shall accompany the proposal through the existing agency review processes;

    (D) any detailed statement required under subparagraph (C) after January 1, 1970, for any major Federal action funded under a program of grants to States shall not be deemed to be legally insufficient solely by reason of having been prepared by a State agency or official, if:

    (i) the State agency or official has statewide jurisdiction and has the responsibility for such action,

    (ii) the responsible Federal official furnishes guidance and participates in such preparation,

    (iii) the responsible Federal official independently evaluates such statement prior to its approval and adoption, and

    (iv) after January 1, 1976, the responsible Federal official provides early notification to, and solicits the views of, any other State or any Federal land management entity of any action or any alternative thereto which may have significant impacts upon such State or affected Federal land management entity and, if there is any disagreement on such impacts, prepares a written assessment of such impacts and views for incorporation into such detailed statement.

The procedures in this subparagraph shall not relieve the Federal official of his responsibilities for the scope, objectivity, and content of the entire statement or of any other responsibility under this chapter; and further, this subparagraph does not affect the legal sufficiency of statements prepared by State agencies with less than statewide jurisdiction.

(E) study, develop, and describe appropriate alternatives to recommended courses of action in any proposal which involves unresolved conflicts concerning alternative uses of available resources;

(F) recognize the worldwide and long-range character of environmental problems and, where consistent with the foreign policy of the United States, lend appropriate support to initiatives, resolutions, and programs designed to maximize international cooperation in anticipating and preventing a decline in the quality of mankind's world environment;

(G) make available to States, counties, municipalities, institutions, and individuals, advice and information useful in restoring, maintaining, and enhancing the quality of the environment;

(H) initiate and utilize ecological information in the planning and development of resource-oriented projects; and

(I) assist the Council on Environmental Quality established by subchapter II of this chapter.

LAWRENCE W. LIBBY AND
RODNEY L. CLOUSER

30 Population and Global Economic Patterns (1990)

Natural resources are the physical context for all human activity. They facilitate, constrain, embody what we as human beings do with or to each other. With population changes over time come inevitable changes in the natural resource context, exerting new constraints or providing new opportunities for people. The purpose [here] . . . is to help clarify future natural resource consequences of two major forces—population and global economics. Beginning with an identification of key concepts, it reviews evidence of demographic and economic patterns and identifies policy needs of highest priority for the 21st century.

Futurist Daniel Bell has observed that the only real "time bombs" associated with people and natural resources of the future are polity and demography. The former concerns how people in meaningful public entities such as counties, states, provinces, or nations organize themselves to solve natural resource problems. The latter concerns both the number of people and their distribution relative to natural resource systems. More people within any natural resource setting implies a greater frequency of interaction with resources, greater likelihood of scarcity or conflict, and greater challenge for political and economic institutions.

From Lawrence W. Libby and Rodney L. Clouser, "Population and Global Economic Patterns," in *Natural Resources for the 21st Century*, ed. R. Neil Sampson and Dwight Hair (Covelo, CA: Island Press, 1990), 7–9. © 1990 by the American Forestry Association. Reprinted by permission of Island Press.

Importance of Resources

The inevitable controversies over natural resource policy will center on the various ways in which those resources generate utility for people. Resource conflict means a difference of opinion about the rate, form and spatial character of resource-based utility. The apparent tautology needs restating—natural resources are relevant to policy only because of what they do for, or to, people. No one truly speaks for resources. They argue to protect resource use patterns that they prefer. Resource utility comes in many forms.

Resources as Production Inputs

Farmers and foresters have learned how to facilitate the conversion of soil, water, sunlight, and various added nutrients into a product that has value to people. Effective economic demand for the natural resource, then, is derived from demand for the product resulting from organized resource conversion. Food, building materials, and the ornamentals that grace the home or landscape are broad categories of valued products that convert or consume available resources.

Resources as Consumer Goods

Some resources or systems of natural resources are consumed directly with little physical conversion—fish, firewood, coal, or natural gas—though there are costly and essential services added to the resource to make it usable. These services generate jobs and political support; they consume additional resources. Other resources create on-site utility. They are valued *because* they are not consumed, converted, or altered by human action, as with wilderness, wetlands, groundwater recharge areas, shorelands. People are willing to bear considerable cost or inconvenience to keep these resources as they are and petition governments to enact programs to protect them. Accessibility of these systems will affect the quality of utility generated. Some are subject to the cost of excessive enjoyment of people—congestion or deterioration. For others, private ownership may restrict access.

Resources as Store of Wealth

Because they are limited in supply, many resources are valued for the likelihood that greater contact with people will increase their monetary value. People buy land or minerals in anticipation of physical and economic scarcity. They anticipate conversion or consumption at some future time.

Natural resource issues and policies of the 21st century will involve conflicts among these sources of human utility as world populations increase and redistribute, technologies develop, and preferences change. Conflict will not be uniformly distributed throughout the landscape or across political boundaries.

Economics of Scarcity

In their seminal work at Resources for the Future, Barnett and Morse (1963) established the essential distinctions between physical and economic scarcity. As the physical supply of a particular resource becomes harder to find or develop, its price is bid up. Users have an incentive to find substitutes, and they do. New production technologies alter the required resource mix for a given output. Agricultural development programs, for example, focus on getting more product from a land unit and substituting other inputs for land. Economic scarcity is a central ingredient of resource conflict as competing users bid for resource services or petition governments to protect certain natural systems.

Institutional Context

Conflicts in the use of natural resources are resolved (some more successfully than others) through specific institutions. Resource markets, for example, can handle much of the allocation problem, with direct government action when needed to allocate resource services that are not handled well by markets. We know from experience that markets are inadequate to allocate access to an ocean fishery, a fragile eco-system, or the waste-processing capacity of land. People request that governments exercise the powers to tax, to regulate, or to spend funds in the public interest on behalf of forms of natural resource utility not handled well by a market. The choice among available and acceptable policy instruments becomes the substance of natural resource policy. An individual or political group will lobby for or against a particular natural resource policy proposal, based on the resource utility being acquired *and* distribution or the potential distribution of the burden. Even when there is agreement on the resource service desired (e.g., protect a fragile wetland), there may be sharp differences over whether that resource should be acquired with tax money or protected through regulation.

We contend at the outset that people and resource imbalances in the United States are at their root institutional or policy problems rather than matters of physical scarcity. Differences of opinion over the form or rate of resource conversion, the importance of protecting fragile eco-systems, the need for controlling frequency of interaction between people and resources, even the rate of population increase, will define the natural resource issues of coming decades.

RON ARNOLD

31 Wise Use: What Do We Believe? (1996)

It was 1964, the year of the Wilderness Act. Historian Leo Marx began his classic, *The Machine in the Garden*, with the assertion that "the pastoral ideal has been used to define the meaning of America ever since the age of discovery, and it has not yet lost its hold upon the native imagination."[1] A little more than thirty years after, we have the present volume, *A Wolf in the Garden*, echoing Marx less than tolling a sea change in American notions of exactly what is meant by the pastoral ideal Marx saw it as a cultivated rural "middle landscape," not urban, not wild, but embodying what Arthur O. Lovejoy calls "semi-primitivism"; it is located in a middle ground somewhere between the opposing forces of civilization and nature.[2] . . .

Since 1964, the rise of environmentalist ideology has pushed the pastoral ideal increasingly toward nature, striving to redefine the meaning of America in fully primitivist terms of the wild. Eco-ideologists have thrust their metaphoric raging Wolf into every rank and row of our civilized Garden to rogue out both the domesticated and the domesticators. The Wolf howls "wild land, wild water, wild air." Whether Wild People might have a proper place in Wolf World remains a subject of dispute among eco-ideologists.[3]

Public-policy debate over the environment and the meaning of America has been clamorous these thirty years. Its terms were succinctly put by Edith Stein:

From Ron Arnold, "Wise Use: What Do We Believe?" in *A Wolf in the Garden: The Land Rights Movement and the New Environmental Debate*, ed. Philip D. Brick and R. McGreggor Cawley (Lanham, MD: Rowman and Littlefield, 1996), 15–19, 23–26. Reprinted by permission of Rowman and Littlefield.

The environmental movement challenges the dominant Western worldview and its three assumptions:

- Unlimited economic growth is possible and beneficial.
- Most serious problems can be solved by technology.
- Environmental and social problems can be mitigated by a market economy with some state intervention.

Since the 1970s we've heard increasingly about the competing paradigm, wherein:

- Growth must be limited.
- Science and technology must be restrained.
- Nature has finite resources and a delicate balance that humans must observe.[4]

That fairly delineates the public debate. However, in order to critique an ideology, one needs an accurate statement of that ideology. The environmentalist ideology striving to redefine the meaning of America was expounded most realistically by author Victor B. Scheffer in a *Northwest Environmental Journal* article, "Environmentalism's Articles of Faith." The five tenets Scheffer proposed appear to be the core of shared beliefs actually held most widely by environmentalists:

1. *All things are connected.* "[N]ever will we understand completely the spin-off effects of the environmental changes that we create, nor will we measure our own, independent influence in their creation." . . .

2. *Earthly goods are limited.* "As applied to people, carrying capacity is the number of individuals that the earth can support before a limit is reached beyond which the quality of life must worsen and *Homo*, the human animal, becomes less human.". . .

3. *Nature's way is best.* "Woven into the fabric of environmentalism is the belief that natural methods and materials should be favored over artificial and synthetic ones, when there's a clear choice.". . .

4. *The survival of humankind depends on natural diversity.* "Although species by the billions have vanished through natural extinction or transformation, the present rate of extinction is thought to be at least 400 times faster than at the beginning of the Industrial Age.". . .

5. *Environmentalism is radical* "in the sense of demanding fundamental change. It calls for changes in present political systems, in the reach of the law, in the methods of agriculture and industry, in the

structure of capitalism (the profit system), in international dealings, and in education."[5]

One can see the Wolf skulking in each of Scheffer's five tenets of eco-ideology. Actual organizations and individuals comprising the environmental movement stress different clusters of these tenets. Although the environmental movement's structure is complex and amply textured, three distinctive axes of influence dominate environmental politics in America:

1. Establishment interventionists—acting to hamper property rights and markets sufficiently to centralize control of many transactions for the benefit of environmentalists and their funders in the foundation community, while leaving the market economy itself operational, they tend to emphasize the need for natural diversity and in some cases to own and manage wildlife preserves. Notable organizations in this sector are the Nature Conservancy, National Wildlife Federation, and National Audubon Society.

2. Eco-socialists—acting to dislodge the market system with public ownership of all resources and production, commanded by environmentalists in an ecological welfare state, they tend to emphasize the limits of earthly goods. Greenpeace, Native Forest Council, and Maine Audubon Society are representative groups.

3. Deep ecologists—acting to reduce or eliminate industrial civilization and human population in varying degrees, they tend to emphasize that nature's way is best and environmentalism is radical. Earth First!, Sea Shepherd Conservation Society, and Native Forest Network are in this category.[6]

The Wolf in these varieties of sheep's clothing is rapacious, not simply protecting nature but also annihilating the livelihoods of dwellers in the middle landscape. Today the Wolf is firmly entrenched in Washington, D.C., where important environmental groups have established headquarters or major operating bases. Eco-ideologists have written many laws, tested them in the courts, and pressured many administrative agencies into compliance with their ideology. They have, in brief, become the Establishment. . . .

As the environmental debate developed during the late 1980s, the "dominant Western worldview" gained an organized constituency and advocacy leadership: the wise use movement. Incipient and gestating more than a decade in the bosom of those who had been most wounded by environmental ideology, the new movement congealed at a conference in Reno, Nevada, in 1988. It was centered around a hodge-podge of property-rights groups, antiregulation legal foundations, trade groups of large industries, motorized recreation-vehicle clubs, federal-land users, farmers, ranchers, fishermen, trappers, small forest holders, mineral prospectors, and others who live and work in the middle landscape.[7]

It came as a shock to environmentalists. The "competing paradigm" unhappily found itself confronted with a competing paradigm. The free ride was over. A substantial cluster of nonprofit grassroots organizations now advocated unlimited economic growth, technological progress, and a market economy. They opposed the eco-ideologists' proposals using the tactics of social-change movements, such as mobilizing grassroots constituencies, staging media events including protest demonstrations, and orchestrating letter-writing campaigns to pressure Congress.

It was a pivotal shift in the debate. No longer were eco-ideologists able to face off against business and industry, pitting greedy for-profit corporations against environmentalism's nonprofit moral high ground. Now it was urban environmentalists defending their vision of the pastoral ideal against those who actually lived the pastoral ideal in the middle landscape.

This simple structural rearrangement of the debate went virtually unnoticed, but was crucial: it was nonprofit against nonprofit, one side promoting economic growth, technological progress, and a market economy, the other opposing.

The emergent wise use movement held up a mirror to the embarrassing questions posed by the "competing paradigm": Just *who* will limit our economic growth? Who will restrain America's science and technology? Who will decide what "delicate balance humans must observe"? The answer was clear: only environmental ideologists, and not those who create economic growth, science, technology, or the market economy. . . .

Although it would be rash to propose wise use's articles of faith—it is a diverse movement—some of the following principles would probably find wide agreement among those who provide the material goods to all of humanity:

1. *Humans, like all organisms, must use natural resources to survive.* This fundamental verity is never addressed by environmental ideology. The simple fact that humans must get their food, clothing, and shelter from the environment is either ignored or obliquely deplored in quasi-suicidal plaints such as, "I would rather see a blank space where I am—at least I wouldn't be harming anything."

If environmentalism were to acknowledge our necessary use of the earth, the ideology would lose its meaning. To grant legitimacy to the human use of the environment would be to accept the unavoidable environmental damage that is the price of our survival. Once that price is acceptable, the moral framework of environmental ideology becomes irrelevant and the issues become technical and economic.

2. *The earth and its life are tough and resilient, not fragile and delicate.* Environmentalists tend to be catastrophists, seeing any human use of the earth as damage and massive human use of the earth as a catastrophe. An environmentalist motto is "We all live downstream," the viewpoint of hapless victims.

Wise users, on the other hand, tend to be cornucopians, seeing themselves as stewarding and nurturing the bountiful earth as it stewards and nurtures them. A wise use motto is "We all live upstream," the viewpoint of responsible individuals.

The difference in sense of life is striking. Environmentalism by its very nature promotes feelings of guilt for existing, which naturally degenerate into pessimism, self-loathing, and depression. Wise use by its very nature promotes feelings of competence to live in the world, generating curiosity, learning, and optimism toward improving the earth for the massive use of future generations.

The glory of the "dominant Western worldview" so scorned by environmental ideologists is its metaphor of progress: the starburst, an insatiable and interminable outreach after a perpetually flying goal. Environmentalists call humanity a cancer on the earth; wise users call us a joy.

If there is a single, tight expression of the wise use sense of life, it has to be the final stanza of Shelley's *Prometheus Unbound* [1819]. Wise users, I think, will recognize themselves in these lines:

> To suffer woes which Hope thinks infinite;
> To forgive wrongs darker than death or night;
> To defy Power, which seems omnipotent;
> To love, and bear; to hope till Hope itself creates
> From its own wreck the thing it contemplates;
> Neither to change, nor falter, nor repent;
> This, like thy glory, Titan, is to be
> Good, great and joyous, beautiful and free;
> This is alone Life, Joy, Empire, and Victory![8]

3. *We only learn about the world through trial and error.* The universe did not come with a set of instructions, nor did our minds. We cannot see the future. Thus, the only way we humans can learn about our surroundings is through trial and error. Even the most sophisticated science is systematized trial and error. Environmental ideology fetishizes nature to the point that we cannot permit ourselves errors with the environment, ending in no trials and no learning.

There will always be abusers who do not learn. People of goodwill tend to deal with abuse by education, incentive, clear rules, and administering appropriate penalties for incorrigibles.

4. *Our limitless imaginations can break through natural limits to make earthly goods and carrying capacity virtually infinite.* Just as settled agriculture increased earthly goods and carrying capacity vastly beyond hunting and gathering, so our imaginations can find ways to increase total productivity by superseding one level of technology after another. Taught by the lessons learned from systematic trial and error, we can close the loops in our productive systems and find innumerable ways to do more with less.

5. *People's reworking of the earth is revolutionary, problematic, and ultimately benevolent.* Of the tenets of wise use, this is the most oracular. Humanity is itself revolutionary and problematic. Danger is our symbiote. Yet even the timid are part of the human adventure, which has barely begun.

Humanity may ultimately prove to be a force of nature forwarding some cosmic teleology of which we are yet unaware. Or not. Humanity may be the universe awakening and becoming conscious of itself. Or not. Our reworking of the earth may be of the utmost evolutionary benevolence and importance. Or not. We don't know. The only way to see the future is to be there.

As the environmental debate advances to maturity, the environmental movement must accept and incorporate many of these wise use precepts if it is to survive as a social and political force. Establishment interventionism, as represented by the large foundations and their grant-driven client organizations, must find practical ways to accommodate private property rights and entrepreneurial economic growth. Eco-socialism's collectivist program must find practical ways to accommodate individual economic liberties in its bureaucratic command-and-control approach. Deep ecology's biocentrism must find practical ways to accommodate anthropocentrism and technological progress.

To accomplish this necessary reform, environmentalists of all persuasions will have to face their ideological blind spots and see their own belief systems as wise users see them, that is, in a critical and practical light. This is a most difficult change for ideological environmentalists. Failure to reform environmentalism from within will invite regulation from without or doom the movement to irrelevancy as the wise use movement lives the pastoral ideal in the middle landscape, defining the meaning of America.

NOTES

1. Leo Marx, *The Machine in the Garden: Technology and the Pastoral Ideal in America* (New York: Oxford University Press, 1964), 3.
2. Arthur O. Lovejoy et al., *A Documentary History of Primitivism and Related Ideas* (Baltimore: Johns Hopkins University Press, 1935), 369.
3. Bill Devall and George Sessions, eds., *Deep Ecology: Living as if Nature Mattered* (Salt Lake City: Peregrine Smith Books, 1985).
4. Edith C. Stein, *The Environmental Sourcebook* (New York: Lyons & Burford, 1992), 6.
5. Victor B. Scheffer, "Environmentalism's Articles of Faith," *Northwest Environmental Journal* 5, no. 1 (1989): 99–108.
6. Rona Arnold and Alan Gottlieb, *Trashing the Economy: How Runaway Environmentalism Is Wrecking America*, 2nd ed. (Bellevue, Wash.: Free Enterprise Press, 1994), 57–67 et passim. This analysis of the environmental movement's structure is part of the larger analytical treatment throughout the text.
7. Alan M. Gottlieb, ed., *The Wise Use Agenda* (Bellevue, Wash.: Free Enterprise Press, 1989). This document was the result of the 1988 Wise Use Strategy Conference and consists of recommendations for natural resource use from 125 of the 250 conference participants.
8. Percy Bysshe Shelley, "Prometheus Unbound," in *The Works of Percy Bysshe Shelley* (Roslyn, N.Y.: Black's Reader Service, 1951), 180.

ANDREE COLLARD WITH
JOYCE CONTRUCCI

32 | Women and Ecology (1988)

Introduction

Susan B. Anthony once asked why women did not burn with outrage and protest at the discrimination of rights and privilege they faced because of their sex. In the past fifteen years, feminists have developed methodologies with which to analyse sexism, fuel protest, and foster liberation. In reclaiming the power to name ourselves and our experiences, women have exposed patriarchy as a disease. The treatment of nature and animals is the vilest manifestation of that disease. Nature and animals communicate their plight in ways this culture refuses to understand. This book is a burning protest against the violation of nature and animals which in patriarchy is inextricably connected with the oppression of women. Feminists must articulate this oppression as part of our holistic, biophilic vision.* For it is a fact that no woman will be free until all animals are free and nature is released from man's ruthless exploitation.

In patriarchy, nature, animals and women are objectified, hunted, invaded, colonised, owned, consumed and forced to yield and to produce (or not). This violation of the integrity of wild, spontaneous Being is rape. It is motivated by a fear and rejection of Life and it allows

---

*'Biophilic', as originally used by Mary Daly, literally means 'life-loving'. See Mary Daly, Gyn/Ecology: The Metaethics of Radical Feminism (Boston: Beacon Press, 1978; London: The Women's Press, 1979), p. 10. For an expanded definition, see Mary Daly, Websters' First New Intergalactic Wickedary of the English Language (Boston: Beacon Press, 1987; London: The Women's Press, 1988), p. 67.

From Andrée Collard with Joyce Contrucci, "Women and Ecology," *Rape of the Wild: Man's Violence against Animals and the Earth* (Bloomington: Indiana University Press, 1988), 1–3, 137–38, 168. Reprinted by permission of Indiana University Press.

the oppressor the illusion of control, of power, of being alive. As with women as a class, nature and animals have been kept in a state of inferiority and powerlessness in order to enable men as a class to believe and act upon their 'natural' superiority/dominance.

I have used animals as a window to the death-oriented values of patriarchal society partly from a deep concern for their well-being and partly because man's treatment of them exposes those values in their crudest, most undisguised form. I have taken the position that it is morally wrong to kill for pleasure, to inflict pain for the thrill of discoveries nobody needs, to colonise other creatures' minds and bodies, to make a fetish of those very animals the culture as a whole is bent on eliminating, and to conserve wild animals in parks, zoos and game reserves, thereby destroying their integrity of being. Likewise, apathy, thoughtlessness, and the denial of responsibility and choice are moral transgressions; they allow for the overall pollution and destruction of the earth, the oppression of people, the atrocities committed on animals in laboratories in the name of scientific progress, and the objectification of wildlife in general through conservation programmes and domestication.

Because rape of the wild and the free spirit of nature is complex and painful, a number of emotions which I have made little attempt to disguise have gone into this book. I am first of all always on the side of nature. Her innocence (in the etymological sense of 'not noxious') may derive from the fact that she acts not from choice but from inherent need. Whatever nature does that seems cruel and evil to anthropomorphising eyes is done without intent to harm. Nature has worked out a self-regulated flow of birth and decay, striking a balance between death and rejuvenation which human beings in their propagating folly ought to have taken as a model. Where the human hand has not greedily tinkered, nature is spontaneous, awesome, refreshingly unselfconscious, magnificently diverse. For thousands of years, nature has been the measure of our humanity, providing much of our self-identity.

I do not believe in trying to reverse time and 'go primitive', but it is important to broaden our understanding of the past and learn from other cultures and other times the way of universal kinship. By universal kinship I mean a recognition on the part of all individuals of our common bond with all that exists. This recognition would lead to an understanding/feeling that the most 'insignificant' part is indispensable to the harmony and well-being of the whole. In other words, it would put human beings back into the concept and reality of nature as similar, and leave behind the concept of nature as different and inferior. It would impart dignity to our dealings with all creatures by dissolving the patriarchal separatist mentality that fractures life into inimical factions. It would abolish all divisive 'isms'—sexism, racism, classism, ageism, militarism, etc. In short, acting upon the concept of universal kinship would start the cultural revolution that would be the undoing of patriarchy.

Women and ecology

We are the rocks, we are soil, we are trees, rivers, we are wind, we carry the birds, we are cows, mules, we are horses, we are Solid elements . . . matter. *We are flesh, we breathe, we are her body: we speak.*
Susan Griffin, Woman and Nature

The identity and destiny of woman and nature are merged. Accordingly, feminist values and principles directed towards ending the oppression of women are inextricably linked to ecological values and principles directed towards ending the oppression of nature. These values and principles are distilled from women's experiences everywhere and of all times. Their realisation for women and the earth is predicated on women and men refusing to endorse the destructive values that drive sexism, racism, classism, and speciesism. It is ultimately the affirmation of our kinship with nature, of our common life with her, which will prove the source of our mutual well-being.

Ecology is woman-based almost by definition. *Eco* means house, *logos* means word, speech, thought. Thus ecology is the language of the house. Defined more formally, ecology is the study of the interconnectedness between all organisms and their surroundings—the house. As such, it requires a thorough knowledge and an intimate experience of the house.

Good women have kept good houses on the model of Mother Nature for as long as there have been mothers. They have seen to it that their children were fed, clothed, sheltered and safe. They have kept the budget (eco/nomics) delicately balanced between extravagance and thrift, often at incredible cost to themselves. Starvation and squalor have occurred only under extreme patriarchal control of the production of the land and children. Even then, as under less stringent degrees of oppression, many women have weathered abuse just as many creatures of the earth, air and water have survived man-made cataclysms, with resilience and regeneration. Like weeds and pests that have become immune to chemical poisoning, they have kept their wildness, that is, their strength and insubordination to outside control by maintaining their ties to each other.

Women's experience with oppression and abuse, as well as their experience of mothering, can make them more sensitive to the oppression and abuse of nature, as well as better situated to remedy it. Feminists in particular can enrich the base of ecology with their own theoretical analyses and intimate experience of the house. Love and anger drive feminists to achieve the goals of non-violence, reproductive freedom, creature rights for all, and rigorous house-cleaning. For women, this means an understanding and sweeping rejection of all behavioural debris that keeps us divided and makes us complicit in our oppression. It means rescuing our wildness and being proud of it. As it concerns nature, it means cleaning up the existing messes we have made through thoughtlessness and greed as well as taking off our shoes before entering the house, the ecosphere of our activities, as if we were entering a sanctuary, for the sheer joy and celebration of it.

In *Woman and Nature* (1977), Susan Griffin draws on this deep, life-sustaining interconnection between women and the earth. Her words, harsh and accurate when she addresses the facts of man's violence against nature, impassioned and grieving when she speaks of the experience of those facts, stir 'what is still wild in us', moving us along with her to a profound sense of loss and a vibrant reclamation of the earth, our sister/mother. She writes

> This earth is my sister; I love her daily grace, her silent daring, and how loved I am *how we admire this strength in each other, all that we have lost, all that we have suffered, all that we know: we are stunned by this beauty,* and I do not forget: what she is to me, what I am to her.* . . .

Historically, our destiny as women and the destiny of nature are inseparable. It began within earth/goddess-worshipping societies which celebrated the life-giving and life-sustaining powers of woman and nature, and it remains despite our brutal negation and violation

*Susan Griffin, *Woman and Nature: The Roaring Inside Her* (New York: Harper & Row, 1978: London: The Women's Press, 1984), p. 219.

in the present. Women must re-member and re-claim our biophilic power. Drawing upon it we must make the choices that will affirm and foster life, directing the future away from the nowhere of the fathers to the somewhere that is ours—on this planet—now.

SUGGESTIONS FOR
FURTHER READING

PART I   INDIAN ECOLOGY, AMERICAN CONQUEST

Beginning in the 1960s, a growing body of Native American scholarship and literature has helped to reveal the range of Indian mythologies in which beliefs about "nature" are centered. Among the many works in this broad category are John G. Neihardt's moving *Black Elk Speaks* (1961) and John (Fire) Lame Deer and Richard Erdoes, *Lame Deer: Seeker of Visions* (1972). These biographies of distinguished tribal leaders broke through Indian stereotypes and offered a rich portrait of native existence. Compiled by T. C. McLuhan, *Touch the Earth* (1971) featured Edward Curtis's Indian photographs accompanied by excerpts of native voices, many of which speak poignantly of dramatic environmental change. Paula Gunn Allen, *The Sacred Hoop: Recovering the Feminine in American Indian Traditions* (1982), is a highly revered synthesis of folkloric myth and social history that goes to the nurturing, matriarchal heart of the Indian world view. For a useful overview of Indian beliefs and traditions, see Alice Marriott and Carol K. Rachlin, *American Indian Mythology* (1972).

An increasing number of environmental historians and anthropologists have surveyed or examined particular episodes of the ecological encounter of native and European Americans. Among the best overviews are J. Donald Hughes, *North American Indian Ecology* (1983), and Christopher Vecsey and Robert W. Venables, eds., *American Indian Environments: Ecological Issues in Native American History* (1980). See also the special topic issue of *Environmental Review* (vol. 9, summer 1985) devoted entirely to American Indian environmental history. Books examining the larger conflict of Indians and Europeans include James Axtell, *The European and the Indian: Essays in the Ethnohistory of Colonial North America* (1981), and Karen Kupperman, *Settling with the Indians: The Meeting of English and Indian Cultures in America, 1580–1640*

(1980). Both Francis Jennings, *The Invasion of the Europeans* (1976), and Calvin Martin's edited volume, *The American Indian and the Problem of History* (1987), challenge the underlying falsehoods and nationalistic assumptions that had heretofore veiled the American conquest of Indian peoples and their lands.

Case histories of environmental change in New England begin with William Cronon's important study, *Changes in the Land: Indians, Colonists, and the Ecology of New England* (1983). Innumerable historians had studied the epic clash of Indians and English colonists, but, until Cronon's work, none had looked closely at the landscape upon which it unfolded. Mining a wealth of previously untapped primary sources, Cronon gives voice not only to Indians and the English but also to the environment itself. He paints an intimate picture of the changing landscape of Indian fields and forests as well as of English rock walls, fences, and cattle pastures, and he offers keen insight into what it all meant for both the invaders and the vanquished. Howard Russell's *Indian New England before the Mayflower* (1983) examines primary accounts thoroughly to explore further the subjects of Indian horticulture and society before the arrival of the English. Also useful are Lloyd C. Irland, *Wildlands and Woodlots: The Story of New England's Forests* (1982), Calvin Martin, *Keepers of the Game: Indian-Animal Relationships and the Fur Trade* (1978), and Peter N. Carroll, *Puritanism and the Wilderness* (1969). On Puritan consciousness, the best work may still be Perry Miller's edited *The New England Mind: The Seventeenth Century* (1939). Cultural-environmental histories of the Southwest include Edward Holland Spicer's survey, *Cycles of Conquest: The Impact of Spain, Mexico, and the United States on the Indians of the Southwest, 1533–1960* (1962), and William De Buys's excellent case study, *Enchantment and Exploitation: The Life and Times of a New Mexico Mountain Range* (1985).

Related studies of other regions include Leonard A. Carlson, *Indians, Bureaucrats, and Land: The Dawes Act and the Decline of Indian Farming* (1981). Carlson reveals the distressing reality that after the historic Dawes Act of 1887, designed ostensibly to encourage Indians to become independent yeoman farmers, Indians farmed less and lost hundreds of thousands of acres of more land to whites who exploited the law for their own self-interest. See also Richard White's *Roots of Dependency: Subsistence, Environment, and Social Change among the Choctaws, Pawnees, and Navajos* (1983). A distinguished environmental historian and scholar of the West, White weaves a history of the forces that worked in various combinations to devastate or transform ancient social, cultural, and environmental relationships among these three tribes.

The larger story of the environmental transformation of public lands in the West in the nineteenth century can be explored further in Everett Dick, *The Lure of the Land: A Social History of the Public Lands from the Articles of Confederation to the New Deal* (1970), Hildegard Binder Johnson, *Order upon the Land: The U.S. Rectangular Land Survey and the Upper Mississippi Country* (1976), Roy M. Robbins, *Our Landed Heritage: The Public Domain, 1776–1970* (1970), Russell McKee, *The Last West: A History of the Great Plains in North America* (1972), and Frederick Turner, *Beyond Geography: The Western Spirit against the Wilderness* (1980). Henry Nash Smith's brilliant *Virgin Land: The American West as Symbol and Myth* (1958) remains the most probing, interdisciplinary examination of the entwined mythologies of untainted wilderness and Manifest Destiny.

The middle stage of colonial farming in the capitalist ecological transformation has drawn increasing attention from environmental and social historians. Were all white farmers rapacious exploiters of the land whose attitudes toward nature stood in absolute contrast to the natives they were displacing? Of course not; the story is far more complex, the values of early white farmers more organicist than capitalist. Beyond Carolyn Merchant's *Ecological Revolutions* (1989), among the works exploring the subject further are Christopher Clark, *The Roots of Rural Capitalism: Western Massachusetts, 1780–1860* (1990), and Steve Hahn and Jonathan Prude, eds., *The Countryside in the Age of Capitalist Transformation* (1985). See also James A. Henretta, "Families and Farms in Pre-Industrial America," *William and Mary Quarterly* 3rd ser. 25 (1978): 3–31; and Carol Shammas, "How Self-Sufficient Was Early America?" *Journal of Interdisciplinary History* 13 (1982): 247–72.

Finally, good histories of the social-environmental impact of mining in California and elsewhere throughout the West include J. S. Holliday's highly acclaimed *Rush for Riches: Gold Fever and the Making of California* (1999), Raymond F. Dasmann, *California's Changing Environment* (1988), George H. Phillips, *The Enduring Struggle: Indians in California History* (1981), Robert Kelly, *Gold vs. Grain: The Hydraulic Mining Controversy in California's Sacramento Valley* (1959), and Duane Smith's fine overview, *Mining America: The Industry and the Environment, 1800–1980* (1987).

PART II NATURE'S NATION: THE AMERICAN LANDSCAPE AND THE NATURE WRITING TRADITION

On the emergence of nature as a focal point in the development of American culture in the nineteenth century, see Hans Huth's pathbreaking *Nature and the American: Three Centuries of Changing Attitudes* (1957). Huth's study was followed by Arthur A. Ekirch, Jr., *Man and Nature in America* (1963), Perry Miller, *Nature's Nation* (1967), Peter J. Schmitt, *Back to Nature: The Arcadian Myth in Urban America* (1969), Lee Clark Mitchell, *Witnesses to a Vanishing America: The Nineteenth-Century Response* (1981), and William Howarth, *Nature in American Life* (1997). On the central importance and shifting conceptions of wilderness in particular, see Roderick Frazier Nash, *Wilderness and the American Mind* (1982), and Max Oelschlaeger, *The Idea of Wilderness: From Prehistory to the Age of Ecology* (1993), examining the philosophical and religious origins of American attitudes toward the wild.

Excellent studies and collections of either nature writers or the theme of nature in American literature include Frederick Turner, *Spirit of Place: The Making of an American Literary Landscape* (1989), Pamela Regis, *Describing Early America: Bartram, Jefferson, Crèvecoeur, and the Rhetoric of Natural History* (1992), John Elder, *American Nature Writers* (1996), Alfred Kazin, *A Writer's America: Landscape in Literature* (1988), Cecilia Tichi, *New World, New Earth: Environmental Reform in American Literature from the Puritans through Whitman* (1979), and Norman Foerster's often overlooked *Nature in American Literature: Studies in the Modern View of Nature* (1923). Each of them surveys and analyzes the central place of nature and landscape in American literature.

Where nature writers "fit" within the canon is the point of Thomas J. Lyon's taxonomy of environmental literature—a feature of his encyclopedic compendium, *This Incomparable Lande: A Book of American Nature Writing* (1989). Although fraught with overlapping boundaries and arguable identification, Lyon's ordering of the vast field is nevertheless quite useful. While recognizing that division in eco-literature is a difficult proposition, he places within genres and subgenres the major works. Among the wide range of exemplary nature writers Lyon includes are Hector St. John de Crèvecoeur, *Letters from an American Farmer* (1782), John D. Goodman, *Rambles of a Naturalist* (1828), Olaus Murie, *A Field Guide to Animal Tracks* (1954), Roger Tory Peterson, *A Field Guide to Western Birds* (1961), John Hay, *Spirit of Survival* (1974), Wendell Berry's brilliant essays on country life, John McPhee's *Coming into the Country* (1977), and Barry Lopez's *Arctic Dreams* (1986).

The significance of nature imagery and the American landscape painting tradition in particular is the focus of two books by art historian Barbara Novak, *American Painting in the Nineteenth Century: Realism, Idealism, and the American Experience* (1969), and *Nature and Culture: American Landscape and Painting, 1825–1875* (1980). On the importance of the Hudson River School painters, see Raymond J. O'Brien, *American Sublime: Landscape and Scenery of the Lower Hudson Valley* (1981).

On the deep symbolism and impact of pastoralism in American culture, see Leo Marx's classic, *The Machine in the Garden: Technology and the Pastoral Ideal in America* (1964). Among works exploring the psychological, cultural, sociological, and historic roots and more universal dimensions of a human sense of place are Yi-fu Tuan, *Space and Place: The Perspective of Experience* (1977) and *Topophilia: A Study of Environmental Perception, Attitudes, and Values* (1974), Neil Evernden, *The Natural Alien: Humankind and Environment* (1985), and Paul Shepard, *Man in the Landscape: A Historic View of the Esthetics of Nature* (1967).

The evolution of American urban ideals and attitudes toward the city and its peripheral suburban green space has received increasing attention in recent decades. Among the representative studies are Robert Fishman, *Bourgeois Utopias* (1987), Kenneth T. Jackson, *Crabgrass Frontier: The Suburbanization of the United States* (1985), and James Machor, *Pastoral Cities: Urban Ideals and the Symbolic Landscape of America* (1987). Much of the new history of suburbia has critiqued the homogenized, white middle-class landscapes of asphalt and neon, the loss of prime farmland and open space, and the abandonment of the urban core, all of which have accompanied our embrace of the suburban ideal. A somewhat contrary view is taken by Craig Whitaker in *Architecture and the American Dream* (1996), who argues that suburbanization and its strip mall culture are not reckless destructive forces but rather quintessential expressions of American ideals of freedom and mobile independence.

Regarding the writers who are the focus of Part II, see Lawrence Buell's *The Environmental Imagination: Thoreau, Nature Writing, and the Formation of American Culture* (1995), a riveting theoretical exploration of Thoreau's seminal place in the development of American nature writing and the national culture. With Thoreau as the point of departure, Buell embarks on a larger examination of American nature writers. Notable among the innumerable other studies of Thoreau are Walter Harding, *The Days of Henry Thoreau: A Biography* (1993), and Robert L. Rothwell, *Henry David Thoreau* (1994) and *Henry David Thoreau: An American Landscape* (1995).

Exploring the biography and work of John Muir are Stephen R. Fox, *The American Conservation Movement: John Muir and His Legacy* (1986), Phil Arnot, *High Sierra: John Muir's Range of Light* (1996), Sally Miller, *John Muir: Life and Work* (1995), William Cronon's edited collection of Muir's *Nature Writings* (1997), and Michael Cohen's *The Pathless Way: John Muir and American Wilderness* (1986). Studies of naturalist John Burroughs include Edward

Renahan, *John Burroughs: An American Naturalist* (1998), Ginger Wadsworth, *John Burroughs: The Sage of Slabsides* (1997), and *John Burroughs's America: Selections from the Writings of the Naturalist* (1997). Mary Hunter Austin's *Earth Horizon: Autobiography* sheds light on the formation of her nature sensibility and her years in the southwestern desert. Melody Graulich and Elizabeth Klimasmith's edited collection, *Exploring Lost Borders: Critical Essays on Mary Austin* (1994), offers an insightful analysis of Austin's writings about the West. Finally, for more on the life and mind of Annie Dillard, see Dillard's *The Annie Dillard Reader* (1995) and *American Childhood* (1999) as well as Scott Slovic, *Seeking Awareness in American Nature Writing* (1992).

A number of critics work to position the early literary naturalists of Europe and America as essential to the development of ecology. Most notable is Jonathan Bate, *Romantic Ecology: Wordsworth and the Environmental Tradition* (1991). Bate's book helped to revive a twenty-year-old discussion of the relationship of the literature of western civilization to the ecological crisis begat by the scientific and technological paradigm. That dialogue commenced with Joseph W. Meeker's *The Comedy of Survival: Studies in Literary Ecology* (1972). Broadly defined by Meeker as writing that contains "biological themes and relationships," "literary ecology" or "ecocriticism" has been an openended inquiry into the relationship of language and the natural world outside.

Deconstructionist ecocritics came to challenge more traditional literary critics such as Bate, arguing that their focus on the transcendent romanticism of nature writers ignored the political and social-environmental context of their work. Beginning in the 1970s and obviously influenced by the environmental crisis of the era, a wave of eco-literary critics countered that impulse. They argued essentially that romanticism offered a refuge and excuse for industrialism, not a challenge to it. Writers and critics such as William Rueckert, Wendell Berry, and Paul Brooks probed the layered meanings of eco-literature for their own time, often asking troubling questions. For the larger outlines and specific arguments of this dialogue, see Cheryll Glotfelty and Harold Fromm's excellent compendium, *The Ecocriticism Reader: Landmarks in Literary Ecology* (1996), and Karl Kroeber, *Ecological Literary Criticism: Romantic Imagining and the Biology of Mind* (1994). The emerging field of literary ecocriticism has prompted several scholarly journals, particularly *Western American Literature*, to devote increasing attention to the subject. Glen A. Love and SueEllen Campbell are among the scholars whose work is found there and in other literary journals such as *ISLE: Interdisciplinary Studies in Literature and the Environment* and *ASLE News*. The arrival of the journal *Terra Nova: Nature and Culture* in the mid-1990s perhaps best announced the flowering of the interdisciplinary impulse. *Terra Nova* brought together writers from a wide variety of disciplines who cross the boundaries of the natural environmental sciences, politics, society, and culture.

PART III SCIENCE, NATURE, AND THE EMERGENCE OF AN ECOLOGICAL ETHIC

The most comprehensive work on the history of ecological thought is Donald Worster's *Nature's Economy: A History of Ecological Ideas* (1977). Deftly placing the intellectual history of ecology in broader context, this study marked Worster as one of the most distinguished environmental historians in the field. In a later essay for the *Pacific Historical Review* (vol. 53, February 1984), Worster made the theoretical case for the use of "History as Natural History," helping to solidify the growing legitimacy of environmental-ecological study. Other strong overviews of the evolution of ecology include Anna Bramwell, *Ecology in the Twentieth Century* (1989), Ronald C. Tobey, *Saving the Prairies* (1981), and Leslie A. Real and James H. Brown, *Foundations of Ecology: Classic Papers with Commentaries* (1991). See also Leo Marx, "American Institutions and Ecological Ideals," *Science* 170 (1970): 945–52. Also relevant is *Minding Nature: The Philosophers of Ecology* (1996), edited by David Macauley, which examines the ecological thought of some of the giant thinkers of western civilization, including Thomas Hobbes, Martin Heidegger, and Hannah Arendt. Frank Benjamin Golley's *A History of the Ecosystem Concept in Ecology* (1993) links the work of numerous ecologists across decades of time in formulating that essential concept of the field.

Among the landmark works in the development of ecology in the twentieth century are Frederic Clements, *Plant Succession: An Analysis of the Development of Vegetation* (1916), Paul Sears, *Life and Environment* (1932), Adolph Murie, *Wolves of Mount McKinley* (1944), Raymond Lindeman, "The Trophic-Dynamic Aspect of Ecology," *Ecology* 23 (1942): 399–418, Eugene Odum, *Fundamentals of Ecology* (1953), and Barry Commoner, *The Closing Circle* (1971). Published at the zenith of the new environmental movement just after the first Earth Day, Commoner's work helped to popularize the word "ecology" and put forth its so-called Four Rules of interconnectedness and human ecological responsibility.

Biographies of the central figures examined in Part III include Thomas P. Slaughter, *The Natures of John and William Bartram* (1996), a biographical double portrait of the character and nature sensibilities of these early naturalists. Slaughter's probing and keen insights into the men themselves reveal just as much of the American landscape when it was still wild. Gregory A. Waselkov, ed., *William Bartram on the Southeastern Indians* (1995), is also noteworthy. On the life and work of George Perkins Marsh, see David Lowenthal and William Cronon, *George Perkins Marsh: Prophet of Conservation* (2000), and Jane Curtis et al., *World of George Perkins Marsh* (1982). Not surprisingly, perhaps, less has been written about the central role of women in the urban public health movement of the turn of the century. See, however, Martin Melosi, *Garbage in the Cities: Refuse, Reform, and Environment, 1880–1980* (1981), and *Coping with Abundance: Energy and Environment in Industrial America* (1985). Robert Clarke's *Ellen Swallow: The Woman Who Founded Ecology* (1974) is a worthy biographical study. On Aldo Leopold, see Susan L. Flader, *Thinking Like a Mountain: Aldo Leopold and the Evolution of an Ecological Attitude Toward Deer, Wolves, and Forests* (1974). On wildlife generally, see Peter Matthiesen's classic *Wildlife in America*. Linda Lear's *Rachel Carson: Witness for Nature* (1997) offers an excellent biographical sketch of the scientist, while Craig Waddell's edited *And No Birds Sing: Rhetorical Analyses of Silent Spring* (2000) sheds greater light on the arguments and long-term results of Carson's daring work.

Among the outstanding histories of the early formative years of the conservation movement are Samuel P. Hays's classic, *Conservation and the Gospel of Efficiency: The Progressive Conservation Movement, 1890–1920* (1959), which first revealed the utilitarian, growth-oriented ideology of Gifford Pinchot and the first generation of conservationists. See also Elmo R. Richardson, *The Politics of Conservation: Crusades and Controversies, 1897–1913* (1962).

PART IV POWER AND PLACE: THE MEETING OF SOCIAL AND ENVIRONMENTAL HISTORY

Barely touched upon in this volume but central to the history of power relations and environmental change in the United States is the subject of slavery and the exhaustion of soils in the South. For outstanding overviews of that history, see Albert Cowdrey, *This Land, This South: An Environmental History* (1983), and Timothy Silver, *A New Face on the Countryside: Indians, Colonists, and Slaves in the South Atlantic Forests, 1560–1800* (1990). Silver penetrates the changing relationships of culture, class, and race as well as the ideology of the conquerors to reveal the profound social and environmental transformation of that forested region over time. In the same vein is *"What Nature Suffers to Groe": Life, Labor, and Landscape on the Georgia Coast, 1680–1920* by Mart A. Stewart (1998), an excellent study examining the links between the power structures and different perceptions and uses of the environment by masters and slaves on Low Country plantations. See also the still vital study by Hugh Hammond Bennett, *The Soils and Agriculture of the Southern States* (1921).

Histories of the environmental movement in the United States speak not only of the ever-widening scope and increasingly dire nature of problems in the twentieth century, but they reveal also the class, gender, and racial dimensions of many of those issues and of the movement itself. Particularly noteworthy is Benjamin Kline's *First Along the River* (1998); epic in scope, the book begins with the fifteenth-century roots of environmental change and concludes with the antienvironmental backlash of the 1990s. Robert Gottlieb in *Forcing the Spring: The Transformation of the American Environmental Movement* (1993) is more focused on the modern era, offering solid historical background on the white, middle-class urban roots of both the resource conservation and wilderness preservation movements. Gottlieb makes a compelling argument that throughout most of the twentieth century, there were two distinct strands of "environmentalism": one focused on preserving wilderness and national parks by exercising their increasing national stature and political power, the other more centered at the grassroots community level and fixed on issues of public health.

Only in the 1970s, Gottlieb argues, did mainstream environmentalism begin forcefully to respond to issues such as clean air, clean water, and hazardous waste and, even then, were slow to engage the grassroots. The major groups learned to speak the regulatory language of cost-benefit analysis and risk assessment in order to influence government on public environmental health issues. Relevant to the history of the increasing scientific-technical professionalization of environmental concerns is Joel A. Tarr, *The Search for the Ultimate Sink: Urban Pollution in Historical Perspective* (1996). Tarr surveys technology's impact on urban America since 1850, specifically the overarching impulse of modern society to impose highly technical solutions to managing (though not resolving) the mounting problems of waste disposal and air and water pollution control.

The focus of mainstream groups, as discussed in Part IV and illustrated by David Brower's testimony, was elsewhere: preservation of wilderness and national parks. Russell Martin, in *A Story that Stands Like a Dam: Glen Canyon and the Struggle for the Soul of the West* (1989), has chronicled the full story of preservationists' struggle to challenge dam building in the Southwest.

Samuel P. Hays's *Beauty, Health, and Permanence: Environmental Politics in the United States, 1955–1985* (1987) provides an overview of the political struggles of the post-World War II era.

Among the many outstanding social-environmental histories of particular regions of the country are Andrew Hurley's *Environmental Inequalities: Class, Race, and Industrial Pollution in Gary, Indiana, 1945–1980* (1995) and *Common Fields* (1997), the latter centered on the social and political structures of environmental problems in St. Louis, Missouri. Also of note is Susan Flader's *The Great Lakes Forest: An Environmental and Social History* (1983), one of the first works to unravel the layered story of environmental change in any region. In a more polemic vein, Lynn Jacobs in *Ranching Wastes the West* (1992) delivers a damning critique of cattle ranching in the West—its mythical cowboy roots, the ecological damage it does to riparian and arid habitats, and the power politics and bureaucracy that perpetuates it.

For more western environmental history, see Ed Marston, *Reopening the Western Frontier* (1989), which chronicles the 1970s and 1980s Sagebrush Rebellion of western development interests who bitterly challenged growing environmental regulation of public lands. The most outstanding books on the history of water in the West are Mark Reisner, *Cadillac Desert: The American West and Its Disappearing Water* (1993, 2d ed.), and Donald Worster, *Rivers of Empire: Water, Aridity, and the Growth of the American West* (1985). Both tell how technology and capitalism, as Reisner puts it, "moved water from where it is, and presumably isn't needed, to where it isn't, and presumably is needed." The history of water is key to any environmental history. It does not begin in the arid West, as Theodore Steinberg makes clear in *Nature Incorporated: Industrialization and the Waters of New England* (1991).

On the related agricultural-environmental history of the region, see Donald Worster, *Dust Bowl: The Southern Plains in the 1930s* (1979), as well as his article in the *Journal of American History* (vol. 76, no. 4, March 1990), "Transformations of the Earth: Toward an Agroecological Perspective in History." Also useful as a good overview is David B. Danbom, *Born in the Country: A History of Rural America* (1995), and R. Douglas Hurt's survey, *American Agriculture: A Brief History* (1994). For further reading on the selections included here, see Adeline Gordon Levine, *Love Canal: Science, Politics, and People* (1982), which reveals more of the horrific political machinations behind Lois Gibbs's story. Michael Brown's *Laying Waste: The Poisoning of America by Toxic Chemicals* (1979) revealed the continental, nightmarish scope of the problem unearthed at Love Canal. Both Robert F. Durant, *When Government Regulates Itself: EPA, TVA, and Pollution Control in the 1970s* (1985), and William U. Chandler, *The Myth of TVA: Conservation and Development in the Tennessee Valley, 1933–1983*, shed light on the power structure of the Appalachian region that is the villain of Harry Caudill's chronicle. For an excellent overview of the emerging movement for environmental justice, see Daniel Faber's edited collection, *The Struggle for Ecological Democracy: Environmental Justice Movements in the United States* (1998). Scholars and activists in the book indict global capitalism as the leading villain that links the struggles of poor people, workers, and peoples of color around the globe who face severe ecological crises.

Many of the writers in Faber's book bring an eco-Marxist framework to their analysis, among which are Ted Benton's edited collection, *The Greening of Marxism* (1996), and James O'Connor, *Natural Causes: Essays in Ecological Marxism* (1997). Both books argue that despite (and in some ways, because of) the defeat of Soviet-style communism, other brands of Marxist ideology have survived and in many places around the world have begun to merge with the movement toward green politics. If capital is the enemy of nature, and Marxism the anticapitalist ideology, then the notion is at least worth considering. The journal *Capitalism, Nature, Socialism* continues to bring these theoretical and political arguments together.

On these broad issues of the relationship between the structures of political power and environmental and social change, two scholarly journals are of particular interest. *Organization and Environment* encourages discussion of the social and political roots of environmental problems from a wide perspective of voices, and *Environmental History* (formerly *Environmental History Review*) is the outstanding journal of the American Society of Environmental History.

PART V   THE ENVIRONMENTAL ERA: RESPONSES TO NATURE IN DISTRESS

For good overviews of the onslaught of environmental problems that mounted in the postwar era and provoked the range of responses surveyed in Part V, see Kendall E. Bailes, *Environmental History* (1985), Kirkpatrick Sale, *The Green Revolution: The American Environmental Movement, 1962–1992* (1993), Roderick Nash, ed., *American Environmentalism* (1990), Donald Worster, ed., *The Ends of the Earth: Perspectives on Modern Environmental History* (1988), and David Pepper, *The Roots of Modern Environmentalism* (1985). Important landmark works that brought issues to light during the period include Stewart Udall, *The Quiet Crisis* (1963), which appeared just after Rachel Carson's *Silent Spring* and echoed its sobering critique of reckless human environmental activity. Also important was Paul Erlich's *The Population Bomb* (1968), which forecast a grim global future without limitations on rising population and its concomitant demands on resources. A number of books in the early 1970s reflected a sense that the free-for-all paradigm of limitless resource consumption was dissolving. These include Donella Meadows et al., *The Limits to Growth* (1972), and E. F. Schumacher, *Small Is Beautiful* (1973). In the context of the 1970s energy crisis, when Americans paid higher prices for dwindling supplies of gas and oil and with their confidence in large technocratic institutions generally weakened, the message of these books resonated.

With respect to the themes and authors in Part V, David Ehrenfeld's *The Arrogance of Humanism* (1978) is helpful in better understanding the philosophy of Robinson Jeffers. Also relevant for reading Jeffers is John Elder's previously cited *Imagining the Earth*. Fine syntheses of the life and writings of Edward Abbey are James Bishop's *Epitaph for a Desert Anarchist* (1994) and James Hepworth and Gregory McNamee's edited collection, *Resist Much, Obey Little: Some Notes on Edward Abbey* (1985). As he surely would have agreed, Abbey's other writings are the best additional sources. See, for example, Abbey's novel of eco-defenders, *The Monkey Wrench Gang*, along with *The Journey Home* and *Abbey's Road*. Bob O'Brien's *Our National Parks and the Search for Sustainability* (1999) offers an overview of the contemporary effort to achieve the impossible: make the national parks more environmentally sustainable while encouraging continued increases in visitation. Good histories of the national parks include Alfred Runte's classic, *National Parks: The American Experience* (1987), and Richard West Sellars, *Preserving Nature in the National Parks* (1997).

For clear and compelling insight into deep ecology, see Bill Devall and George Sessions, *Deep Ecology: Living as if Nature Mattered* (1985), Murray Bookchin, *The Ecology of Freedom* (1982), and the anthology compiled by George Sessions, *Deep Ecology for the Twenty-First Century* (1994). The latter is a compilation of writings by leading deep ecology thinkers from Arne Naess to Gary Snyder, who argue that the true value of nature is intrinsic.

For further considerations of the connections between religion and ecology that are raised by Lynn White, Jr., see the surveys by Roger Gottlieb, *This Sacred Earth: Religion, Nature, and the Environment* (1995), and Max Oelschlaeger, *Caring for Creation: An Ecumenical Approach to the Environmental Crisis* (1994). For strong challenges to the long-standing presumption of Judeo-Christianity's supposed antinature teleology, see Calvin B. DeWitt, *Caring for Creation: Responsible Stewardship of God's Handiwork*, Ellen Bernstein's collection of essays, *Ecology and the Jewish Spirit: Where Nature and the Sacred Meet* (1998), and Helen Waddell, *Beasts and Saints* (1996).

For excellent overviews of the broadening range of ecofeminism, see Patrick D. Murphy, *Literature, Nature, and Other: Ecofeminist Critiques* (1995), and Irene Diamond and Gloria Orenstein's collection, *Reweaving the World: The Emergence of Ecofeminism* (1990). A compendium of ecofeminism, *Reweaving the World* delivers both damnation and vision from the field, revealing ancient, revitalized female ideas about nature. In *Made from This Earth: American Women and Nature* (1993), Vera Norwood traces the lives of various American women—scientists, horticulturalists, naturalists, and writers—and concludes that their work and their views of the natural world were informed to some degree by their lives first as women. Norwood's earlier collection of women's nature writing, *The Desert Is No Lady* (with Janice Monk, 1987), argues that the masculine response to the Southwest became the popular perception of that region, obfuscating the different and varied responses of women. Susan Griffin's *Woman and Nature: The Roaring Inside Her* (1978) and Alan W. Watts's *Nature, Man, and Woman* (1958) remain classic works in the field.

The latest and perhaps most comprehensive historical analysis of environmental policy making in the United States is Richard N. L. Andrews, *Managing the Environment, Managing Ourselves* (1999). Andrews takes the long view and places the wave of environmental laws of the last third of the twentieth century in the context of all that had gone before. A more provocative critique of the technical-scientific model of environmental management is S. Robert Lichter and Stanley Rothman, *Environmental Cancer: A Political Disease* (1998), who suggest that an obsessive American fear of cancer and a determination to manage an increasingly carcinogenic environment have driven much of the environmental debate and policy making since the early 1970s. Taking further aim at the failure of legal-scientific-bureaucratic regulatory structures to protect society from the dangers of toxic chemicals is John Wargo, *Our Children's Toxic Legacy* (1998). Pointing toward a more ecological future for environmental management is *Thinking Ecologically: The Next Generation of Environmental Policy* (1997), edited by Marian R. Chertow and Daniel C. Esty. From land use to global trade and market-based environmental incentives for industry, this book brings together new directions in environmental policy. Many of them have the potential to bridge the ideological divide between those who favor increased government regulation and those on the "wise use" end of the environmental debate.

On the wise-use movement, see its proponents' arguments well summarized in Phillip D. Brick and R. McGreggor Cawley's edited volume, *A Wolf in the Garden: The Land Rights Movement and the New Environmental Debate* (1996). In *The War against the Greens: The Wise Use Movement, the New Right, and the Anti-Environmental Violence* (1997), David Helvarg documents the growing use of intimidation, vandalism, and violence employed by an increasing number of wise-use advocates against environmentalists and government workers responsible for environmental regulation. He chronicles the deep historical roots of wise users as well as the corporate financial supporters, grassroots activists, and political connections of the contemporary movement. This increasingly bitter, polarizing struggle recalls the historical fault line between advocates of America's unfettered development and those seeking to restrain it.

For serious critiques of the dominant technocratic values of modern America that have helped to propel environmental change, read Lewis Mumford's classic, *Technics and Civilization* (1934), and also Ian G. Barbour, *Technology, Environment, and Human Values* (1980), Langdon Winner, *The Whale and the Reactor: A Search for Limits in an Age of High Technology* (1986), and Joan Rothschild's collection, *Machina Ex Dea: Feminist Perspectives on Technology* (1983).

Finally, on the real and rhetorical questions of "What is nature?" and "Is nature necessary?" in postmodern America, see the works by SueEllen Campbell and Jennifer Price cited in the text. Also relevant is Gary Snyder, *The Practice of the Wild* (1990), provoking readers to reconsider highly privileged definitions of nature, language, and civilization. Similarly, Susan Sontag's *Against Interpretation* (1961) helps readers to deconstruct and better understand the preconceived meanings of images in western culture, and Jack Solomon's *Signs of Our Time* (1988) offers a very useful lesson in semiotically decoding the universe of popular culture images, not the least of which (both in volume and loaded significance) are environmental.